CW01465120

MOTHER TONGUE TIED

MOTHER TONGUE TIED

On Language, Motherhood & Multilingualism – Disrupting Myths & Finding Meaning

MALWINA GUDOWSKA

FOOTNOTE

First published in 2024 by
Footnote Press

www.footnotepress.com

Footnote Press Limited
4th Floor, Victoria House, Bloomsbury Square, London WC1B 4DA

Distributed by Bonnier Books UK, a division of Bonnier Books
Sveavägen 56, Stockholm, Sweden

First printing
1 3 5 7 9 10 8 6 4 2

Copyright © 2024 Malwina Gudowska

The right of Malwina Gudowska to be identified as the author of this
work has been asserted in accordance with the Copyright,
Designs and Patents Act 1998.

All rights reserved. No part of this publication may be reproduced, stored in
a retrieval system, or transmitted in any form or by any means without the
written permission of the publisher, nor be otherwise circulated in any form
of binding or cover other than that in which it is published and without a
similar condition being imposed on the subsequent purchaser.
All permissions have been sought.

A CIP catalogue record for this book is available from the British Library.

ISBN (hardback): 978 1 804 44079 7
ISBN (ebook): 978 1 804 44078 0

Printed and bound in Great Britain
by Clays Ltd, Elcograf S.p.A.

MIX
Paper | Supporting
responsible forestry
FSC
www.fsc.org FSC® C018072

For my son and my daughter,
my mother and my father,
and most of all, for C.H.

There is one O in God and one O in mother.
— Deborah Levy, *Things I Don't Want to Know*

Perhaps any language, if pursued far enough, leads to exactly the same place.
— Eva Hoffman, *Lost in Translation*

Contents

Note on Language   ix

Introduction: Interfaces   1

An Interruption: The Comma   19

Part 1:   Beginnings & Ends   25

Part 2:   The Familiar & the Foreign   61

Part 3:   Bodies & Borders   109

Part 4:   Love, Literally & Language, Emotionally   161

Part 5:   Departures & Returns   197

Acknowledgements   215

Bibliography   217

Notes   235

About the Author   259

Note on Language

Not all mothers give birth to their children, and not all people who give birth are mothers. *Mothering* should not be defined by gender, and certainly not all families have *mother(s)* and/or *father(s)*. But when I use *mother* and *motherhood*, it is because those terms still predominantly signify a childbearing parent more obviously than *parent* or *parenthood* do, especially because mothers continue to be held up to higher standards and endure more judgment and scrutiny than fathers. Think how the terms *mothering* and *fathering*, or *to mother* and *to father*, differ in their definitions, and in both their societal, and many cultural expectations. Using *parent* or *primary caregiver* does not always capture the burden of societal expectations placed on *mothers*. The word *mother* in *mother tongue*, with its underlying semantic link to motherhood and gendered caregiving roles, may even play a part in perpetuating these kinds of stereotypes, something I explore in Part 1. Gender and race are social constructs but language, and often linguistic injustice, intersects with both, as it also does with socio-economics, class, ethnicity, and many other factors in complex ways, some of which are explored here. Research on multilingual families has predominantly not only focused on heteronormative two-person families, but also mostly on language outcomes. But that is changing as many scholars exploring multilingualism in the family are calling for more diverse definitions of *family* and *multilingualism*, as well as a focus on the lived experiences of a variety of families in many different languages.[1] Family identity is formed by its members through countless ways, including language and language practices.[2]

Language is multisensory, multimodal – spoken, written, signed, other visual modalities like gesture, tactile, digital – and multilingual. It is personal and political and never neutral. Our language(s) and the way we use them are a fundamental part of who we are. Like the multitude of spoken languages in the world, there are hundreds of sign languages with different varieties, dialects, and accents. Although I mostly use the terms *multilingual* and *multilingualism* to signify the use of two or more languages or varieties regularly, there is an argument they highlight the separation of languages and are used as a form of 'pluralization of monolingualism' – means of thinking about language we need to move beyond.[3] (*Pluralingualism* is suggested instead, as well as *translanguaging*, a concept I explore in Part 3. Some research is specific to *bilingualism*, the use of two languages, as opposed to *multilingualism*, but here, I mostly use the latter term to signify two or more languages.)

A similar contradiction permeates ideas around *linguistic diversity* in that discussions on the topic may in fact contribute to injustice by masking inequality while at the same time creating it by considering one group as 'normal' or 'standard' and anything else as 'diverse'.[4] Although multilingualism and linguistic diversity is often proclaimed to be more prevalent than ever, so in fact is linguistic inequality. One of the issues I explore throughout the book is the idea of who is 'allowed' to be multilingual and why some people and groups are praised for knowing, using, and learning multiple languages while others are scrutinized, shamed, oppressed, and even persecuted.

I mainly use the term *heritage language* throughout to signify a language, primarily learnt in the home, that is not the majority/societal language of where the person resides or grew up. (*Minoritized* language also comes up in contrast with *majority* or *societal* language: *minoritized* instead of *minority* as it is the way the language is perceived as opposed to its true value.) I discuss in Part 3 why *home language* is problematic but why *heritage language* is also not without complex connotations. In some families, including my own, there is a cultural element to the notion of *heritage language*.

There are a multitude of ways to use language, to *language*, 'an ongoing process of interactive meaning-making'[5], and to exist and communicate in the world. Every language and experience is important and valid. The title, terminology, pronoun, moniker someone chooses to use, and identifies with, should be respected and acknowledged, and it is up to each individual to decide, and for everyone else to respect. Language, and using it in a respectful and affirming way, is a form of love and care. When I think about the people who oppose 'newer' inclusive terms like *chest-feeding* and *birthing people*, arguing they exclude *mothers* and *women*, the opposition often includes those who say they cannot get behind a singular *they* because the term is so 'new'. The use of singular *they* in English dates back hundreds of years.

Inclusive language *includes* and language change is perpetual. As I tell my children, words and language matter, and what you say and the way you communicate with others in the world is powerful and carries with it a responsibility. It is estimated more than half of the world's population is multilingual and many people live their lives in multiple languages so there is nothing *diverse* about multilingualism. And yet, in places like the UK, where I reside, parts of Canada, where I grew up, and its neighbour, the US, multilingualism is still often considered *diverse* and with that come many repercussions, including linguistic inequality (often in the guise of celebrating multilingualism). Inclusive language and optimistic notions around multilingualism and linguistic diversity alone, without structural and societal change, do not equal justice and equality.

And yet, I begin with words because we must begin and, more importantly, keep going and continue bringing these issues to light. I hope I convey a message of inclusivity and accuracy in these pages as much as possible. Where my words have failed, I hope others continue this conversation, because language is fluid and unfailingly changing.

Introduction: Interfaces

Morphology: *the study of the internal structure of words.*
Morph *from Greek, meaning* shape *or* form

'*You* comes later than *it*,' said my linguistics professor. I wrote down the sentence and suddenly felt its crushing weight. The module, titled, 'Interfaces in Syntax', was about how syntax and semantic interpretation of person, causation and information structure interact. That day's lecture was on how children learn pronouns. My first child, not yet two years old at the time, was learning pronouns at a crowded and costly London nursery, filled with echoes of baby babbles and other children's first words, while I sat in the badly lit, windowless classroom, attempting to reinvent my career. In English first-language acquisition, *you* comes later than *it* because second-person pronouns are acquired after third-person pronouns. But in that moment, during a class about boundaries and interactions, causation and relation, and asymmetric coordination, it was also the perfect analogy for motherhood.

I was a pupil of linguistics, 'the science of language', and a novice at motherhood, the art of caregiving. The modules I was studying, the same ones introducing each part of this book, went far beyond the classroom, permeating my day-to-day caregiving. To me, sociolinguistics was not only the study of language

1

in relation to society, it was how motherhood and language corresponded for me and my child, especially in public spaces. The semantics and pragmatics of early motherhood eluded me, and syntax exemplified how small fragments of the everyday, not unlike words and morphemes, the smallest units of language that have meaning, form a whole. I was the *you*, my baby was the *it*, and I had only begun to discover what the world expected from mothers, and what it condemned them for, in caregiving but also in language.

I began an MA in Linguistics shortly after my son turned one, and suddenly, I was a new student, learning about Wugs, a well-known experiment to investigate the acquisition of the English plural in children, and William Labov's fourth floor, the 1966 study about language and social class. After nursery drop-off, I mastered syntax trees, struggled to memorize the International Phonetic Alphabet, and barely made it through a semantics course. A year earlier, I was a new mother, deciphering the language of motherhood: meconium, colostrum, nipple shields, fourth-degree tear, annihilating emotions and unadulterated love. You know, same, same. As my son was born in London, where my partner and I had moved to from Canada two years earlier, my baby-related lexicon was British English: nappy for diaper, dummy for soother and pram/pushchair/buggy for stroller. (I am still unsure of the difference between the three.) When I called the doctor in London to make my first pregnancy appointment, I had a momentary back-and-forth with the receptionist: he kept asking if I was calling about an *antenatal* appointment, I kept insisting I wanted to book a (Canadian English[6]) *prenatal* appointment. Although the pregnancy was a surprise, I did not want to terminate, I told him, and an *anti-natal* appointment was not what I required. Ohhh, *ante-* not *anti-* I ultimately realized. Whether literal or figurative, everything in my new world was about language.

Once my son was born, I was not only living the parallel lives of a linguistics student and a new mother, but I had simultaneously begun a crash-course in raising a multilingual child. Polish, my first language, the one I grew up speaking at home with my parents, had become, through English socialization after our immigration to Canada when I was five, despite my fluency, my non-dominant language. When I became a mother, I also began to mother my first language[7], to coax her out, at times coerce. I had to untangle her from English, the language she was forever entwined with, and one that threatened to devour her for years. Motherhood made me question my cultural and linguistic identity in ways I never had before. My identity as a woman was at times, especially at first, at odds with my identity as a mother. My multilingual and multicultural identities, ones I had considered throughout my life often, but not for some time, and not at the same scale, or with the same urgency, were vying for my attention. In early motherhood, I lost the language of self, and was unsure for a long time how to find it, or how to create something new from the fragments of my past life in any language. In the words of Julia Kristeva, my child's language acquisition implied I too had to re-learn language[8], a maternal vernacular but also a day-to-day conversational Polish, one I had not used regularly since moving out of my parents' home fifteen years earlier.

Before our baby was born, my monolingual English-speaking partner and I both knew we wanted him to be multilingual. Living in the United Kingdom, my children – a daughter was born nearly three years later – would learn English because that is the societal language and the language spoken between me and their father. But Polish was the language I alone was responsible for, no matter the cost, I told myself. Having lived most of my life between, beyond and across three languages (I attended French immersion school in Canada until I was seventeen), I knew raising a multilingual and multicultural child would not be a simple endeavour, but I never imagined how exhausting and emotional it could be.

I come to this topic as both a child of immigrants and an immigrant myself, two distinct but inextricably linked experiences, hoping to pass on a heritage language to my children. It is a language that binds me to my parents, my extended family, my birth country, and my childhood. Although I always felt an in-between or, rather, a between life in two languages and cultures as a child, I was too young when I immigrated to Canada to feel a sense of loss or an acutely conflicting identity between the new and the old. It felt more as something that just was, I was simply multilingual *and* multicultural. But motherhood was my rebirth into a language and culture I already knew, or thought I knew. I became intimate with Polish and parts of the Polish culture in a way I had never felt before, caring for them, nurturing them, making them my own and my children's. In some ways, I also returned to French, not to teach my children, but to feel my own childhood coincide with my children's. I began to read books in French again as I did at school. But the more my languages (re)surfaced, and I attempted to (re)create cultural moments and ties, the more lost I felt trying, looking for answers in language, in notions of home and cultures that were meant to be *mine*, only to steadily find more questions.

This book is about parallels and paradoxes, contrasts, and contradictions, in language, multilingualism and in motherhood. Through the study of language and my experience thus far as a woman and mother raising multilingual children, I've come to realize that so much of what we think we recognize, or are told to know or to feel, is in opposition. In *Of Woman Born*, Adrienne Rich famously begins the book by outlining the two meanings of motherhood she will attempt to distinguish between: the experience of motherhood and the relationship of a mother to her children, and the patriarchal *institution* of motherhood. After having children, I immediately understood the institution predominantly worked against caregiving, especially for mothers attempting to create meaningful work beyond, and in addition to, the momentous work of mothering. Mothers are meant to move effortlessly between a maternal language we share with our children and with the world in the role of Mother, to a language of personhood that must never reveal our motherhood and sometimes not even our womanhood. The dichotomies of mothering, as I felt and recognized them, began to mirror the contradictions in language and multilingualism, especially in my experience of raising two multilingual children. Both caregiving and the use of a minoritized language, a language considered in opposition to a majority one in *and* of the community, or deemed less *valuable*[i], if it is judged to have any 'value' at all, are habitually believed to be part of the private, domestic sphere. This, in turn, forces both caregiving and a multilingual family's use of a heritage language, even when acknowledged, to be made invisible, pushed into a metaphorical but also private space.[9]

As a new mother, I was, and continue to be, entrenched in discourses about raising multilingual children, especially the benefits, strategies, frustrations, but also the many misconceptions that astonishingly refuse to die after incredible runs.[ii] I am inundated with conversations and headlines about *the gift* of multilingualism, a welcoming sentiment – who does not love a gift? – but ultimately complex, double-edged and commonly intertwined with notions around language as a commodity. A gift can easily become a burden – the distinction rarely straightforward, especially when it is not ours alone to make but influenced heavily by society and nation-state ideologies. But I rarely come across conversations about how linguistic diversity goes hand-in-hand with linguistic inequality, or the way languages are assembled hierarchically, or why some multilinguals are praised while other are criticized and even discriminated against. Why do mothers continue to feel they are the ones 'failing' or tell themselves, and others, they are 'lazy' or at fault when their children do not acquire a heritage language (all sentiments I have heard before), considering mothers not only often lack support, but encounter obstacles, and monolingual ideologies, at every turn.

---

[i] The idea of language having value, or one language, but also variety or dialect, being more valuable than another is something I return to throughout the book. The subjectivity of this label is especially jarring *within* a language where multilingualism and linguistic diversity is celebrated from the outside, but certain varieties of the same language, in a sense on the inside, are scrutinized and oppressed.

[ii] There are so many misconceptions and myths I note throughout the book but perhaps the most prevalent one I hear from other mothers, often something they have been told by a professional, is that multilingualism causes language delays or will confuse children.

'The word "mother" hardly appears in bilingual-childrearing books except when referring to a specific mother. In indexes, "parent" is listed with lots of sub-sections, and "father" appears, but not "mother", except for "mother tongue,"' writes Toshie Okita in her seminal 2002 study, *Invisible Work: Bilingualism, Language Choice, and Childrearing in Intermarried Families.*[10] It was only when I read Okita's work that I began to fully appreciate and recognize my experience of multilingual childrearing in its form of invisible work, a domestic labour predominantly performed by mothers like me that is also highly emotional but rarely acknowledged. Okita's words echoed my lived experience of constant monitoring, reminding, ensuring my children were, and still are, using their heritage language, a minoritized language constantly living in the shadow of a dominant majority language of the society but also one that is equally prominent in our home.

More than twenty years after the publication of Okita's study, the word 'mother' appears more often in research on multilingual childrearing. Just recently, I came across an academic article examining parents' individual language use and how it was a better predictor of language exposure than family language strategies. The article, titled 'Like Mother Like Child', reported on a study that found that mothers had, 'at least double the impact on language exposure than fathers, likely due to gendered caregiving roles'.[11] The 'mother' was there, in the title (!), as was the nod to gendered caregiving roles, and the study uncovered valuable information that could inform recommendations and policy, and yet I felt apathy. Mothers who are transmitting and maintaining a heritage language continue to face a paradox of scrutiny and praise: invisible mothers performing invisible work until it is time to assess their success or, especially, their failure.

Mothers raising multilingual children regularly have their identities as *good mothers* called into question[12] whether they are, or they are not, transmitting a heritage language: consider the *good mother* who is giving *the gift* of multilingualism, but also the *bad mother* who is said, invalidly, to be compromising a school or societal language in the process. Or she is the *bad mother* for *not* passing on a heritage language, blamed by family members living in another part of the world, unable to communicate with the children abroad. When mothers consider heritage language maintenance their responsibility, they often believe language loss reflects poorly on their choices and practices as mothers[13] and irrespective of their multilingual proficiency, mothers become 'guardians of their children's "true" bilingualism'.[14] Sometimes, grown children blame their parents for not passing on a heritage language, despite themselves pushing back against it when they were children. As Okita notes in her study on Japanese mothers raising bilingual children in America, mothers who fail in their 'language work' are made to feel they are having a negative effect on their children, unlike fathers who are praised for at least trying.[15] Even in situations where minoritized languages like Scottish Gaelic, Welsh, Sámi and Breton were for years oppressed and colonized, and their speakers persecuted, oppressed and sometimes punished for using the languages by those in government and societal power, mothers were still blamed for 'killing' the languages by not using them with their children.[16]

In her work examining mothers transmitting and maintaining heritage languages in Australia, Hannah Irving Torsh notes that the pressure to raise bilingual children arises from discourse around 'intensive mothering' and calls mothers 'cultural brokers' for their children. This goes hand-in-hand with notions around language as capital, an investment into the child's future, an asset and yes, that *gift*. But it does not apply to *all* languages because, again, some languages are still considered more *valuable* than others. When a language or a language variety is not considered prestigious, the *gift* may be invalidly identified as a burden and the paradoxical image of the mother providing either an investment, or, if it is the *wrong* language or variety, hindering success, takes shape. By way of an example, Polish is the most common language in the UK after English and Welsh, according to the 2021 census, and yet, in my experience, it does not hold the same prestige in this country as a language like French. And unless you have familial or heritage ties to the language, it is highly unlikely one would choose to learn it. In the US, where Spanish is widely spoken, many of the language's varieties, like Puerto Rican Spanish, are consistently and continuously unduly stigmatized, something I return to in Part 3.

Numerous studies show that mothers are the ones who have more influence when it comes to passing down a heritage language, even when it is the partner's language the family wants the children to learn. For immigrant mothers, often new to a societal language and culture themselves, and who not only want to, but need to maintain and transmit a heritage language to keep an emotional connection with their children, there is an even greater burden. They have to be 'the keeper' of one culture and language, the 'recipient and supporter' of another, and the 'mediator between the two cultures when they clash'.[17] And there is a lot at stake. When children and parents do not share a language, both parents and children may feel a sense of loss of identity, culture and emotional bonding.[18] As a multitude of posts on any online multilingual parenting forum will attest, and from my own experience, when mothers believe they have *failed* because their children are not using a heritage language *enough*, or they believe their children's fluency is not at the level it should be, or they realize they (I!) should have started *earlier* (in the womb!) or done *more*, the guilt begins to seep through our veins. And if someone like me – who is familiar with multilingualism research, of what is needed to become 'proficient'[iii] in a language, how there are a multitude of factors influencing language, while also being acutely aware even in the best-case scenario there are no guarantees, feels a substantial responsibility, and often excessive remorse – how do others fare?

Even in monolingual contexts, motherhood and language are often pitted against one another in a multitude of ways: mothers are judged, sometimes shamed, for their children's language. Mothers are told they are to monitor their children's language development, to count words, to save their children from deficit-based outcomes, when so often society fails families and especially mothers repeatedly. The blame is placed on the individual – the

---

iii 'Proficiency' and 'fluency' are subjective terms and in many ways impossible to measure. What is proficient and fluent for one person may not be considered the same for another, especially depending on domain and context.

mother – as opposed to the system and the many pervasive social inequities. As Allen Ansgar and Sarah Spencer write in *Regimes of Motherhood: Social Class, the Word Gap and the Optimisation of Mothers' Talk*, 'the mother is firmly positioned in terms of her personal responsibility.' Motherhood needs to be endlessly optimized by academia and research, in the context of children's language development, and mothers are confined in a 'permanent labour' where the expectation is they will better themselves, in a way that is quantifiable by what others can observe in the development of their children's language.[19] There is rarely recognition of 'broader sociocultural factors', argue Ansgar and Spencer, nor the importance of 'privileging the expertise and agency of mothers.'

I want to pause here and acknowledge fathers because I know there will be readers who will argue I am unfairly painting *all* fathers with the same brush. I wish I didn't have to say this, but of course not *all fathers* and many fathers – my partner included, who is incredibly supportive in every possible way – play a pivotal role in their family's multilingual childrearing. But the research shows mothers continue to be held more responsible, and bear most of that immense responsibility, for their children's multilingualism.[20]

When you become a mother, suddenly the debates and dilemmas come at you like tidal waves: bottle or breast, sleep train or attachment parenting, disposable diapers or reusable ones. But these 'choices' do not happen in a vacuum. You quickly realize you are part of a wider conversation where everyone has an opinion. The same holds true when you decide to raise multilingual children.

'Why wouldn't you pass on another language?'
'Are you sure they are not confused?'
'Are three languages too many?'
'How will they fit in with their peers?'
'A second language is such a gift.'
'Have you counted how many words your child is saying?'
'It sounds like they are behind.'
'I can't believe you wouldn't give your child the gift of multilingualism.'
'I can't believe you would stress your child out with another language.'
Give the fucking gift!

Language ideologies and practices within families and between mother and child intersect with socio-economic, historical, and political factors in everyday life, and it is impossible to separate one from the other. I have heard from mothers with neurodiverse children, or those whose children have speech delays, how they are made to feel their use of a heritage language is silly, at best, or at worst stressful and detrimental for the child. Multilingualism does not cause speech delays and, although there is some variability in the rate of language acquisition for multilingual children, the development of two languages follows the same pattern as that of one language. If a multilingual child has a speech delay, they will have that delay in multiple languages, or in one language if they are monolingual, and it is not one language negatively affecting the other or 'causing' a speech delay.

When my son was a toddler, I wrote an article for a major Canadian newspaper on how unexpectedly challenging my experience of raising a bilingual child had been up to that point. In response, I received mostly messages of support, as I have throughout the years when I write something about how emotional and hard multilingual mothering can be, especially from other mothers. But one letter was not like the others. It was from a man who said he did not understand why raising bilingual children was so hard for me. Both of his children were 'perfect bilinguals', he wrote, who had a command in both of their languages and could move effortlessly between them. It had *never* been an issue for the family and bilingualism was *never* a challenge (emphasis my own). As the letter went on, it became apparent that this man was, in fact, monolingual and the person predominantly responsible for his children's bilingualism was his bilingual wife.

Around the same time, at a developmental check for my toddler, I was told by a health visitor I should only speak English to my son, and only when he has a 'good grasp' of that language should I introduce Polish. I calmly explained to the woman that this is not how multilingualism works and that she must stop giving this erroneous advice to caregivers. And then I wondered how many mothers had heeded the advice already, stopped using a heritage language and changed their lives and possibly their relationship with their children forever. When I first began to recount this infuriating story to others, I used to call this health visitor 'well-meaning', but I don't anymore. When more than half the world's population is multilingual, every practitioner working with children and families should be aware and trained in research on multilingualism and language acquisition in multiple languages.

The cognitive benefits – multitasking skills, working memory, metalinguistic awareness – of multilingualism, often called the 'cognitive advantage', are well documented, albeit also more recently disputed.[21] Although they are major selling points, and I am here for anything encouraging multilingualism, there is a tendency to emphasize studies where multilingual children are compared with monolingual ones. The comparison, even in studies praising bilingualism, perpetuates ideas that monolingualism and multilingualism are, at worst, at odds with one another or, at a minimum, something to be compared. In the words of linguist François Grosjean, who coined the phrase in a seminal paper in 1989, 'a multilingual is not two monolinguals in one body'.[22] Vivian Cook referred to this as 'multicompetence', defining it as 'the compound state of a mind with two grammars'[23], and later expanded the definition to the knowledge of more than one language in the same mind. Ofelia García calls it 'dynamic bilingualism', and not simply 'additive', where the language practices of bilinguals are complex and interrelated and they do not emerge in a linear way or function separately since there is only one linguistic system.[24]

In other words, the knowledge of multiple languages is multifaceted and complex and not at all equivalent to a double monolingualism. One of the many reasons comparing monolingualism to multilingualism can be harmful is that for many multilingual families, multilingualism is praised if it does not interfere with a school or societal language. Bilingualism is perceived as great only if you are in a privileged position, if English, or another societal language, is 'strong', if you are white and have high socio-economic status, if you sound and look a specific way. But in other situations, it is incorrectly and dangerously perceived as hazardous, damaging or as an interference to a language that is deemed more important than the heritage/home/minoritized language. These notions are tied to racist, classist, colonialist, and capitalist ideologies. All languages are equal, and all languages are important, and one does not interfere with another. Multilingualism should not have to prove its worth to be considered important and its value is as simple as generations of a family being able to communicate with one another. The perceived value of a language, or even the supposed value in its perceived fluency, can also have detrimental effects for a family when the attitudes of caregivers, often influenced by society and monolingual and standard language ideologies, influence whether the parents will transmit and maintain a heritage language.

And then there are the prevailing myths, the oh-so-many myths, many of which we heard above – multilingualism causes speech delays, children will be confused by multiple languages, parents need to ensure one language is 'strong enough' before introducing another – around bilingualism that will not die despite the abundance of research debunking them. Although discredited for years, the myths continue to be passed on, often causing irreversible damage to families who adhere to the incorrect advice from those propagating the myths. For those families, the moment they accept this harmful advice, it is the beginning of an end that is hard to come back from. There are also the misconceptions that seem harmless in that they live *inside* multilingualism, but they too can wreak havoc. For example, that bilinguals have *perfect* or *balanced* knowledge of their languages, that multilinguals do not have accents in each of their languages, and that mixing languages is *bad* for multilingualism. 'What is particularly interesting is the way that myths are used to justify social order, and to encourage or coerce consensual participation in that order,' writes Rosina Lippi-Green in *English with an Accent.* 'Myths are magical and powerful constructs; they can motivate social behaviors and actions which would be otherwise contrary to logic or reason.'[25]

There is a multitude of incredible books and resources about multilingual parenting that report on the research in an accessible way and help caregivers make the right decisions for their families by providing evidence-based facts. But often, the most vital and newest research takes time to make it down to caregivers and mothers who need it most. When it does it can get lost or misinterpreted by media (more on this in Part 1) or by those sometimes helpful, often bothersome online parenting forums where everyone has an opinion and is an expert (beware!). Sometimes, even knowing all the strategies and the most up-to-date information can just as easily be a burden as a gift, or at least the burden of the fear of failing at multilingualism with your children.

If you are reading this thinking how easy it is to raise multilingual children, how your community is supportive of multilingualism, how you have access to multilingual resources or education[26], how your heritage language is not oppressed or persecuted, how you are not discriminated against for using one language over another, how you do not have to die for your language[27], you are extremely lucky. But like everything in life, it should not be about luck. We all need to be advocating for one another, not only for multilingualism but for the end of linguistic injustice and linguistic inequality.

It is an incredible privilege and a luxury to be able to choose what languages I want my children to learn, and which language I use with my children, as it is a privilege that my children know me in both of my languages. Not all families, especially those who are new to a societal language because of migration, or who continue to be persecuted for their use of a minoritized language, have a choice. There are many devastating examples of language being forcibly stolen and violently denied that continue today. It is a freedom I do not take for granted to have access to multiple languages when so many others have lost that right or are too afraid to use a language, variety, dialect, because of linguistic prejudice, linguistic discrimination, linguistic racism, colonialism, white supremacy, accentism and linguicism. But there are parallels in the varied experiences for mothers swimming against a current of the majority language threatening to consume us and our children. And the more we bring these experiences to the forefront, to amplify the voices of others, to share the stories of hardships and challenges, the more we bring attention to the social consequences of linguistic diversity and, in turn, how 'linguistic disadvantage' is a form of structural disadvantage.[28] In *Linguistic Diversity and Social Justice*, Ingrid Piller reminds us:

> 'Linguistic diversity is widely regarded as a novelty of our age when in fact, it has been the normal human experience all along. We do not just fail to see linguistic diversity in the historical record because of ideological blinkers but also because it has oftentimes been actively expunged from the historical record in an attempt to deny legitimacy to subordinated groups.'[29]

Children learn a first language, or multiple languages in the case of simultaneous bilinguals who are learning more than one language from birth, by being exposed to language. But at some point, especially when a child goes to school, or when a societal language begins to infiltrate the home, there may begin an element of *teaching* the minoritized language, or rather a minoritized language maintenance begins because the societal language, the school language and that of the peer group will likely become the dominant one for the child. Children need exposure, input, and a sense of need to maintain or learn a language other than the one they are using in wider society. A linguist I admire once said she feels as if she is clipping her son's wings no matter which language she speaks with him.[30] If it is German, her heritage language and one she wants to pass on to her child, the context or the meaning of certain concepts gets lost and a conversational flow may be compromised. If she uses English, her dominant language, her son's dominant language and the community language, she gives up the opportunity for input in the heritage language, a vital component of language transmission. Plus, children, like her son, may not view their heritage language as part of their identity like she, the mother, might. If there is no connection with a language, it is a pointless endeavour to try and force it.

The landscapes of motherhood and language can be familiar, or foreign, as if you've known mothering and *languaging*[iv] all your life, but in the same breath are a beginner at both. Language and motherhood are the beginnings of every story: complex, fluid, layered and, above all, emotional. Language happens in relation to one other, as does the act of mothering. Fluency in language and in motherhood can come easily or with great effort. And in both, without warning, you might regress. Both language and motherhood are often considered common and predictable. Terms like innate and instinct are incessantly thrown around when describing both language and motherhood. If we pause and consider each, beyond the Chomskian debate of innateness[31], both language and mothering are extraordinary, complex, and unique to everyone. Language and notions of mothering, especially when considered beyond the institution of motherhood and society's idea of what a mother *should* be, can both offer solace: children and language bind us to our past and our future in inexplicable ways while keeping us humble and sometimes even conflicted in the present. What I craved the most in those early days of raising a multilingual child was to hear the stories of other mothers like me, especially how others were *feeling*, stories about the highs, lows, the frustration, the joy, and everything in between. I didn't want to hear about the possible cognitive benefits *again*, but rather how language was inextricably linked with belonging, identity, home, ethnicity, heritage and how linguistic diversity and social justice were intertwined, and how any and every language is valuable

---

[iv] The concept of 'languaging' was first introduced by Chilean biologists Humberto Maturana and Francisco Varela in 1973 in the theory of autopoiesis: that 'we cannot separate our biological and social history of actions from the ways in which we perceive the world'. The term has been reinterpreted over the years to identify how language is more than what is communicated verbally or through sign, but also includes gestures and expressions, ultimately *being* and *doing* language, *making meaning* and *becoming*. For a discussion, see García, Ofelia and Li Wei, *Translanguaging: Language, bilingualism and education* (United Kingdom, Palgrave Macmillan, 2014): p. 7–8.

simply because someone uses it to communicate. I hope my words here offer comfort, and especially recognition, to anyone needing it, like I once did and frequently still do.

When I travel, I take photos of hanging laundry: out windows, on clothing lines, draped over railings. Usually, these photos are taken in incredibly romantic destinations, far from my own piles of dirty clothes and other chores. They represent the domestic, a sign that someone lives an everyday life in these dreamy cities. The private becomes public, and people air their (clean!) laundry for everyone, including tourists, to see.

When my son was a newborn in London and doing laundry was my new hobby, I would hang his tiny baby clothes out to dry on our balcony in the blazing summer sun. One day, someone in our building slipped a note under the door. On it, scribbled in barely legible handwriting, were a few lines informing us that hanging the laundry on our balcony was making the entire building look 'cheap' and 'unsophisticated'. Who hates seeing adorable tiny baby clothes that much, I thought. I later learnt it was a building rule not to hang laundry on the balcony. A few years later, in a different building, I noticed most tenants hanging laundry on their balconies, especially during the many heatwaves London was enduring one summer. Sensible people and sensible building management, I thought. That is, until all the tenants received a letter stating action would be taken against repeat offenders who hung laundry on their balconies. According to an online search, reasons include the prevention of accidents from falling objects but also, that laundry on display lowers the resale value of flats. The private cannot become public, and everyday lives, and everyday domestic labour of laundry, must be hidden behind closed doors, or at least the threshold of the balcony. Hidden, unpaid, domestic labour, often also maternal labour, runs parallel to the hidden domestic labour of heritage language learning. Raising multilingual children is work, often also maternal work that is pushed into the home. We say we value what happens in the home, how we take care of family and those in need, but often society does not want to see caregiving work in the public eye, to pay for it, to value it in more ways than lip service. The same occurs with heritage languages, especially in immigrant families. One of the most prevalent and perpetuated myths around raising multilingual children is that a heritage language used in the home will have a negative effect on a language used in school. Multilingualism continues to be misunderstood by so many, especially in societies where monolingualism mindsets prevail.[32]

A few years after the '*You* comes later than *it*' moment during my linguistics seminar, I took part in a webinar on multilingual parenting. The speaker, a distinguished professor in the field whose work I know well, finished her talk by stating the most important part of multilingual parenting is the well-being of the child. Even though my research on the emotions of mothers raising multilingual children has taught me otherwise, it still floored me that the prevailing notion of mothers and their well-being as second-tier had infiltrated even linguistics. The most important part of multilingual parenting, like the most important part of mothering in general, is the well-being of *both* mother *and* child. My laundry-on-display ban analogy is only one example of the division of what is considered private versus public in both domestic and maternal work but also with language maintenance and transmission of a heritage language. The separation and sometimes conflict between private spaces, like the home and the maternal body, and public ones, in language and in motherhood, is a reoccurring theme throughout this book. When the laundry, the mothering and the language(s) are *seen*, it is an acknowledgement of not only the labour that it all entails, but the everyday, individual lives people are living all over the world in a multitude of languages.

Years before I had children, I wrote a magazine article about multilingualism and raising bilingual children. I interviewed Canadian families who were raising children in multiple languages and one mother who, although she had initially planned to, decided to stop speaking Swedish to her children because, after years of trying, the overwhelming resistance and the lack of support became too much to bear. I wrote about that encounter again years later, after having my own children and being in the throes of multilingual parenting. I admitted I had judged that mother harshly during our encounter, silently telling myself back then she had missed an opportunity and thinking how sad it was she 'gave up'. I now know, as I did when I realized my initial (mis) judgment, she did not give up. She was consumed by language, by motherhood, by raising children in multiple languages, likely by people telling her to *do it*, to *not do it*, do it *differently*, this way, that way. She did what she had to do to survive. Some days, when I think of that mother, I envy her for making that decision. And yet, I am sorry she had to *give in, give up, give, give, give*.

The prevailing myths around language, especially bilingualism, are unequivocally related to illusions and assumptions of motherhood and mothering. In the end, nothing remains unchanged after we become mothers, and every time we make a choice, a choice in motherhood or language, we naturally lose something else. Both language and motherhood can play a fundamental role in forming a sense of self and, most importantly, both mothering and the language(s) offer the radical potential to find meaning, create connection and advocate for change in the world. But it is not always either/or and language lives within us and between us, within mothers and children but also between them. When something is lost, it can also be found, but not always in its original state, and that too is a fundamental part of our changing linguistic, cultural, and mothering identities.

When my children were very young, I remember reading somewhere about a mother who would say to her children in English before bedtime that she loved them more than all the stars in the sky. I loved the imagery of the sentiment and the way you could extend the 'alllll' as if it was possible to truly reach across the entire sky and wipe away the stars, so insignificant compared to the love you have for your children. I tried to say the same thing in Polish, but it sounded choppy and not beautiful or romantic at all. The phrase was not mine to take and translate. Whether we mother in one or multiple languages, in the end, or really from the beginning, we hope our children will remember us by a gesture, a song, a saying or a sign – a minor or mundane moment that will have nothing to do with the institution of motherhood but only with the act of mothering and, often, language.

An Interruption: The Comma

Applied Linguistics: *the study of real-life applications of linguistics*

When my son first began to write, his commas were breathtakingly beautiful. First, he would make a small dot and go around and around until he was satisfied with its size: a whorl of a snail's shell, his little fingerprint, the way a newborn baby's hair grows. The top part of the comma was as wide as half the letter next to it. Then, he would flick the pencil to create the bottom of the comma, an exaggerated loop, or I came to think of it as an anchor. The pause was firmly placed and could not be moved except to signal something beyond, something further: a steady navigation. Perhaps it is not a coincidence the first word my son, the comma-conscientious child and now devourer of texts, said was *more*. I wrote it down, along with *hot, mama* and *dada* in his baby book, on the page where it commands you write down 'the firsts'. Even though I knew *mama* and *dada* were not really my son's first words as much as they were early sounds[33], I was grasping at the recognition, just like every other caregiver I knew. At the front of this baby book were four gleaming blank pages. Four pages representing the first four months of my son's life when I was so traumatized by childbirth and having a newborn, I did not, *could not* write a single word. After he was born, there was so much *more* of everything: more sweat, more blood, more pain, more despair, more love, more life but also more (fear of) death.[34] My baby cried a lot; I cried a lot. The blank pages haunted me for a long time until I began to appreciate their representation of a pause, a break, a breakdown, a rebuilding of words and, eventually, myself. In art, negative space[35] is used to define the shape or boundary of a form. In conversation, and often life, pauses make us uncomfortable. But there is beauty and meaning in a pause, especially in dialogue and often in a new form.

,

There are four types of commas – listing, joining, gapping, bracketing (interrupter) – with eight uses. The comma represents both interference and continuity. Stop and start.

In (my) mothering and (our) multilingualism, the listing comma is simple: a to-do list, or a list of things to remember. Brush teeth, bring a water bottle and a hat, book a dentist appointment. *More* Polish input, *more* Polish exposure, read five pages of the Polish book, FaceTime with grandparents so kids speak *more* Polish.

The joining comma connects two complete sentences into one using, for example, *and, but, while, yet.* 'You are Canadian, *and* you are Polish, *and* you are a Londoner,' I tell my children when they ask. 'And yet, you are just you in any way you want to be, communicate and live in the world. All of your languages are a part of that.' The gapping comma appears when there is an omittance, a choice not to repeat something that was already said. It is the hardest one for me as I fill the gaps and I ask for my children's repetition: 'Now say the same thing in Polish.' I offer my own repetition: 'And in Polish, you say . . .' so that there is *more* exposure, *more* input, *more* practice. Finally, the bracketing or interrupter comma. A pregnant pause. I worry as I write this book the interruption my children have to their Polish language input and exposure. They spend time with their father or other English speakers while I write, a punishing irony for a mother writing about worrying about her children's multilingualism because of a lack of input and exposure to the minoritized language. She, *I*, am the input and when I am not there, I am also the interruption. Lisa Baraitser writes that the interruption of the continuum or the flow creates a break and an in between that itself creates something new, often a segment: '. . . this intervention into flow shows up flow as flow . . . a series of segments with breaks between.' What might be if we '. . . understand relentless interruption as not just depleting but generative?' Baraitser asks.[36] I must trust my absence is an interruption to a movement that will continue, despite the interlude.

,

This book was written in, and with interruptions between, and during parenting, academic research, day-to-day life, between reminders to speak a minoritized language and the frustrations of, like so many other mothers raising multilingual children have shared with me, feeling as if I was failing. It is written in segments and fragments, nothing unsaid, but like silence, intervals in space. Units of conversation. The thoughts are anecdotes, research summaries, interviews, lists, reporting and narrative, positioned one next to another often separated by a single comma, in all its glorious significance – an ode to my son's anchor and the spiral of a snail shell with its drawn-out movement, complete with the whorl of my own fingerprint.

In mothering, and in language, there is a reoccurring deficit-based rhetoric that will reappear time and time again in these pages because it appears time and time again in life. What is missing? Where is there not *enough*? Am I doing all I can? My language(s) are never *good enough*. How do I fill a space, a crack, a pause? But a space is an interruption, a segment that is part of a bigger whole. Mothering changes and moves on, just like language flows and transforms. Even within languages, there are fragments and interruptions. But people find their way back to something lost in language and caregiving all the time; the in-between segments create their own narratives. Nothing is really lost in translation because something can always be found, be heard, be understood. It is worth considering these pauses, these fragments and segments in both mothering and language. We weave through and in between language, between caregiving, between ideas. 'We may learn from spaces of silence as well as spaces of speech,' writes bell hooks in *Teaching to Transgress: Education as the Practice of Freedom.* The notion of interruption of flow, a pause in the form of being self-conscious in the language we use, is also something English speakers need more of, not less, argues Julia Penelope when writing about what she calls a 'patriarchal universe of discourse': 'Being aware of the cognitive significance and social ramifications of the linguistic choices we make is both necessary and constructive, because it ensures that we won't accept misogynistic language as "normal".'[37]

Alastair Pennycook considers language and repetition in relation to time and space and, in turn, language use within a concept of flow and repetition as 'an act of difference, relocalization, renewal'.[38] Language as a 'local practice' is the result of repeated social activity, as opposed to structure. But repetition is also difference. Pennycook draws on the idea of repeated sameness as opposed to observable difference and how the modest, repetitive, everyday uses of language are a 'central aspect of human difference'.[39] In other words, what appears to be the same through time, list after list, comma after comma, becomes, through its repetitions, different. (As a mother and caregiver, I think about this often, in many contexts.) My family's repetitions, our 'everyday talk' in multiple languages, over and over and back again, create meaning and identity.[40]

,

It is not lost on me that I write here about using Polish with my children, describing the events and experiences predominantly in English, a colonial language, the language I am persistently condemning when I want my children to use Polish. And yet it is the only way I know how to share this story and the stories of so many others who are trying not to lose a language, or to gain one back: an interruption of a flow that will idyllically, in one way or another, continue to flow. Consider it a joining comma. I have written before about how translation also occurs in fragments: word-level equivalence, grammatical equivalence, textual and pragmatic equivalence. In these parts of translation, the collection of fragments creates a continuity. I translate myself into motherhood, and as a multilingual mother, I translate between my languages and those of my children. Back and forth, back and forth: mothering and translation changing the rhythm of a narrative. Translation, not unlike mothering, is about choice and sacrifice: both a joining and an interrupter comma. I hope you too consider the interruptions, the pauses, the fragments, and segments as something unbroken, something to be considered, when joined together, a whole.

,

PART 1

Beginnings & Ends

Pragmatics: *the study of how context contributes to meaning and how human language is utilized in social interactions; the relationship between the interpreter and the interpreted*

Bite Your (Mother) Tongue

I am at the doctor's office to discuss chronic hip and groin pain. I begin to tell the doctor perhaps the scar tissue from procedures related to the births of my children are at the root of the pain and offer a self-diagnosis of nerve damage. I am cut off. 'Are you American?' the doctor asks. 'No,' I answer. I ask to be referred for a scan. 'I don't think you need one,' says the doctor. I look down and on the desk I see a box of *tongue suppressors*. The metonym for language is tongue. The tongue is the only muscle that is not connected to a bone at both ends. At one end only, it is connected to the hyoid bone, the only bone not connected to any other bone in the body. The hyoid bone holds up the tongue, above, and the larynx below. The lingual frenulum is located under the centre portion of the tongue, anchoring the tongue in the mouth and stabilizing its movements. When the frenulum is uncharacteristically short or thick, it is called ankyloglossia or tongue-tie.[41] The idiomatic use of the term tongue-tie dates to the 1500s and means someone is unable to speak momentarily. I look closer. No, they are tongue *depressors*, not *suppressors*. The words on the box blur and the meaning of a contraction of a muscle that pulls down on a part of a body morphs into silence instead. The (mother) tongue is both free and restrained.

Statistics Canada defines the 'mother tongue of a person' as the first language learnt at home in childhood and still understood by the person at the time the data is collected.[42] The definition continues (all emphasis my own):

'. . . if the person no longer understands the first language, the mother tongue is defined as the second language. If a person learnt more than one language at the same time in childhood, the mother tongue is the language this person spoke *most often* at home before starting school. The person has more than one mother tongue *only if* they learned these languages at the *same time* and still understand both languages. A pre-verbal child has more than one mother tongue *only if* the languages are spoken to them *equally*, so the child learns the languages at the *same time*.'

The 2021 census in England asked, 'What is your main language?' Only one answer permitted. The printed version of the census offered this guidance, emphasis again my own: 'If you're not sure what your *main language* is, think about the language you use most *naturally*. It *could be* the language you use at home.' *Could be. Naturally.* I have neither a mother tongue nor one main language. I speak and understand multiple languages, but not always equally. I speak English most often but *only if* I am not alone with my children or my parents. English could be the language we use at home *most often,* but I am trying my hardest for Polish to keep up while also introducing other languages. Polish is not my mother tongue, not *really*, because Poland is one of the few places where the term *father tongue (język ojczysty)* and *fatherland (ojczyzna)* are used.[i] I am mother-tongue-less, devoid of a *main*

---

[i] *Język ojczysty* is commonly translated as *native language* while *ojczyzna* is considered a *homeland* but in Polish, the word for father is *ojciec* and therefore, unlike other languages these terms are closely linked to *father* as opposed to *mother* as in, *mother tongue* or *motherland*. For a closer translation of *mother tongue* in Polish, it would have to be *język macierzysty* from *matka* (*mother*) but that term is not used.

language, without *only one* allegiance, like so many others around the world who have multiple mother tongues or main languages.

In its eminent definition, a 'mother tongue' is the language of birth, a first language, sometimes stretched out into childhood, but almost always born of a small fraction of someone's life. And yet, when a reference to the mother tongue is made, it is in a context that is vast, encompassing and often done so many years after childhood has ended. Its brevity carries a weight beyond its measure, a power it can rarely contain, and sometimes immeasurable pain.

'What signifies a "mother tongue"?' asks a mother on a popular online multilingual parenting forum. The question relates to someone attempting to persuade her that her son's *mother tongue* cannot be English, because his mother's *mother tongue* is a different language. The mother is raising her son in English, a language she is fluent in but that is not her first language, in a country where English is not the majority language. The child only knows a few words of his mother's first language but is fluent in English, the language the mother uses to communicate with him. And yet, according to a stranger with a strong yet highly flawed conviction of what a *mother tongue* must be, the child is mother-tongue-less because his mother communicates with him in a language she learnt later in life. A mother-tongue suppressor.

I once read a social media post by a woman who said her mother only spoke to her and her siblings in Mandarin when they were growing up. The mother was, in the words of the now-grown daughter, 'so desperate to preserve our language that she lost out on a relationship with us'. The children were bullied at school and when they came home, they wanted to share their experience with their mother, but she insisted on Mandarin only. If the children spoke English, she would punish them with handwriting assignments. As the children attended a school where English was the main language, it is likely they did not have the vocabulary to recount their school days in Mandarin, even if they were fluent. Bilinguals use their languages in different contexts and therefore often have different vocabularies in each language.[43] Now grown, the siblings are fluent in Mandarin and use the language professionally, but at what cost? The daughter who posted about the experience is a Mandarin immersion teacher. She has taught hundreds of children Mandarin but because of her childhood experience and the lack of an emotional and linguistic relationship with her mother, she can't teach her own children the language. Her question for the parenting group: 'How do I balance Chinese and a relationship [with my children]?' 'In one of its popular senses, the term "mother tongue" evokes the notion of mothers as the passive repositories of languages, which they pass on to their children,' writes Suzanne Romaine.[44] I am saddened for this adult daughter and her children, but I also deeply empathize with the mother's desperation at feeling she was the repository for her children's Mandarin.

As unaltered and often romanticized as the idea of a *mother tongue* is, colonialism and Christianity are at its roots. The term was allegedly first used by monks to identify a language used other than Latin when 'speaking from the pulpit' while the mother is 'the holy mother the church'.[45] In *Mother Tongues and Nations: The Invention of the Native Speaker,* Thomas Paul Bonfiglio examines the ideological history of the metaphors *mother tongue* and *native speaker*. The terms arose in the early Renaissance when nation states began to form, and the people began to write in the vernacular: French instead of Latin, Italian instead of Latin, and so on. To prove the worth of the spoken language, 'naturalized attributes' were invented around the idea of the body and the family (*native* and *mother*): language was said to be learnt at the mother's breast but at the time, the nursing mother figure was the Virgin Mary and therefore religion and the idea of Mother God were interwoven into the meaning.

In linguistics research, *mother tongue* is rarely used. Instead, the less poetic but also less emotional and less presumptuous L1 is the first language, most often defined as the language learnt before the age of three. L1 is not problem-free either as simultaneous bilinguals, those who learn more than one language from birth and before the age of three, have multiple L1s. How we identify languages and which one(s) we consider our first, our second, our *mother tongue* has consequences for how we think about the languages of the world in connection with nationalism and colonialism. '. . . mother tongue is often not merely associated with mothers' role in transmitting culture, but serves as the embodiment of that culture, ethnicity, or sense of nationality,' writes Jean Mills.[46] Internally or externally, a hierarchy is created that may affect our linguistic identity, but also how we perceive others and their language(s).

If *mother tongue* has a connotation with a mother, *native speaker* is a child of a particular *motherland*. Native speaker is often thrown around carelessly, or at least without pause, especially in educational contexts, when the term is increasingly hard to define. Who is, and by which definition, defined as a *native speaker*? By the meaning of a first language and being born in a place where the language in question is widely used, I am a Polish native speaker. And yet I would have an incredibly challenging time teaching Polish beyond an intermediate level. (I use the teaching example because educational contexts are predominantly where the notion of *native speaker*, especially of English, is prevalent.) It takes me longer to read and write in Polish than it does in English, also my *native language*, even though I learnt the latter at the age of five. It is unjust to judge someone's linguistic competence based on where they were born, and the divide between what and who is a *native speaker* versus *non-native speaker* emphasizes a deficiency, one that a large part of the world's population possesses.[47]

Native speakerism is intertwined with nationality but especially race and ethnicity, for example, when calls for English teachers proclaim 'only *native speakers* need apply' but what that means is that the person should have a specific look (white) and a specific accent, or variety of English ('standardized English' or Received Pronunciation). As educator and researcher Vijay Ramjattan examines in his work on the intersection of language, race, language learning and work, sounding *native* predominantly depends on one's racial categorization.[48] 'The "native speaker" of linguists and language teachers is in fact an abstraction based on arbitrarily selected features of pronunciation, grammar, and lexicon, as well as on stereotypical features of appearance and demeanor,' writes Claire Kramsch, noting how the abstraction is monolingual and monocultural, deeming it even more unrealistic considering most people live in multiple languages and multiple cultures.[49]

A *mother tongue*, in the context of multilingualism, only looms when there is an *other*, or a presumption of something else, often carelessly perpetuating a monolingual ideology. And yet the romanticized but consequential version of *mother tongue* is synonymous with the language of *a* or *the* mother. But do languages have a beginning and an end?[50] Beginnings are more difficult to establish because one does not know from the start if something will be worth recording. And yet, when it comes to *mother tongue*, the beginning is the *only* thing that is recorded because we associate the first language with the primary caregiver, predominantly a mother. This creates a false sense that this is it, there is only one allegiance, one true love, one identity, all to be used as juxtapositions beside a separate language, a separate culture, a separate identity. But for simultaneous bilinguals or those growing up with multiple languages like my children and like populations that make up a large part of the multilingual world, it is simply untrue. The multiple languages, or many mother tongues, are not always in conflict with one another.

In *Beyond the Mother Tongue: The Postmonolingual Condition*, Yasemin Yildiz calls the idea of one mother tongue part of a 'monolingual paradigm' and describes how the term is part of our obsession with the 'invocation of the maternal, affective and corporeal intimacy'. Although linking the mother tongue to the maternal body and, in turn, against male authority (of a *father tongue*) is praised by feminists, writes Yildiz, some feminists consider this going against the mother being separate from language and preceding it. The idea that the mother tongue comes from the mother – physical or figurative – plays into the narrative about origin and identity, often to the detriment of a mother and a language-learner, and becomes far more than a metaphor. Even when the mother in *mother tongue* is an abstract, it is overwhelmingly linked with a primary caregiver. There is a historical fantasy behind the term linking *mother* and *tongue*, writes Yildiz, who references the work of media theorist Friedrich Kittler on how bourgeois mothers around 1800 began teaching their children phonetics, the mother's mouth becoming 'the central conduit in the production of proper sounds in the mother tongue'.[51] Yildiz doesn't argue that a *mother tongue*, as defined by a first language and not necessarily one that came from a mother's body, can offer a sense of belonging and connection to a language, and perhaps a place, but, 'it combines within it a number of ways of relating to and through language,' she writes. More than one language can offer connections to family, society, identity, linguistic skill, and emotional attachment.[52]

Both the *mother* and the *tongue* in *mother tongue* are also problematic in that they, in their definitions of first language and one that comes from a mother, do not account for the different modalities of languages, or the different types of families. Many forms of language are not performed using the tongue[53] and families where the first language is not learnt from a mother, or where the caregiver does not identify as a *mother*, are excluded from this metaphorical phrase. For hearing mothers of deaf children who learn one of the many sign languages, or deaf mothers of hearing children, the idea of a *mother tongue* or a *mother language* as defined by a first language learnt from a primary caregiver like a mother leaves them behind.[54] It is a similar situation for mothers with history of trauma that may be associated with a language of the past, their heritage or home language, and one they want to avoid when raising their own children. The idea of a mother tongue linked to a mother is elusive in communities, especially Indigenous ones, where an entire generation of mothers was brutally and violently forced to stop speaking an Indigenous language. Some children in Indigenous communities, now grown, are taking it upon themselves to revitalize their Indigenous language(s), to learn and communicate with grandparents and elders who know and possibly still use the heritage language. But the generation in the middle, the generation of the mothers of the adult children, is often lost to this linguistic knowledge because it was stolen from them. Notions around first languages being 'fundamental' or strongest may also perpetuate misconceptions around what is 'true bilingualism' and the idea that to be a 'real bilingual' one must learn their multiple languages in childhood.[55]

I have my own internalized attachments to the idea and ideal of a *mother tongue*. (Look no further than the title of this book!) I am torn between how the term brings people closer to a language, much in the same way *heritage language* often does, and will never refute the lexical power of *mother tongue* with its poetic, symbolic, idealistic connotation, especially if it encourages and supports multilingualism. But idealism is the language of poetry and prose, and it is impractical in the day-to-day of raising multilingual children. I praise the beloved term for offering a deep sense of attachment, to a language, to a maternal figure, and most importantly, to multilingualism or the possibility of it. But idealism and realism must meet in the middle to allow for the multilingual paradigm of not only *mother tongue* but multiple first, dominant (some non-dominant) and heritage languages, all modalities of language, and the many caregivers a child encounters throughout their life, especially those who play a pivotal role in their multilingualism.

Tick Tock

I take my children to the Yayoi Kusama Infinity Mirror Rooms at the Tate Modern in London. The exhibit includes two rooms, both made up of mirrors, one that represents Kusama's vision of endless reflections, and the other titled 'Chandelier of Grief'. I take photos of the four of us – me, my partner and our children – amid the twinkling lights, our reflections repeating endlessly in the photograph: a deception and heartache captured in an image of time standing still, while also gone forever immediately after the photo is taken. Infinity and grief. While waiting in line for the exhibit, we start a conversation with a couple standing in front of us. They moved from the United States to London more than a dozen years earlier, when their only daughter, now in her twenties, was primary-school age. There are many great things about having an adult child, the woman tells me after hearing me lament how fast I feel my children are growing. I nod and say I am trying to cherish every moment because it is happening *too fast*, the kind of ubiquitous phrase often thrown around to make mothers feel like shit rather than to empower them. 'Oh yes,' she replies. 'I cherished every moment with her when she was young too, but it still all went by too quickly.'

,

In George Lakoff and Mark Johnson's *Metaphors We Live By* the discussion around how we conceptualize the passing of time with metaphors is two-fold: time is either a moving object or time is stationary and we move through it. In both instances 'time passes us,' the difference being that in one, we are the ones moving while it stands still, and in the other, time is moving and we are standing still. Most people believe metaphor is 'a device of the poetic imagination and the rhetorical flourish – a matter of extraordinary rather than ordinary language'.[56] But metaphor is ordinary, present in not only language but thought and action. When time is a moving object, there are different ways in which something can shift. Time flies, time creeps along, time speeds up, and yet metaphorical concepts are not about concrete images like flying, speeding, creeping, but in more general categories, like simply passing.

While mothering in the early postpartum days, I felt I was neither moving nor was I standing. Like many mothers, I dreaded night-time in the newborn phase. It was during those dark middle-of-the-night hours that time dragged on, when my body would ache, my skin would itch, and I felt like throwing up. Even now, as a mother of two young children who no longer wake me multiple times every night, it is not clear what feels more accurate: is time flying or am I the one running out of it? Mothers are continuously bombarded with phrases about losing time with their children. Even with the best intentions, the warnings are ineffective because no matter what you do, how you feel, or how much and how intensely you cherish it, time simply passes. *The days are long, but the years are short; Blink and you will miss it; Enjoy it while it lasts; Where did the time/years go?* Time, the most used noun in the English language[57], is a motherfucker.

When raising multilingual children, there is an additional clock ticking next to the standard blink-and-you-will-miss-it one. I once heard an American journalist living in Paris, when asked how raising bilingual kids was going, say, 'it is a race against time'. She had only learnt French as an adult after meeting her partner, and what the response likely meant was that the bilingual children, born and raised in France, were gaining on her French. The children would soon, as expected, since their community language from birth was French, feel more comfortable in their mother's second, likely non-dominant language. I heard a similar sentiment about running out of time from another American mother also living in France with young children who were becoming more confident in their mother's second language, surpassing her language ability in the community language, for better and for worse. The worse when there is the potential, because of a linguistic disconnect between the dominant language of the child and the dominant language of the mother, of a breakdown in emotional connection. Immigrant mothers especially fear this happening and endure it often: the child's dominant language becomes different than the mother's, sometimes when the mother is still herself learning the community language in a new country. And then there is the potential for not only a parental power imbalance between mother and child, a parent lacking authority in a minoritized language, but a loss of emotional connection[58] and often a copious amount of anxiety[59] for everyone thrown into the mix. When immigrant parents and their children communicate in a common language, studies have shown they report a higher family relationship quality, but when the dominant language of a parent and a child differs, there is less cohesion in the relationship.[60] Immigrant mothers face the pull between the heritage language and the community one all the time, because they are meant to learn a new language themselves and maintain the home language for their families, while also moving effortlessly between the two. A common thread of many diaspora-themed essays by children of immigrants, now adults themselves, and especially by those who do not speak their parents' first, and often still dominant, language is the notion of not really knowing their parents in the same way they might if they shared a common first or dominant language. But even with my own parents, in a language we share, I often think I have only ever known fragments of their beings and cannot begin to comprehend the trauma and complexity of their immigration. This is not so much a linguistic injustice, but one centred around the pain and loss as a result of assimilation and acculturation, something so few children of immigrants truly know, notably if they were very young when the family immigrated. The thought of not being able to access a caregiver because of a linguistic barrier is heart-breaking, but when I read these essays by adult children lamenting on not *truly* knowing their parents, I always think about the mothers. The immigrant mothers, whose loss of identity after not only motherhood but something as life-altering as immigration was already so great, only to be intensified by a linguistic loss of a language they should have shared with their children.

In interviews with Syrian mothers who had recently arrived in Canada, Laila Omar found that after their immigration, the mothers what she calls 'foreclosed' on their own timelines in favour of their children's futures in a new country. The mothers felt their own growth could only happen in their previous home. Time had stopped for these mothers, in some sense as women pre-motherhood, or at least mothers in their previous homes, while their mothering and caregiving roles continued through the lives of their children.[61]

In *Identity and Language Learning*, Bonny Norton highlights a study on mothers, migration, and language learning, looking at how an immigrant woman's gendered identity as mother is implicated in her investment in the target, predominantly societal language, and her interaction with speakers of that language. One of the study's participants, Katarina, immigrated to Canada with her husband and young daughter from Poland and worried immediately her daughter would grow up in a language she, the mother, did not know well. '. . . the Polish language meant more to Katarina than a link to the past. It was an essential link to her future: her ongoing relationship with her daughter and her identity as a mother,' writes Norton on the temporal connection Katarina had with Polish.[62] But English was also vital for Katarina to reclaim her professional identity and she was torn with how to balance her English language learning in the present – she noted that she felt uncomfortable speaking English in front of her daughter, who had quickly surpassed Katarina's English level – with keeping Polish as the language of the home. Katarina's story not only reminded me of my own childhood in

Canada and in the ways I could, or felt I couldn't, connect with my parents in both Polish and English, but also of the conflict between the two languages in our home with my own children. I am not learning a new societal language like Katarina or many other immigrant women, so our experiences are vastly different, but there remains a present-day conflict of how to achieve some sense of equilibrium of life in multiple languages, especially when the scales are endlessly tipped in favour of the societal language.

,

Some of the most frequently asked questions in multilingual parenting forums online consider the notion of time:

'Is it too late?'
'When is too early?'
'When will he respond in the heritage language?'
'When will she speak English?'
'How long before he is fluent in my mother tongue?'
'How long before the school language takes over?'
'When will they speak?'
'When will this feel easier?'
'When will this be easier?'
'When?'
'How long?'
'When?'
How long?

There are a few myths, misconceptions, and misunderstandings to blame for the outpouring of questions on this topic. The first being that children are sponges and *absorb* languages. This statement is often paired with *the earlier, the better* or the myth that the earlier a child acquires a language, the *more* fluent[i] or

---

[i] It is worth repeating here that 'fluency' and 'proficiency' are subjective terms. What is fluent and proficient for one person may not be considered the same for another, especially depending on domain and context.

proficient they will be later in life. Introducing a new language early on or using more than one language from birth with a child is wonderful and if it works for the family, parents should proceed without listening to any erroneous suggestions they need to wait to introduce more than one language. But as is the case with so many contradictory and paradoxical aspects of raising multilingual children, ideas around the value of early multilingualism may be just as undermining when parents fear they are running out of time or, worse, the clock has stopped, and they blame themselves for their children's lack of bilingualism.

The Critical Period Hypothesis (CPH) is largely responsible for the echoes of earlier is better, the critical acting as a synonym, for me at least, for parental anxiety, despite my knowledge around the complexity of such a hypothesis. CPH is the theory that there is an age when language acquisition crosses over a threshold to become more difficult for children, or at least in what is deemed as 'native-like' proficiency in a language. This often has to do with proficiency but also pronunciation, or, if I refer to the concerned parents on multilingual parenting forums, a 'native-like accent' in both languages.[ii] CPH is highly debated in the research, with some studies putting the cut-off at puberty, while others conclude there are too many variables to offer a clear age where this sort of change occurs. Ideas around CPH often go together with the ubiquitous *children are sponges* phrase. It is fairly common for older learners of an additional language to lack the fluency achieved by young learners, although they may progress faster than children in language learning. Children put more effort into learning a language than adults and it takes them longer; they just do it differently and have more time than adults. Children's brains do make more neural connections and there is the question of pronunciation and accent for children versus adult language

---

[ii] Accents, or rather, notions around accented speech, in all their glorious complexity, are explored in Part 2, but it is important to note here that it is a misconception that (only) 'proficient', 'fluent', or the dreaded 'true' multilinguals do not have accents in any of the languages they use.

learners, but nothing is straightforward, and each experience is singular. It is never too early and never too late to (re)learn a (new) language.

Another common myth is that simultaneous bilingual children are speech delayed, especially if they are not producing as many words as their monolingual peers. But what is usually occurring is that the bilingual children use just as many words as their monolingual peers but spread over multiple languages. The idea around critical periods are also ableist in that 'abled people expect language acquisition to take place on a very specific timeline, with limited investment from themselves. Children are expected to achieve linguistic benchmarks by certain ages . . . Then when those children fail to meet those temporal linguistic benchmarks, they are labeled with disordered language,' write Jon Henner and Octavian Robinson.[63]

There is a growing body of evidence in research that shows multilingualism has no negative effects on children with autism. And yet many families are still instructed by institutions and practitioners to drop a home language. When autistic children are denied access to learning a home language, they do not have access to the cultural and linguistic identity other children may have, and 'the consequences of imposed monolingualism on an autistic child could have detrimental effects on communication and inclusion within a bilingual family or in fact community.'[64] Imposed monolingualism also makes participation in the family social life in a home language impossible and may have harmful effects on communication and inclusion. And here too, parents and children may not only miss out on an emotional connection but the parent–child relationship may be devastatingly compromised. Ideas around the cognitive advantages of bilingualism can also be harmful for autistic individuals and their families, research argues. If the monolingual autistic person is compared with a bilingual autistic person in a cognitive experiment and the former performs *better* no matter how small the difference, the additional language(s) may be blamed, 'as if the bilingual experience does not have its own value and is not worthy of exploration unless it can offer particular cognitive advantages.'[65] Instead, the focus must be on the lived experience of the multilingual autistic person, free from deficit-based assumptions and ideologies and timelines that are preconceived and prejudiced (something I explore further in Part 3).

,

I google 'How many hours does a child need to be exposed to a language to be fluent?' It is something I have been asked before and a question I do not know, or want to know, the answer to. At least, not really. The common answer found online is a child needs to be exposed to a language 30 per cent of their waking time to acquire it. A typically developing[iii] child learns a first, or multiple first languages, by being exposed to that, or those, languages. It is not something most caregivers necessarily quantify because language acquisition happens with exposure to a language. And yet multilingual mothering in a minoritized language that is competing with a societal one, especially if there are multiple home languages, is a constant game of choose-your-own-exposure adventure. With my own children, I feel a race against time acutely, especially as my older child is speeding toward double digits. Have I exposed him to *enough* Polish? Could I have done *more*? Why didn't I do, say, teach *more, earlier*? Despite knowing that CPH is exactly that, a hypothesis, despite knowing that children learn languages at different ages, and adults learn new languages all the time and *faster* than children, my role as a *good mother*[66] is one that passes on a heritage language, that ensures my children learn and speak Polish, from the beginning. I am not exempt from the panic caused by notions of time running out.

[iii] I use 'typically developing' here with caution and hesitation. If something or someone is identified as 'typical' it means something or someone else is 'atypical' and we must move beyond these assumptions because all languaging is valid (see more in Part 3). However, in linguistics research, this term is often still used to signify a specific type of development trajectory in children.

Plus, I have a child-of-immigrants debt to pay, early enough so my parents can see the fruits of my labour of love!

,

We depend on two interrelated linguistic systems to 'anchor events in time,' writes Aneta Pavlenko.[67] The first is a lexical system that includes temporal adverbs (earlier, later), time units (day, week, year), and spatiotemporal metaphors (time flies). The second system is a grammatical one of temporality, determined through morphosyntactic categories such as aspect and tense. Languages differ in how they consider time (think: linear versus cyclical). Historically, *female time* in Western society is associated with cyclical time (biological rhythms, cycles, gestation) whereas *male time* is seen as linear, writes Lisa Baraitser, who examines the maternal experience but also how we perceive time in relation to practices of care in *Maternal Encounters*.[68] However, today everyone is dominated by linear time, even when cyclical time is still at the forefront of many women's lives (read: the impossibility of being a mother today). Women's time, or anyone with care work or caregiving responsibilities, is predominantly seen in connection with the time of their significant others. Caregiving work, like that of mothering, is continuous. Office work, in contrast, is discontinuous because there are typically set hours with breaks in the evening and on weekends. For caregivers like mothers, there is no break from responsibilities because those obligations are often in relation to other human beings who themselves cannot wait while the caregiver takes a break.[69]

For multilingual mothers, language maintenance and transmission of a heritage or second language in the home is also a form of care work that never stops. The mental load of always considering which language is being used in and outside the home, how much input and exposure is necessary and ideal, how to balance heritage and societal and school languages, and so much more is time-consuming and, often, overwhelming. In her work on Japanese American mothers raising bilingual children, Toshie Okita noted the constant monitoring of conflicts around time organization, social environment and making progress with language projects, while also allowing children to learn 'naturally'.[70] In addition to other maternal and domestic demands, language transmission is another form of supervision, even when the mothers are not physically with the children. Even for monolingual mothers, there is a constant and exhausting awareness, mostly due to societal pressures and especially in the early days of a child's language acquisition, of monitoring, repeating, counting words, engaging with a child.

Mothering children in multiple languages is cyclical and linear: the act of caregiving coupled with the way we perceive language acquisition, language development, and learning in a straight line. But language, and especially languaging, like mothering, is never direct, neat, without ups and downs, moments of pause and then revival. And yet the instructional part of language maintenance and transmission of a heritage language from mother to child is considered predominantly linear, rarely accounting for the emotional. The concept of maintenance is a 'durational practice' that keeps things – relationships, connections, networks – going, writes Lisa Baraitser, but one that is often devalued: 'Maintenance is in part generated by conditions of vulnerability that we all share, and in part by the excesses and internal logics of capitalist cultures that make maintenance so necessary.'[71] Heritage language maintenance is both vulnerable and, for some, capitalistic especially evident in what is called 'elite bilingualism' when some languages are considered 'prestigious' while others are devalued.

,

A synonym of *monitoring* is the noun *nursing*. In 2019, the artistic duo of Conway and Young created the *Milk Report*, a print piece recording the hours and minutes one of the artists, Jesse Young, spent breastfeeding for the first six months after giving birth. The total was 720 hours and seven minutes, documented line-by-line as the artist and mother clocked in and clocked out, tallying the seconds, minutes, hours. The artists printed 720 copies to be sold at £8.21 per copy, the price equal to the 2019 National Living Wage, for a total of £5916.95 once all the copies were sold. I searched how many hours it takes to learn a language. The top response: The Foreign Service Institute research indicates it takes 480 hours to reach basic fluency in group one languages and 720 (!) hours for group two to four languages.[72] The work of breastfeeding and chest-feeding and the work of language-learning (and transmitting a heritage language to children) takes time, effort, labour and is never *free*. Both are part of the economy of care, and both are predominantly performed by people who identify as *mothers*. But both are also often considered personal responsibilities and if a caregiver 'fails' to breast- or chest-feed in the same way someone, especially someone who is new to a country, 'fails' to learn a language it is the personal responsibility of that individual. In both, many factors are often at play, predominantly ones out of the control of the individual. If we consider learning a language, especially the narrative that a 'good immigrant' learns the language of the new country, it takes on average twelve years to learn a first spoken language: the first five or six from birth are for acquiring oral fluency, the next handful of years to learn reading and writing, to expand their vocabulary, to learn grammatical structures and improve pragmatic conventions.[73] And yet, in the 'fallacy of personal responsibility in language learning', it is the linguistically privileged who perpetuate linguistic domination, and in turn subordination, by considering their privilege as a personal effort and not one intertwined with and within a system of inequality.[74]

The Paradox of Loss

After my first day of Canadian kindergarten, I came home and told my parents when I spoke Polish to the other kids in the new class, they did not respond. So I tried Swedish, a language I learnt in preschool during our year in Sweden before moving to Canada. The children still did not respond. I was lucky as the class was mostly little boys so when I joined two months into the school year, when the teachers asked who could show me around, another little girl, likely relieved I was not a boy, volunteered to be my friend. This was the mid-1980s and at the time, there were no English as an additional language (EAL, but then called ESL, English as a second language) programs for children like there are now across Canada, at least not in elementary schools. I was in the classroom with all the other English-speaking children and, although I do not remember much from that time, I was likely meant to get on with learning the school language through immersion. Perhaps this was my moment of transposing myself entirely, at least for a short time, until my classmates finally understood what I was saying. Or maybe it was an early lesson on the power of having multiple languages to draw on, different cultural identities, modalities, and persisting until some sort of communication was achieved.

By the end of the school year, I had learnt English, or at least enough to carry a kindergarten-level conversation. The following

September, my parents enrolled me in a French immersion program at a different school because, my mom tells me, she thought I had a knack for languages. I wish I remembered the last Swedish word I uttered before I lost the language, moving from fluency to hesitancy to nothing at all. Was it *adjö* (goodbye)? Or perhaps *godis* (candy)? I used Google translate to find these Swedish words as the only thing I remember is *hur mår du?* (*how are you?*) and *va heter du?* (*what is your name?*) Language shift, language attrition, language forgetting, language loss, language erosion, all labels, albeit with differences, especially in the study of language attrition, for the same, non-linear, and often invisible, experience. When a language environment changes at a young age, like it did for me, there was an overlapping area of Swedish acquisition that waned, and attrition began. And since I no longer used Swedish either at home or at school, I lost it quickly. One of the great paradoxes of language loss is that, although studies have shown the languages we are exposed to as babies, even for a short period of time, stay with us perhaps forever,[75] the loss of a language, at least in its productive and active capacity, happens gradually but in the utmost deceiving way in that what seems an unhurried erosion is faster than a family realizes. Just as *effortlessly* and *quickly* as a child can appear to learn a language, a child can also, just as effortlessly and quickly, forget or lose it.

In *Life as a Bilingual*, François Grosjean writes about *dormant bilinguals*, those who revert to using only one of their languages, essentially putting the other language to sleep. It is only when the slumbering language does not wake, perhaps ever, that a language is forgotten. I could have been a dormant Swedish user for some time after our immigration to Canada but, after so many years of not being exposed to the language, it is truly lost to me. But what I love about Grosjean's take on language attrition and loss is that it is 'simply the flip side of language acquisition . . . just as interesting linguistically,' despite the attitudes toward it.[76] Language forgetting begins when the domains of its use are reduced or become absent. Eventually, the forgetting becomes a source of insecurity and people simply use it less and less. Researchers agree that before the age of twelve, language is more vulnerable, in that attrition is more likely to occur if there is a change in language situation before then. There are various factors that influence the attrition, forgetting, or loss of a language including length of residency in a new country, age of onset of the attrition, exposure, and input, but they are difficult to verify. Throw in personal attitudes, emotional factors and experiences, and things get even more complicated. The only factor that has a straightforward influence on language attrition is age of onset because there is a space in time, around puberty, researchers note, where a first language is fully acquired by a child and attrition will be less likely afterward.[77]

In *Flights*, Olga Tokarczuk describes a scene where two people, one far from home, meet in a video rental shop. One character overhears the other swearing in Polish and shares that she too is Polish. However, she recounts as she begins to cry, she married a Hungarian and forgot the language. After the Polish woman leaves, we hear from the narrator: 'It's hard for me to believe that you could forget the language thanks to which the maps of the world were drawn. She must have simply mislaid it somewhere. Maybe it lies wadded up and dusty in a drawer of bras and knickers, squeezed into a corner like sexy thongs acquired once in a fit of enthusiasm that there was never really an occasion to wear.' I wish I could say there is a tiny trace of my Swedish somewhere in one of my drawers, or in the back of the closet, but I think it is far more likely, like my sexy thongs, also acquired once in a fit of enthusiasm or more likely because I was conditioned to think I needed a pair, to be long gone.

❧

My experience with Swedish is both vastly different, considering the language was part of my life for such a short time with no emotional connection, and similar in its intensity and speed of the loss, to the way children *lose* first or home languages after immigration to a new country and to a new linguistic community. But for families where the caregivers still use the language, where it has ties to a familiar, cultural, and emotional past, forgetting or losing a language has devastating consequences for the child and the family. Sometimes, the devastation is felt most acutely, especially by the children themselves, when they become adults.

In *Cultural Memory of Language,* Susan Samata interviewed older adults who found themselves at 'the far side of language shift' (where language attrition becomes language shift). The author examined the effects of what is absent in the lives of these adults who do not know their parents' first language (PL1), whether they never learnt it as children, never fully acquired it or lost it as they grew up. The respondents all shared feelings of exclusion from language communities and an associated sense of ambivalence, but especially a general search for explanation of why things did not turn out differently for them linguistically. This at times manifested as blame, either directed at parents for not promoting bilingualism, or at themselves for not learning their parents' language.[78] In the book's introduction, Samata writes about her personal experience as a mother of multilingual children who, after a move from Japan to England as a result of their parents' separation, lost their Japanese. 'As they grew older and more aware of their linguistic position vis-à-vis Japanese, they felt this as a loss and blamed me for it; it was not until they were adults themselves that they came to appreciate more fully the circumstances that had led to our move to England,' she writes.[79]

It may seem contradictory to focus on language shift and attrition here when my goal is to maintain and transmit a heritage language but, as Samata notes, there are wider implications for looking at language shift and loss with a broader lens, and how participation in a parents' first language can occur with little language ability. A bond with a language, whether through ability or cultural memory, matters for feelings of identity, emotionality and connection within families and cultures. The acknowledgement matters for those who desire to move beyond a feeling of 'failed multilingualism' as evidenced by the many essays on the topic.[80] 'There is a celebratory attitude concerning multilingualism evident not only in popular but also in academic discourse which tends to ignore, or effectively denigrate, the individual of a migrant background who does not become bilingual,' writes Samata.[81]

But these experiences are valid and vital for understanding the results and consequences of language shift and loss, and not solely as a warning. It bears repeating that caregiving *and* multilingual childrearing do not happen in isolation. Bearing witness to stories of loss, whether they conclude with feelings of ambivalence and acceptance, or of anger, frustration, blame and a deep sense of defeat, is our collective responsibility. Feelings of isolation from a language community, or reflecting on what may have been, can be present in both caregivers and children, especially when children are older and have more of an awareness of the loss. But loss rarely occurs without sacrifice and any blame must extend to the wider systems at play, to society, to unyielding myths, ideologies, mother blaming, to how caregiving is already undervalued with or without the added element of multilingualism. We must examine all sides and levels of language shift and loss to appreciate the immeasurable consequences of treating language and human connection as if they did not matter. The cost of devaluing language and not handling it with the utmost care is tremendous and lasts a lifetime for many people.

How Does a Language *Die?*

Buried under a pile of my son's *Ninjago* magazines, I recently came across my old sociolinguistics module notes. In the pile were pages from a class on multilingualism with a section on why some languages remain strong amid social change while others are abandoned within a few generations. The answer was ethnolinguistic vitality: 'a group's ability to protect and maintain a language through intergenerational transmission, cultural practices, social cohesion, and emotional attachment to collective identity.'[82] The three pillars of ethnolinguistic vitality are status, demography, and institutional support. Also in the notes was a photo of Chief Marie Smith Jones, who died in January 2008 and was the last speaker of Eyak, an Indigenous language. When a reporter from *The New Yorker* visited Smith Jones in Alaska and asked her how she felt about Eyak 'dying' with her, she famously responded: 'How would you feel if your baby died? If someone asked you, 'What was it like to see it lying in the cradle?'[83]

Joshua A. Fishman's three-generation theory is often presented as a model of immigrant language shift. The first generation of immigrants adds knowledge of the new environmental language to their home language, the second generation grows up bilingually, and the third is commonly monolingual. Sometimes, the process is faster or slower depending on whether there are older siblings, if there is a strong language loyalty or if immigrants do not assimilate. But take away those ifs, and a language can be lost from only one generation to the next. One generation – like mother to child. But whether in immigrant or Indigenous communities, languages never simply die, and never without a multitude of factors affecting their demise. In the most devastating, yet all too common, circumstances, language users, speakers, cultures, and communities are intentionally oppressed and persecuted, overtly or covertly, writes Paul J. Meighan. Meighan examines how dominant and colonial languages are privileged over Indigenous, endangered and minoritized languages in education and policy, what he terms 'colonialingualism'. Not only are acts of oppression and repression at the root of language loss, but so too are the multigenerational and psychological aspects of the trauma associated with that oppression and the internalized deficit ideologies that govern the *value* of a language.[84]

In an overview of studies on the connection between attitudes toward a first language and attrition of that language, the authors show that nothing is as straightforward as it appear at first glance. Sometimes, immigrants may feel a powerful connection with their first language and the country they left behind, and their first language will still show signs of attrition. Or feeling *at home* in a new country may in some cases mean the affiliation with the former country is weakened. Other research has shown there are always exceptions. The overview included studies on parental attitudes, noting the role parents play in heritage language maintenance. Although the study acknowledged 'parents' emotional connection to their native language', there was no mention of 'fathers'. Mothers, however, and mothers' attitudes toward the use of a heritage language was said to have an impact on the child's language development and studies highlighted the crucial role mothers play in heritage language maintenance.[85]

❯

As I was writing this chapter, Pentl'ach, a Coast Salish Indigenous language that had been considered extinct since the 1940s when the last known speaker died, was declared a living language once again. The Qualicum First Nation on Vancouver Island's east coast reconstructed the language, its grammar and vocabulary, using old documentation and recordings and by finding similarities between the language and other neighbouring Indigenous languages. More than anything, the reclaimed and revitalized status of the language, as acknowledged by the province of British Columbia in Canada, was part of affirmative action in recognizing the atrocities of the residential school system and the role it played in the violent language loss of so many Indigenous people. It was also a recognition of identity for many of the members of the Qualicum First Nation.[86]

But language reclamation and revitalization of an Indigenous language does not occur without its own burdens; it is a meeting of the present with a devastatingly painful, colonial past. As Pia Lane writes about the reclamation of Sámi in Norway, language revitalization can be a silencing experience: 'For many, the process of taking the language of their parents and grandparents back is characterized by a strong investment, but also emotional tensions, and this process may be so demanding that they give up and reside in silence.' The process can be both empowering and defeating in a multitude of ways. Self-silencing may even occur when language reclamation is met with memories, or ghosts, of colonialism. And even within communities, those reclaiming a language may feel an overwhelming sense of fear and judgment and being met with criticism for not already knowing, or being fluent, in the language, or speaking it in a 'non-authentic' way.[87] Lane writes about this impossibility:

> 'A sense of belonging and ownership may strengthen a desire to learn an Indigenous language, but it can also be a dual-edged sword. The expectancy of reclaiming what one ought to already possess ... places new speakers of Indigenous languages in a precarious position. When reclaiming an Indigenous language, new speakers find

themselves in a space of tensions and possibilities as they strive to reclaim a language of their roots in order to become a speaker for the future. Through this process, they might be confronted with their own or their parents' silence and feeling of insecurity and shame.'[88]

Beginnings, Again

Stories of communist Poland are my family heirlooms. When I was younger, visiting family in Poland, conversations between my grandfather, father and/or one or both of his brothers inevitably turned to who was and wasn't a communist, who had to pretend they were affiliated with the party to get by or ahead, and who feigned not being one when really they were. I never considered the power and pain of these stories, the resurfacing of past ghosts, until recently, and I know I cannot begin to understand their weight and the trauma of that part of history in Poland. But my favourite story is the one from when I was three years old, still living in Kraków, about a year before we immigrated to Canada via Sweden. My father would take me to shops and we'd do a rehearsed back-and-forth anti-communism performance. In the store, he would ask me what we could buy and to that, I'd answer 'Nothing, because the shelves are empty.' 'Why are the shelves empty?' he'd ask. 'Because the communists are here!' my toddler voice echoed. His other favourite activity, one he now admits was dangerous and irresponsible, was taking me to the main square in Kraków, still one of my favourite places on earth, where, sitting on his shoulders, I would make the peace sign with my small, three-year-old fingers. But that V didn't symbolize peace, it meant victory. Victory over the soldiers patrolling the square, over the communists, and over communism. We would do laps around the main square like that, me with my arms outstretched and my fingers erect, while armed soldiers looked on, he has told me many times. For my parents, immigrating to Canada and escaping communism *was* a victory, but it was also great loss. The triumph was always contingent on my parents' only child speaking, writing, reading and *being* Polish in the new country. Yet victory looks vastly different for many immigrants. Victory over a dangerous regime through immigration sometimes means never speaking the language of the past, of a former home, again.

My parents and I made our first trip back to Poland in 1990, after the fall of communism, more than a handful of years after we left; it was too risky to return before then. The arrival area at the airport was packed with families and friends waiting for loved ones. I imagine many of those passengers were also returning after prolonged absences. There was a cheerful bustling, people were eating ham sandwiches wrapped in paper, yelling across the crowd, running toward loved ones who'd emerge at the gate, ragged and exhausted after long flights. I remember being in awe at all the strangers speaking Polish around me. The only time I was immersed in Polish in Canada was at the Polish church or at the weekly Polish class for the children of immigrants. But there, it was always the same people, I knew all the faces. The crowd in the Polish airport was made up of strangers all speaking the same language. My aunts and uncles were loud, excited, lining up to hug us and all still so young and vibrant.

After that, the three of us made the trip most summers. For years, there was always someone waiting at the arrival gate for us, and the sound of Polish permeated my pores as I stepped off the plane. For a long time, the joke in the family was that the first place I wanted to go after arriving in Kraków was the Main Square in the Old Town, the *Rynek Główny*, the same place where I sat on my father's shoulders while he circled the area to protest communism before we moved. The square was always a bustle of activity: tourists sitting at overpriced restaurants, young people smoking at the cafés that line the square, toddlers holding out tiny fistfuls of breadcrumbs, screaming with joy as pigeons surrounded them, residents making their way somewhere in a hurry cutting through the square. Year after year, I made the pilgrimage to this place, walking the square religiously, buying overpriced amber jewellery and later expensive lattes, soaking in the energy I felt from the place and the language. I imagined my parents sitting in the smoky café off the square they had frequented during their university years, performing at theatres my father pointed out. Most of the buildings and businesses of my parents' youth were still around back then. But, like language, places and people change. Businesses fold, buildings are torn down, family members get older, some die, you have your own children. Fewer and fewer family members wait for you at the arrival gate, if at all. Like language, notions of home are also about time, not just place: a specific moment, a saying, a conversation, a summer in a birth country.

In *Braiding Sweetgrass,* Robin Wall Kimmerer writes about the Indigenous language Potawatomi and how at a yearly tribal gathering, she listened to the last remaining fluent speakers of a language that was stolen from her people. Only nine fluent speakers in the world remain. After the gathering, she felt even more compelled to (re)learn the language and covered her living space with Post-It notes, each one with a new word or phrase to learn and memorize. She likened having so many Post-It notes in her house to the experience someone might have before a trip abroad, learning the basics of a language by matching objects to words in the new language. And yet, as she notes, she was not going away, she was coming home.

)

One summer, for the first time in nearly four years, we visit my parents in Canada and my hope is that a week with them, speaking almost exclusively Polish, will boost my children's non-dominant language. It is not Poland but a similarly immersive environment as we spend most of our days conversing in Polish. More than anything during the visit, I want someone else – my parents – to take on the responsibility, sometimes the burden, of practising my children's non-dominant language with them. My daughter breaks into Polish often, rarely needing to be coaxed. She moves between English and Polish confidently and her vocabulary is vast in both languages. My son is reluctant to communicate in his non-dominant language, often a point of contention between us. As a linguist and multilingual parent, I know the way to encourage your child to speak a heritage language is to make it fun, to create a need and to never push or threaten. The mother in me, desperate for my effort and work to be worth it, to come to fruition, pushes, threatens, begs, pleads. When my son continues to reply in English or when I realize his vocabulary is missing many Polish words I thought he knew, I tantrum and storm out of the room, whispering under my breath that I must do something to fix this before I run out of time. And then I feel ashamed of myself and vow to change and to trust in him, and me. Sometimes my son, who can't remember a word I consider simple, *leg*, for example – 'How do you not know the Polish word for leg,' I want to scream, but stop myself – finishes the same sentence with a word I don't ever remember using myself, *ulga* (translation: relief). *Relief. Sweet relief.* I surrender to the process and promise to never again question his, and my, multilingualism. But of course, never is an unrealistic time frame.

It is equally staggering to see how my children at times are learning my first language far beyond me, and how I learn anew through them. At around three years old, after watching a cartoon in Polish, likely *Bluey*, or *Blue* as the Polish dubbed version is called, my daughter began to call her plastic pull dog toy *bułka z masłem* (bun with butter). I couldn't figure out what it meant until I sat with my kids while they watched Polish cartoons and heard the expression, that means something is easy. The same thing happened with *sorki* and *nawka* when my children began to use the Polishized version of *sorry* and *Satnav* prevalent in children's television programs, especially *sorki*. My son often tries to *Polishize* English words by pronouncing them in ways he thinks sound Polish. It is endearing and adorable. As a parent who uses media to support my children's heritage language learning, I will forever be grateful to the children's television programs and movies that have the Polish language option.

)

In her series on pregnancy, photographer Janet Russek photographs women at close range, their breasts and bellies becoming abstract lines and shapes. In one black-and-white photograph, Russek shows a close-up of a pregnant belly, occupying the entire frame, hands only showing slightly at the bottom of the photo. The bellybutton protrudes and there are faint rings around the bottom of the belly, skin stretched from growing a human, a spiral of delicate marks as evidence. The photo reminded me of another artwork I saw a few years ago with my children at the Hayward Gallery in London. It was at an exhibit about trees and the image was by Giuseppe Penone, a wall drawing, part of his series *Propagazioni* meaning *propagations* or spreading. Tree rings tell us how old a tree is and what sort of climate it endured during each year of its life. Penone begins each drawing with an image of a fingerprint in the centre, a unique representation of every being. It is the act of drawing around the fingerprint, circular line after circular line, like the rings of a tree, that sets the propagation in motion. One of Penone's goals with the time-consuming work, according to show notes, is to 'concentrate time in one space'. Like a pregnant person's stretchmark-laden belly, tree rings symbolize a narrative, a language, gestation, a timeline.

On the left side of my cheek, near my hairline, I have a small patch of melasma that appeared during my first pregnancy. Also known as hyperpigmentation, it is sometimes called the *mask of pregnancy*, as melasma can appear courtesy of the hormonal changes that happen when you're gestating a baby. It is one of my many *birth-marks* of becoming a mother, some visible, others not. Although not apparent at birth, in the first few years of my life, a constellation of moles appeared on the right side of my face. I search for them in photos of me in Poland as a toddler, in Sweden as a four-year-old and finally in Canada as a five-year-old. They appeared or darkened one by one, with every move and every new language: Polish, Swedish, English and two for French. In elementary school, I was teased by a boy named David for having five moles in the shape of an upside-down house on one side of my face. A kind teacher, overhearing the childhood taunting, clarified they were not moles but beauty marks. I think about that upside-down house, a home, a cluster of languages on my face. Both of my children have inherited their mother's predisposition to beauty marks. My children and I often play a game – can you match your beauty mark to mine in the exact same place on our body? So far, my daughter has two beauty marks on her face, one on each side, one for each language she knows.

I learn birthmarks are called *voglie* in Italian, which also means *longings*, after reading an essay by Sabrina Orah Mark in *The Paris Review*.[89] Orah Mark writes that she and her sister, although they have different fathers and a large age-gap between them, have the same birthmark, the same longing their mother had for them. I think about the longing I feel for my children and how I think about them grown, no longer small, and how much I feel that yearning for them the way they are now, the way they were only a few years ago as a toddler and a preschooler. I consider my children's Polish a birthmark because it is mine alone to give, but I also know it may only be my longing and not theirs. Longing comes from the idea of length, a prolonged dwelling in or of something.

Will you love me forever? How long will you love me? Why do we have to die? Will you die before me? One of my children asks at least one of these questions every couple of nights. *Yes. Forever. I don't know. I hope so*, I respond. Then one of them will say something funny and, because they know I write down their sayings and the charming phrases and words they utter, tell me to 'for sure write that down in your special book, it was a good one.' I want to hoard languages for my children, keep count of their words and funny sayings, while also stockpiling for them memories of myself as their mother, as if the two are so tightly bound that unravelling one from the other is unbearable. I maintain a present, haunted by both the past and the future and I record the beginning(s) because I am certain they are worth recording. 'You will teach my children Polish one day,' my son likes to say. To which I always reply, 'I hope so, but you will also teach them yourself.'

PART 2

The Familiar & the Foreign

Phonetics: *the study of the production and perception of sounds, or in sign languages, the equivalent aspects of sign*

Phonology: *the study of sound patterns and their meanings, both within and across languages*

The Sound *of* the Fury

I feel a wave of nausea wash over me as soon as I walk out the door. It is mid-December, and I am rushing off to the university for my phonetics tutorial, a make-up class for the one I missed the week before because of my toddler son's Christmas concert. I am twenty-six weeks pregnant with my second child, my belly deliberately concealed by an oversized sweater and wool coat. During the forty-five-minute tube ride, a strange sensation begins to spread across my abdomen. I make my way to the university, determined, and in hindsight delusional considering how ill I feel, to attend the tutorial. We begin the phonetics class with guttural sounds,[90] common in many languages but rare in English. The tutor asks us to try our deepest 'of the throat' sound, not an easy feat for those unaccustomed to using one, and an unfortunate experiment for someone who is on the precipice of being sick. Before the second go, I get up, run out of the class into a nearby stairwell and vomit behind a fire extinguisher. That evening, I am admitted to the hospital, defeated by pain, and terrified of the unknowns before being diagnosed with a burst appendix and rushed into surgery. I undergo an appendectomy while my daughter remains in utero. For a long time after, I worry about the stress the appendectomy and subsequent complications mean for my unborn baby. After her birth at thirty-nine weeks via caesarean section, and months after, the uneasiness continues. Every cry, although few and far between, is a worry she may be scarred by a memory from that traumatic time (traumatic for me, at least). And then there is the c-section – stay with me for a brief language-related digression – a procedure that is not any less *natural* than a *vaginal* birth. And yet linguistically, it remains on the opposite end of an invisible language spectrum with a caesarean birth *here*, and *natural* birth *there*, rather than the more linguistically and physiologically balanced *abdominal/c-section birth* and *vaginal birth*.

There are endless articles quoting often flawed studies with major limitations about how c-sections affect a child's development. 'Children born by caesarean section could have developmental delays in their grammar, numeracy, reading and writing . . .'[91] proclaims one article. Toward the end of that same piece: 'I think this is one of these things that unfortunately, if taken at face value, without an understanding of the complex methodology that was at stake and the limitations of the data that are in the study – will scare people and upset people unnecessarily.' *Complex methodology. Limitations of the data. Will upset people unnecessarily.* Beyond birth, breast- and chest-feeding also fall victim to this type of publicity: 'Breastfeeding may "rewire" babies' brains in ways that help them acquire language and eventually learn to read, according to a new study' or 'It's no secret that being breastfed correlates to having higher verbal and language function.'[92] *May rewire. Eventually learn to read. Correlates.* I am well versed in how media regularly sensationalizes scientific studies, especially in the headlines, but nevertheless, when a study comes out about how high levels of cortisol, the stress hormone, during the third trimester of pregnancy may improve speech and language skills in the first three years of a child's life, I latch on to the data.[93] I can finally flip the worry narrative. The stress of the appendectomy while my daughter was in utero didn't hurt my baby, it was good for her speech and language skills! The difference between correlation and causation is a mother looking to be absolved, or one surrendering to societal blame.

❧

By around the twenty-eighth week of pregnancy, a fetus may be able to detect sounds, especially its gestational mother's voice from the outside and through vibrations against and in her body. The noise is muffled by amniotic fluid, like listening to voices under water, so prosody, the rise and fall, melody, and rhythm, are the prominent features of what the fetus hears. Prosody separates continuous sound into words and phrases through cues, pauses and stress. Babies whose mothers use sign language are exposed in utero to a similar sing-song rhythmic movement of their mother's hands.[94]

Outside of the womb, newborn babies recognize their birth mother's voice and show a preference for it. Their cries have patterns of intonation like the language they were most exposed to in the womb: French infants cry on a rising note while the cries of German babies have a falling (higher to lower) melody.[95] Babies whose mothers speak tonal languages such as Mandarin (four tones) and Lamnso, the language of the Nso (eight tones), produce more complex cry melodies and higher melodic variation, compared to German babies.[96] A study on multilingual mothers, who used multiple languages while their babies were in utero, revealed that after birth, the babies showed no preference between the languages their mother used.[97]

In the cave-like darkness of the newborn phase with my first baby, so tired and torn to shreds – literally and emotionally – I was less concerned with deciphering which language my baby was crying in, or what his cries meant, and more with, how do I stop them? Contrary to my stunned silence, my newborn would wail uncontrollably, often. My son's cries meant everything and nothing. Often the only thing that would interrupt my baby's cries was turning on a hair dryer, its white noise mimicking the sounds of the womb. My son's language preference was the BaByliss Turbo Power 2200. Before I admitted defeat to the hair dryer, I tried to appease with nipple after nipple – boob, bottle, dummy/ soother – and when sucking didn't work, I tried all four of the other S's: swaddling (helped), side-stomach position (didn't), swing (only if the *swing* was me or my baby's father) and finally, intense shushing (worked!). The international phonetic alphabet

(IPA) symbol for the shhh sound in English is /ʃ/: a curve much too delicate and smooth for the sound I was making; extreme shushing was my maternal language. In Polish, it is more of a ćśś closer to the word for silence (*cisza*). IPA for Polish ć/c(i), /tɕ/: an arc overhead and a complicated bend, turned on itself like I was on myself. A more accurate symbol for what I was doing. I was a multilingual *shusher*.[i]

From the moment babies are born, they face an in-between in language. Babies cry in the patterns that mimic the language they heard in the womb[98] but babies are also universal listeners, or what neuroscientist Patricia Kuhl coined 'citizens of the world', who can discriminate all the sounds of all languages, unlike adults, who are 'culture-bound listeners' who can discriminate the sounds of their language(s) but not those of others.[99] A popular example is Japanese adults who cannot distinguish the difference between an English /l/ and /r/ whereas Japanese babies can. But this changes at around six months, when babies become better at discriminating the sounds of the language(s) in their environment. The language(s) the baby is exposed to take control and others fade away. If a baby is being raised as a simultaneous bilingual, in two or more languages from birth, this occurs for both languages. Sequential bilingualism is when one language is learnt first, followed by another, perhaps at school or after a move. For children who acquire languages simultaneously from birth, dominance in each language will depend on exposure and input: how much they are exposed to the language, how much they use it, where and with whom, and eventually how useful and important they believe the language to be.

Receptive bilingualism (annoyingly sometimes called 'passive bilingualism') is understanding a language but not necessarily being able to produce it. Active or productive bilingualism is understanding and producing two or more languages. There

---

[i] Only recently did I discover there is now a popular product with the same name that mimics the human *shhhh* sound for babies. Clearly, a missed business opportunity on my part!

is a common misconception, or rather a lack of clarity for parents, in that they don't necessarily consider receptive (passive) bilingualism as 'true bilingualism' (a highly subjective moniker I come across often, also sometimes called 'real bilingualism'). This is linked to notions around how 'balanced bilingualism' or communicating in one's multiple languages all at the same level, often in the same way, is the goal for many parents. But balanced bilingualism, at least how many caregivers I interact with define this as a 50/50 split, is highly unlikely because people acquire and use their different languages in different contexts all the time.[100] (I am using 'bilingualism' instead of 'multilingualism' here as often the balance comes down to two languages, but notions around balanced use of languages can also manifest in families where there are more than two languages in use.) And yet 'balanced bilingualism' is the anticipated outcome for most families, especially if the parents believe that if they just do everything right, follow all the 'rules', be diligent about the strategy and effort, things will turn out the way they expect. (Despite knowing as much as I do about multilingualism, I too often still cling to this unrealistic expectation.) And then, when it does not turn out the way caregivers expect, because in most cases it is an unrealistic expectation to begin with, parents, especially mothers, feel guilt, stress and shame about circumstances that are affected by a multitude of factors.[101]

Interpret & Affirm

Jessamine Chan's dystopian novel *The School for Good Mothers* is about a society that punishes mothers for 'parenting mistakes'. Mothers are sent away to look after life-like dolls where they must train to be 'good mothers' before possibly returning to their real children. 'The mothers must pay attention to both pitch and vocabulary . . . the mothers must narrate everything, impact wisdom, give their undivided attention, maintain eye contact at all times . . . The mothers practise like singers running through scales. If the dolls babble, the mothers must try to turn those sounds into words. Interpret, the instructors say. Affirm. Help her make meaning,' writes Chan. A make-believe society that is, as in many dystopian works, too close to reality. The description of the linguistic acts the mothers are forced to perform with the dolls are a form of *motherese*. Like *mother tongue*, the root of motherese is *mother*. Also known as *baby talk, infant-directed speech (IDS), child-directed speech (CDS), caregiving speech*, and *parentese*, I have yet to see *fatherese* included in any list.[102] Moving away from solely the *mother* (again), let's call the high-pitched, slower enunciated type of speech people use when talking to babies and children 'IDS'. IDS has many key features: a sing-song pattern, vowel hyper articulation, slower pace, exaggerated prosody, simple sentences, and high pitch. Vocal timbre, or quality of sound, also shifts for mothers when communicating verbally with their babies, or sometimes other babies, animals (guilty!), even plants.[103] Although at times irritating to the ear, IDS plays a part in language development and occurs across many languages and cultures. It can be a wonderful communication tool and many babies love it, but it is not present in *all* cultures, not in *all* languages, and not *all* mothers use it or should be made to feel they have to. For some neurodiverse children, certain features of baby talk – heightened praising, exaggerated intonation – may even be upsetting if they become overwhelmed by the sensory stimuli.[104]

Alessandro Duranti, Elinor Ochs, and Bambi B. Schieffelin examined how acquiring language is embedded in the act of being socialized to be a member of a social group, and how each process affects the other. They note that in America, parents are told they should sing, speak, and read to their babies in utero, and are encouraged to buy products like a belt with a battery-operated microphone that a pregnant woman straps on with the instructions, 'Speak in a loving tone'; 'Read a story that you will also read to the baby after birth'; and 'Do not speak too loudly or you will disturb the baby.' Babies do become familiar with their mother's voice in utero, but it is muffled, and there is no evidence reading to babies in utero will benefit either mother or child.[105] As Ochs and Schieffelin point out in earlier work, in many communities and cultures, infants are not even considered 'primary addressees' until they produce 'recognizable utterances'.[106] (Ochs conducted field work with Samoan children, while Schieffelin examined the speech activities of the Kaluli people of Papua New Guinea.)

Baby talk is prevalent in many languages and cultures, but it is not universal, or at least not all its features. Speakers of K'iche or Quiché, a Mayan language of Guatemala and Mexico, either make no pitch distinction in speech to young children, or often lower the pitch slightly compared with adult-to-adult interaction.[107] In Quiché culture, a high pitch is often used to address persons of a high status. Quiché form of baby talk does have diminutives, another feature used in IDS across many languages.

Baby talk or IDS becomes highly problematic when conflated with 'quality input' and especially when mothers are made to feel if they do not perform IDS, they are at best not setting their children up for success, and at worst harming them. As I was writing this chapter, yet another headline popped up about motherhood and language, for an article about how being a 'chatty mother' while pregnant could give your baby a head-start in language.[108] (Has there ever been a headline about 'chatty fathers'?) Linguistic interventions, or proclamations that *earlier* or *more* is always better, no matter how well meaning, do not address the bigger societal pressures and problems around support systems, housing, quality childcare, paid maternity leave, discrimination (including linguistic discrimination) and so much more, especially for mothers in marginalized communities. The idea of what is and what is not 'quality input' in children's language development is not only subjective but a dangerously slippery slope. A vital question to consistently ask is how quality is defined, and who decides. Ideas and assumptions around 'quality input' are part of standardized ideologies where marginalized and racialized children and families are the ones consistently told they have linguistic deficits.[109]

Psycholinguist and research scientist in children's language development at the University of Arizona, Megan Figueroa fervently advocates putting an end to notions around what is defined as 'quality input' in children's language development. The features christened 'quality' – one-at-a-time conversational turn-taking between caregiver and child, longer utterances, more words – are not universal characteristics, and 'quality input' is a value judgment, she writes.[110] A judgment about what is and is not quality input is a language ideology mirroring how users of a language are considered by others and society, and not in fact about the language, or the input, itself.[111] Plus, children learn and acquire spoken or signed languages around them without implicit instruction.[112]

Notions around 'quality input' for children go hand-in-hand with the 'thirty-million-word gap' (also known as 'word gap' or 'language gap'), courtesy of developmental psychologists Betty Hart and Todd Risley's claim that by the age of four, some children, predominantly racialized and marginalized children, are exposed to thirty million fewer words than other children (quantity conflated with 'quality'). The 1995 study that launched a multitude of 'thirty-million-word gap' discourses was not only flawed in its design, but the researchers were white while the participating lower-income families in the study were Black, a 'by-product of institutionalized racism'.[113] An example of 'quality input' from the 1995 study I want to share here because of my disbelief that something would be measured in this way, is that if a parent responded to a child's reply to an initial statement within less than five seconds, the interaction was marked as having higher 'quality input'. In addition to how destructive it is to measure caregiver and child interactions this way, and to blame families who need societal support and not linguistic interventions, there is a lack of awareness around how things like the flaws in standardized tests, and how underlying racist and colonial beliefs influence ideas around what is linguistic deficiency.[114]

For Figueroa, who is Mexican American and an outspoken critic of the 'word-gap' rhetoric, her work around dismantling discriminatory and racist ideologies on language and multilingualism is both professional and personal. Figueroa once wrote online about how, when she considers – sometimes daily – she can never have a redo of her childhood to learn Spanish from her father, there is a profound sadness, a 'flesh wound'.[115] Figueroa's father was born to Mexican immigrants and speaks both Mexican Spanish and Chicano English, but did not pass Spanish on to Figueroa, who grew up in the U.S. Her father 'removed Spanish from the equation,' she tells me, because not only did he experience corporal punishment in school in the U.S. for speaking Spanish, but he also considered it an obstacle to success for his daughter.

I ask Figueroa why she thinks deficit-based rhetoric like the word gap is still so prevalent in research. (The morning of our interview, I see the 1995 Hart and Risley research on the word gap cited in a paper by a linguist I respect, and not long ago I also saw it cited in an important book about language loss and revitalization.) 'I think the reason is because we're so used to mother blaming,' says Figueroa, making the link between capitalism and the blame women and mothers endure for not doing what society considers 'their one job'. 'We're convinced that it's the individual that you need to fix and not . . . we need to change our school systems, or we need to change the standardized tests, or we keep measuring individual faults with systemic tools.' The language gap discourse is an easy sell, Figueroa says, in a way that people want to help, but again linguistic interventions are not what marginalized families and those living in poverty need. Notions around a 'language gap' and 'quality input' may do double damage to multilingual families: if families believe children need *more* ('quality') words in the societal language, the heritage/home language will be pushed even more aside in favour of the majority one.

During our conversation, Figueroa reveals a vulnerability around her own English–Spanish multilingualism (she is fluent in Spanish now, having learnt the language at school) that is both unsurprising, because fear and the fear of judgment run deep for many of us, while at the same time startling because she is a linguist well versed in linguistics research. She offhandedly mentions she worries if she has children they will inherit her accented Spanish. 'There's something stopping me from saying I speak Spanish,' she says, 'I feel like I'm much more of a receptive bilingual than productive because I've stopped myself from producing because I'm so ashamed of, you know, my accent.' I am sharing Figueroa's comment here, a comment I will return to later when writing about caregiving and accent, because it is a testament to the fact that no one is immune to the constant messages women, mothers and multilinguals in patriarchal, colonial and monolingual-mindset dominant societies come across. Women and mothers are consistently barraged with messages about what they are perceived to lack, or the damage they may do to their children if they do or if they don't do this or that, as if a multitude of factors do not affect both caregiving and language.

In the UK, Ian Cushing, senior lecturer in critical applied linguistics, also examines how notions around the 'word gap' between economically disadvantaged children and wealthier ones have been normalized in schools, under colonial logics and, often, in the guise of social justice.[116] When marginalized children are forced to change or give up a language or variety, there is both blame and a sense of fault placed upon children and their caregivers. The inequalities faced by children of colour from low-income families are produced and perpetuated by educational inequalities, white supremacy, capitalism, and colonialism and not by, and within, the family and its language practices. The question that is never asked: how and why are educational systems set up to prevent marginalized children from thriving? Deficit-based notions like the 'word gap' maintain racial and class hierarchies prevalent in the UK and elsewhere, and condemn marginalized families and speakers for failing to use *enough* words, or not the *right* words, or for using language that does not adhere to what is considered 'standard language'. Although an in-depth exploration of heritage/home language and the intersection of education/schooling is beyond the scope of this book, it is vital to consider the role schools and education systems play in linguistic diversity by either supporting or, in many instances, impeding multilingualism, often in order to uphold standard ideologies.[117] Putting the onus solely on parents to maintain and transmit heritage language is itself social inequality and a 'denial of inclusive education' and may result in families abandoning the home/heritage language in favour of the societal/school one.[118]

I have mentioned 'standardized language' or 'standardized language ideology' (often referred to as 'standard' but it is worth considering how, rather than it being 'standard', it is, in fact, *standardized* by those in power) a few times now without fanfare or definition, partly to show how easy it is to slip into discourse because it is commonly accepted that 'standard' means 'normal', 'ordinary', 'everyday'. ('Standard' as equated also with 'quality'.) I once had an argument with a friend when she tried to convince me she expected her daughter's nursery teacher to speak a certain variety of English because that was the 'right way' to use the language. When I asked her who decides what is right or wrong and why the way the nursery teacher was speaking

English was not 'right', the only thing she said was 'because it *just is* the right way.'

'The standard language ideology (SLI) is a bias toward an abstracted, idealized, homogenous spoken language which is imposed and maintained by dominant bloc institutions and which names as its model the written language, but which is drawn primarily from the spoken language of the upper middle class,' writes Rosina Lippi-Green.[119] As Rob Drummond outlines in a detailed and thought-provoking chapter on how 'standard' English came to be in *You're All Talk: Why We Are What We Speak*, it was not because of some 'linguistic battle of quality and fitness for purpose', but rather a 'historical accident and business acumen'. The accident being the printing press set up in London by William Caxton and, as a result, a sense of a 'better' language used in print meant perceptions shifted for spoken English.[120] The standard (or standardized) language ideology is prevalent in institutions, especially in educational settings, and linguistically marginalized groups are often convinced they should adhere to a 'superior language', despite the fact that no language or dialect is fundamentally better or worse than another.[121]

In *Linguistic Justice: Black Language, Literacy, Identity, and Pedagogy*, April Baker-Bell explores how standardized ideologies cause language subordination, what she calls Anti-Black Linguistic Racism, and how linguistic hierarchies and racial hierarchies are interconnected:

'That is, people's language experiences are not separate from their racial experiences. Indeed, the way a Black child's language is devalued in school reflects how Black lives are devalued in the world. Similarly, the way a white child's language is privileged and deemed the norm in schools is directly connected to the invisible ways that white culture is deemed normal, neutral, and superior in the world.'[122]

Baker-Bell uses 'White Mainstream English' instead of 'standard English' to demonstrate how white ways of speaking become normalized. When young Black people are told to, or made to feel they must, code-switch into White Mainstream English, for example, it is another form of Anti-Black Linguistic Racism, and a 'justification for racist language policies, practices, pedagogies, and classrooms.'[123]

Growing Up Bilingual: Puerto Rican Children in New York is an expansive multigenerational study of the Puerto Rican immigrant community, *el bloque*, in New York by Ana Celia Zentella. Over twenty years, Zentella examined how multilingualism thrived in this community and how the young women there were multilingual in Puerto Rican Spanish, Puerto Rican English, African American Vernacular English, New York Spanglish. And yet, because standardized varieties of English and Spanish were not part of their linguistic repertoires, the women's multilingualism was considered a failure and detrimental to their futures.[124] It was never about language, code-switching, or language mixing, but about the social, societal, and educational injustices members of this community faced, as well as how varieties such as Spanglish were considered inferior:

'At the root of the inability to validate the range of language behaviours that thrive in communities like *el bloque* is the belief that there is only one correct or 'pure' form of a language that everyone should speak, and that a true bilingual never mixes language. But a language is not a collection of vocabulary, sounds, and grammatical rules divorced from the geographical, ethnic, racial, gender, and class identities of its speakers.'[125]

The participants in Zentella's two-decade study went on to have children of their own and she examined how each of them communicated with their offspring in different ways, drawing on various linguistic repertoires depending on their personal circumstances with partners and extended families. The mothers predominantly used English with their children because, like so many others in their community, they were not immune to 'the messages of linguistic inferiority that bombard working class speakers of Puerto Rican Spanish, and which make the demand of "your language for your children's successful life" seem like a fair trade.' For this reason, and the unexpected enormity of the task of passing on spoken and written Spanish, language attrition was 'predictable' for the next generation in this community.[126]

It is a paradox faced by many caregivers who are barraged with messages about being linguistically inferior in a societal language, while at the same time being expected to nurture multilingual environments. Languages become adversaries, as do experiences from the past and hopes for the future. Caregivers, predominantly mothers, are stuck in the middle:

> 'Those who blame caregivers who do not insist that children respond to them in Spanish ignore the extent to which members of the first generation hope to spare the next generation the educational, employment, medical, and legal problems they endured – problems attributed – often unjustly, to their lack of English skills.'[127]

Is That a British Accent I Hear?

Over three weeks last summer, my children's accents were examined and commented on to an unprecedented degree. This is not new and I have embroiled myself in too many futile discussions on the topic to give it much thought anymore. It is not the discussions themselves that bother me as much as I am left in disbelief at how committed most people are to their opinions even as I share research evidence disproving their ideas. But these three weeks were singular as they highlighted precisely how accent is in the ears of the beholder.

Toward the end of our two-week trip to Canada last summer, a Canadian friend asked me if my London-born and raised children thought it was funny the way everyone around them spoke English while we were away. Considering they hear a version of Canadian English from both their parents every day, no matter where we are, I said not really. This spurred a comment from another friend who noted my children's British-English accents were 'so strong'. Some friends and family singled out one child over another, telling me that this child 'definitely' has an accent but perhaps the other one 'does not as much'. This all despite my explanations that the younger child has yet to master certain

English phonemes because they come with age, and why she sounds different than her brother. During the same trip, another friend, a Canadian-American who has spent considerable time in the UK, told me she was surprised my children didn't have 'more of a British-English accent'. (As we were only in Canada for two weeks, and my children are still young, it is unlikely they were accommodating or shifting their accents to accommodate their interlocutor, a common occurrence.) A couple of days after returning to London from Canada, we ran into American friends. Like us, the couple have resided in the UK for more than a decade and have three children, who to me, sound considerably British English, a contrast from their parents' American-English accents. After hearing my son ask me something in English, my friend turned to me and, unexpectedly, as we were not discussing accents, said she can't believe how he has no trace of a British-English accent. During these three weeks, to my ears, my children sounded the same every time they spoke. Does it matter if my children sound Canadian, British, like Londoners or a mix of everything? Should it bother me if someone expects them to sound a certain way because of where they live? The short answer is no. But the long, and more important, one is about how these encounters in only a three-week period exemplified how differently an accent is perceived depending not on the speaker(s), but on the listener(s), on the context, and even on the geography.

When someone posts a 'funny' meme about someone's accent, when children make fun of the way their immigrant parents sound, when people imitate an accent 'for fun', they likely never take into consideration how for many people, that 'funny/cute accent' prevents them from getting jobs, from accessing parts of society, from living lives free of prejudice and discrimination. Linguicism is the linguistic discrimination based on the way someone speaks, writes, or communicates. Accentism is a part of that discrimination, judging someone and discriminating against them because of the way they sound. Recent studies in both the UK and the U.S. show accent discrimination is prevalent in the workplace.[128] In the UK, there is a hierarchy of accent prestige, something I only learnt after moving to London, a signal of socio-economic status.[129] (This is not unique to the UK and a grotesque example in the media of how this occurs in the U.S. is the now-defunct Gawker Media's 'America's Ugliest Accent Tournament'.) In the UK, it is against the law to discriminate against anyone because of 'protected characteristics' including race, nationality, ethnic or national origin but there is no legislation explicitly stating it is discriminatory to treat someone differently because of their accent.[130]

In *English with an Accent*, Rosina Lippi-Green defines accent as 'loose bundles of prosodic and segmented features distributed over geographic and/or social space', or 'a way of speaking'. Prosodic features include intonation, stress patterns, tempo, pitch contours, upswings, and downswings, while segmental features are how consonants and vowels are pronounced. Accent refers to pronunciation, while dialect or variety refers to pronunciation, but also vocabulary, grammar, and language use. Sets of sounds and sound systems differ between and within language(s). If we consider how children acquire their first spoken language(s), it makes sense these sounds inform and influence a language that is learnt later in life. Many languages do not share sounds, so you can imagine how difficult it is for Mandarin, German, Polish and other language users to say 'th' when that sound is brand new for them in English, or if the English sound is almost the same as one in their language but not exactly. Signed languages also differ greatly and not only is American Sign Language, for example, a different language than British Sign Language or Irish Sign Language, there are accentual differences among sign language users depending on their language communities.[131]

Accents are also multimodal: textural, gestural, visual, inciting questions about difference, order and power, authors of *Thinking with an Accent* argue:

> 'Accent does more than denote; it calls out modes of relation, of speaking and listening, laying bare the very logics of representation, identity, and interpretation. Vocal and visual stresses are typically understood to distinguish particular bodies when, in fact, difference only emerges

through comparison. An accent is an accent precisely because it stands apart from what surrounds it.'[132]

Think of terms like *foreign accent* or *strong* or *thick accent*. And then ask: foreign to whom? Strong or thick for whom? There is no such thing as *bad English* because *good* or *proper English* is indefinable; English cannot be *broken* because what would it mean to speak *whole (unbroken) English*? When someone identities a *foreign accent*, the foreign is contained to the identifier while at the same time, the person with the accented speech, depending on where they are, may also consider themselves, for that instant, unfamiliar. Accents amplify differences and are markers of both belonging and othering. Like *mother tongue*, accent only exists when there is an *other*.

In 'Everything is Accented: Labor and the Weight of Things Unsaid', Anita Starosta writes that rather than people *having* accents, accents are events, linked to labour and temporality.[133] The person *with* the accent is *without* the accent of the other, lacking because they are not from *here* or are from *there*. In speech, the work is of muscles that have been trained for years to pronounce certain words in certain ways, and the accent, or rather accents, are in that moment unique to a time and space and only for those specific interlocutors. Perhaps, the entire idea of *lacking* should be eliminated to consider how each person, with their own accented speech, has something to gain from the other. Both parties have a responsibility to themselves but especially to one another: 'When speakers are confronted with an accent which is foreign to them, the first decision they make is whether or not they are going to accept their responsibility in the act of communication,' writes Lippi-Green.[134] Plus, the judgment of how someone sounds, of someone's language, is 'a covert way of judging not the delivery of the message, but the social identity of the messenger'.[135]

Growing up in an immigrant community, I was acutely aware of how 'foreign' accents in (Canadian) English are judged, scrutinized, and discriminated against. I remember, albeit affectionately, discussing – yes, *judging* – with other Polish friends the 'cute' ways our moms said something in English with their 'Polish accents'. It is a memory I am not proud of as it now feels like every other form of discrimination, but these auditory memories are also a source of immense comfort derived from a childhood immersed in a loving and warm immigrant experience. In Canada, I never considered how I sounded speaking Polish, but when I visited Poland, I was made acutely aware I sounded *different*, my dominant English phonology infiltrating my Polish. I was often warned by well-meaning family members, especially not long after the fall of communism, I might be taken advantage of monetarily because people will place me as being American. I feel a heavy sadness when I remember all the times in the past I apologized for my Polish, especially conversing with someone who had grown up in Poland. It happened frequently when I first moved to the UK and met many other Polish speakers. 'I am fluent, but I might sound different because I actually grew up in Canada,' I would bare my linguistic scars as if to say, I am not whole but please take me anyway. I eventually stopped, after a Polish friend told me the first time we met that she had no idea I hadn't grown up in Poland. I am ashamed I needed the affirmation. It was my internalization of all the native speakerism, mother tongue, accentism, and standard ideology bullshit!

And yet I have immense privilege in that my Canadian-English accent when I speak English, although often questioned or othered and misidentified as American, is not stigmatized in the UK. I have bilingual friends whose Polish phonology permeates their English (some would say they have 'Polish accents' when they speak English) and they have experienced discrimination because of it. Regardless of where I grew up, I could, and do, sound like a multilingual when I speak each of my languages because it is a prevailing myth that 'real bilinguals' have no accent in their different languages.[i]

---

[i] Multilinguals may have accents in all of their languages and, depending on a multitude of factors, not only may a first language influence a subsequent one, but a second language or one learnt later in life may influence a first language. Like a 'non-accent' a 'real bilingual' does not exist. For more of a discussion on this, see: Grosjean, François, *Bilingual: Life and reality* (Harvard University Press, 2010): p. 77.

After nearly a dozen years living in the UK, most of my accommodation, or how I shift my style of speaking to accommodate a British-English interlocutor, is lexical: lift for elevator, football for soccer, coriander for cilantro. As for pronunciation, I remember one embarrassing moment with a neighbour discussing spring gardening when something came over me – a moment of accommodation, or perhaps intimidation as this was a woman who presents herself with an air of superiority complete with an RP English variety – and instead of my regular Canadian English *to-may-to*, I felt my lips and voice working in defying unison to say *to-mahhh-to*. (In)famous in our building for her candour, the neighbour shook her head and, as if I had somehow offended her (maybe?), said, 'Can you *please* not say it that way and just say it the way you normally do.'

Mother May I?

I came across an article in an online parenting magazine recently by a mother who was upset about her young Brooklyn-raised children not having her New York accent.[136] It was an interesting meditation on how we want our children to have something of us, to be part of us, to sound or communicate like us, not unlike how I want Polish for my children. The author noted her children are fifth-generation New Yorkers so they *should* sound like New Yorkers, like she does. The linguists she interviewed explained accents don't work in that way and children are influenced by the way their peers and wider society sound and communicate, even if initially they sound like their primary caregivers. The article analyzed the changing New York accent and how, even though the author's children remain in the same place they were born and raised, they do not sound the same as their mother, who was also born and raised there. (There was lamenting about the old New York versus new New York that, at first, was jarring but made sense when considered in the wider context of how language, culture and a sense of belonging somewhere are rife with nostalgia.) The essay covered accent 101 ground: accents are not inherited, they change and adapt all the time, and the way we sound is often associated with not only generations before us, but also with a place (something I return to later in the book).

I thought of this piece in juxtaposition to the countless times I have come across mothers worried about the opposite: their children will inherit their 'immigrant accent'. Or mothers who worry about passing on a language other than the societal language if they learnt that language later in life and do not consider themselves 'native speakers'. The difference in these examples is the New Yorker who wants her to children to sound like her, because she sounds like many of the people around her, in a place where the New York accent, or a version of it, is prevalent. In other words, she is *allowed* to be proud of her accent. In her neighbourhood, she uses a familiar accent, one that has a covert prestige, as opposed to an overt prestige that, for example, a Received Pronunciation accent has in the UK because it is celebrated by wider mainstream society. When a mother is in a place where the accent is *othered* or *unfamiliar*, or if that mother has experienced discrimination, linguicism or linguistic racism because of an accent that does not possess overt prestige, it is highly likely she will try to help her children avoid a similar experience. And no one can, or should, blame her. This brings up the vast and complex topic of a mother's confidence in her multilingualism, and what happens when something, someone, her lack of confidence or especially fear or worry for her child, stops her from using multiple languages, a new language, or a first language with her children.

I was once told by a family member my use of Polish diminutives with my young children had a time limit. If your children only learn the diminutive form, they said, your kids will eventually sound 'uneducated' when they get older and speak in 'cute' Polish. I was a child when I left Poland and my Polish exposure growing up was predominantly from adults as I used English with my peer group, even in our Polish immigrant community. My linguistic world of Polish is laden with diminutives because in many ways, my world stopped growing in Polish when we left Poland and when English became my dominant language, Although, my lexicon has diversified and grown exponentially since having children, by not only using Polish more than before, but by being exposed to new vocabulary through my children.

After my family member noted my use of diminutives in Polish, I considered how I had never said 'doggie' or 'horsey' to my children in English because, to my ears, it did sound odd and condescending. But in Polish, my childhood had such a grip on my language, a permanent imprint at a specific time and place that *pies* (dog) was almost always *piesek* (doggie). (The English language is also vastly different in its use of diminutives, and in Polish words may even have multiple degrees of diminutivization.[137]) My increased use of diminutives was also a result of mothering young children. I was damned if I didn't, because IDS speech is 'good' for language development, the message is reiterated by researchers and media, and babies love it, but also, damned if I did – for too long.

English with an *English* Accent

Shortly after relocating to London, I began working as a writer at a fashion company. I have few happy memories from that time, except for meeting some excellent people. One of them was Pooja Kalyan, my desk neighbour, who made me laugh daily and whose pronunciation of *water* with its elongated vowels and soft whispered *t* was fascinating for this Canadian new to London. Although I had written about multilingualism many times before and lived in a multilingual and multicultural world my entire life, I was still a few years away from studying linguistics and learning about the significance of regional English variation in the UK. It was only then I began to comprehend what variation *within* a language meant on a lexis level, where different parts of the same country use different words for the same thing, on a sentence level, in the way someone structures a sentence and, especially, in pronunciation.

Pooja grew up in Hounslow, close to Southall, amid mostly first- or second-generation Indian immigrants. Her mother emigrated from Singapore, her father from a small village in India and Pooja and her brother grew up on a council estate (social housing). She attended a school she calls 'the neighbourhood school for bad kids'.

One summer, she attended a drama camp where she learnt how to project her voice, about articulation, tools to express herself, and how to project herself 'eloquently', she says. Through another school program, Pooja interned at the National Portrait Gallery and eventually communicated daily with prospective donors. She became acutely convinced, not only as a person of colour but as someone who is petite, often called 'cute' and considered much younger than she is, she needed to change the way she sounded to 'sound clever or more adult-like', she tells me. Unless she was speaking with her immediate family or accommodating someone else's accent, her code-switching, or rather style-shifting, as it was within one language, took on a more permanent pattern into a Received Pronunciation (a.k.a. the Queen's English and associated with power and prestige in England). She was attempting to fit into a professional world where she felt she needed to sound a certain way, something she had been conditioned to believe. Varieties like RP and the status associated with them maintain an entrenched class system, and language is used to uphold barriers between social classes.[138] Certain accents are perceived consistently as being *more* prestigious, or *more* 'nice-sounding' or *softer* for no reason except many hierarchies and stereotypes of accents are built up and into societies over time, through existing attitudes that are passed on.[139]

What is the most interesting aspect of her accent and style-shifting, says Pooja, is that it wasn't until she moved to New York for four years as an adult that she experienced a type of othering like never before: Americans could not wrap their heads around someone who looked and dressed like her and who had an English accent, of any variety. For Americans, especially in her professional world of tech, Pooja was supposed to sound either American or Indian, but not a variation of British-English.[140] Accent and language are always personal and political. As a successful professional who makes it her mission to take up space in the boardroom and to advocate for other marginalized people, Pooja is proud of her roots but doesn't know how else she could have achieved her professional goals without, at certain times, shifting or *reducing* her *original* accent. (I italicize *reducing* and *original* here because it is vital we consider *reduced to what?* And *original* refers to Pooja's Hounslow accent and the way she sounded as a child growing up there, but the way we sound changes all the time throughout our lives for different reasons.)

It is infuriating and devastating when an accent or language variety change comes as a result of discrimination or being instructed to, as educator, researcher, and advocate against accentism Vijay Ramjattan writes, 'reduce an accent; neutralize an accent; eliminate an accent; lose your accent; control your accent – there is a range of brutal and disdainful ways to describe what can allegedly be done with an accent.'[141] The idea of accent reduction signifies that one accent is 'better' than another in the guise of being 'understood'. It is one accent simply replacing another. But what about someone's identity and ethnicity? Is that too meant to change? It is never about *just* the accent, as Rosina Lippi-Green writes (emphasis author's own):

> 'Accent reduction courses make an implied promise: *Sound like us, and success will be yours. Doors will open; barriers will disappear.* There are two problems here. The first is the claim that it is possible to 'eliminate' an accent, which is reminiscent of magic creams to remove cellulite and electromagnetic belts to make undersized children grow. The second, almost more disturbing, implication is that the discrimination is purely a matter of language, and that it is *first and primarily* the right accent which stands between marginalized social groups and a bright new world free of racism and prejudicial treatment.'[142]

Accents are highlighted while we listen and not when a person speaks. It should never be about accent reduction but rather *accent recognition*. The judgment of someone's accent needs to be turned toward ourselves to examine reasons we are judging in the first place, and instead of focusing on the way someone sounds, concentrating on how we listen. At the same time, I know how unjust it is to expect individuals to not feel they must shift, particularly if they consider themselves outsiders, or especially when their safety is at risk.[143] No one should have to code- or style-switch for the sake of others or to avoid discrimination or linguistic racism. Style-shifting and especially code-switching is a form of oppression, particularly when the discrimination and prejudice runs deeper, as it almost always does, than the way someone sounds. Code-mixing and shifting also sends the message that one language or variety is inferior, and we should all work to dismantle such beliefs. When people enter into dialogue, they both accept a 'communicative burden'. When communication breaks down, it is predominantly due to someone rejecting their responsibility.[144] There is a prevalent myth that there is a 'non-accent or neutral accent', especially for those who have spent their entire lives where most people sound like them:

'Thus, it is not surprising that many individuals do not recognize the fact that for spoken language, variation is systematic, structures, and inherent, and that the national standard is an abstraction. What *is* surprising, even deeply disturbing, is the way that many individuals who consider themselves democratic, even-handed, rational, and free of prejudice, hold on tenaciously to a standard language ideology which attempts to justify restriction of individuality and rejection of the *other*.'[145]

❜

In a lecture given at the New York Public Library, later published in *The New York Review of Books*, Zadie Smith says it never occurred to her moving to Cambridge, 'a smaller, posher pond, and almost univocal', for university would affect her linguistic connection to Willesden, the north-west London neighbourhood of her childhood she calls 'a big, colourful, working-class sea':

'I thought I was adding Cambridge to Willesden, this new way of talking to that old way ... For a while, that's how it was: at home, during the holidays, I spoke with my old voice, and in the old voice seemed to feel and speak things that I couldn't express in college, and vice versa. I felt a sort of wonder at the flexibility of the thing. Like being alive twice. But flexibility is something that requires work if it is to be maintained . . . I regret it; I should have kept both voices alive in my mouth. They were both a part of me, but how the culture warns against it!'[146]

It is Smith's note of being alive twice that moves me, as if one self must die for her to live again, live a *new* life. And yes, the wonder, sometimes the burden of two lives, of two existences, of *here* and *there*, also entails a form of flexibility. Smith's shift was obviously not simply a loss of litheness but was a multilayered modification for reasons that changed her professional and personal trajectory. 'How the culture warns against it!' is the cautionary tale of deviating from 'the standard' English, or rather, from the 'univocal pond' that is considered *better* than the 'working-class sea'.

The Myth of a Monolith

When variation within a language other than English exists, especially in a place where English is a majority language, the discrimination may be deceivingly two-fold, layered one atop of the other: a 'pro-multilingualism' mindset with caveats, and only if it is the *right* variation. 'We are not a monolith,' says Diandra Morse, a social worker, mother raising multilingual children, Black Latina, and an ardent bilingual parenting advocate (@bilingualplaydate on Instagram). Morse is Dominican American based in the U.S., raising her sons with her partner in Spanish, and is prolific online, sharing ideas about how to raise bilingual children, about the mental load of multilingual parenting, while also advocating for what she calls 'humanizing language' or connecting language to culture. 'We think that is part of the humanization of the languages that we present Spanish, as in like every country speaks Spanish the same way, and these are the right ways to speak Spanish, and these are the right words to say,' she says of the many different varieties of Spanish, including her own Dominican Spanish, that are overlooked, ignored and often stigmatized. 'And if you say it any different variation, it's actually wrong and it's not a "good Spanish".'

Morse advocates for moving away from ideas around how language is fixed, or that it must be taught like a math problem in the classroom without taking into consideration cultures, histories, emotions, personal connections, changes, and imperfections. The highly problematic bilingual and dual-language Spanish programs in the U.S. come up in our conversation as an example of where varieties of Spanish are consistently stigmatized. That is if Spanish heritage speakers even make it into a dual-language classroom, a highly unlikely occurrence considering the programs are infiltrated by white middle-class families in gentrified American neighbourhoods looking to add Spanish to their children's resumes. Something similar is happening with French immersion programs in Canada where, according to a report in *The Globe and Mail*, affluent white families drive demand for French immersion programs often as resumé-building capital for their children, while the languages of immigrant diasporas are ignored in educational settings: 'This has created a landscape where officials and parents are struggling to redefine what equitable education looks like,' note the authors.[147]

If heritage Spanish speakers do make it into Spanish-program classrooms, excited to use their home language, they are often told their Spanish variety is not *right*, not *good enough*. 'But the students, who are monolingual English white don't have that. They get the celebration of like, oh my God you said *"amarillo"* . . . so good, but then the other student doesn't get that same praise, and the fact that people are not like, what is going on? Like, why are we OK with that differential treatment?' asks Morse. And this creates not only a sense of shame and frustration for users of the many different varieties of Spanish but can push families into language shift faster if they do not have the educational resources to draw upon and are constantly advised their language, specifically their variety of a language, is *wrong* or *invaluable*.

Nelson Flores, associate professor of educational linguistics, who explores experiences of racialized students in bilingual education programs and examines how language and race are co-constructed, notes that one way to dehumanize Indigenous and Black populations is to call into question their language practices. These ideologies remain prevalent today, and the inadequacies students may already be feeling around their Spanish as they enter school are, devastatingly, often only emphasized. Ironically, the bilingualism of Latinx children is most marginalized and 'belittled' in Spanish classrooms or in bilingual programs:

'You have already, these insecurities that children have been socialized into, not through any fault of their own, but through broader societal discourses around language and the fact that oftentimes, they're made to feel that Spanish is an inferior language. Then, they come into a classroom where a Spanish teacher is using Spanish in ways that seems completely foreign to them and suggests that the Spanish that seems familiar to them is somehow wrong, or incorrect, or other negative deficit frames. That sends a message to a child that their use of Spanish isn't good.'[148]

Not long ago online, a clip was going around after Mexico's men's soccer team won the Gold Cup. An ESPN Deportes reporter in California went over to a young boy wearing Mexico's green jersey to interview him about the game. He called the boy the future of Mexico and asked him his name in Spanish. The boy looked confused and, in English, asked if the reporter was asking his name. In the background, producers could be heard saying in Spanish the child doesn't understand, 'This is a generation that does not speak Spanish.' The clip went viral, and people quickly began blaming the child's parents for not teaching him Spanish. Other people made fun of the young boy, calling him a *'no sabo* kid', a common phrase meant to shame English-dominant Latinos and Latinas. The phrase has gained popularity, especially online, and is a play on the ungrammatical form of *'no sé'* (*I don't know*), insinuating a child who is not proficient in Spanish would likely conjugate the verb incorrectly. When the clip of the boy at the football game went viral, people added, 'Don't be like this *no sabo* kid, teach your children Spanish,' as if parents, in any heritage language minoritized in a society, don't agonize over this constantly. The *'no sabo* kid' is another example of blaming individuals for language loss or attrition when the systems at play are much bigger and stronger than one immigrant family, especially in a monolingual-minded country like the U.S. (There are even posts online of parents shaming their own children, calling them '*no sabo* kids'.)

'Capitalism has ingrained us with, if you work harder, you'll get there; if these parents who speak Spanish *really* wanted their kids to speak Spanish, they would work really hard at it . . . they would find a way,' says Morse. 'And no, it's not *they*. It's not a personal family, familial problem. It's a societal problem and I feel like that's where we need to shift.' Languages are not an addition for most families, they are part of the human lived experience and identity. 'They don't see it as like, imagine if everything was in Spanish and you were the English speaker,' says Morse. 'What would you do to make sure that your child had access to English because you are in a Spanish speaking [environment]?'

Interpret Me

French artist Camille Henrot's 2019 watercolour was on display at Goldsmiths Centre for Contemporary Art in London, as part of an exhibition titled *Unruly Bodies*. I had seen the work online before, part of a different exhibit, titled *Mother Tongue*, and part of a series called *System of Attachment*. The mother is all head and breasts, reminiscent of a serpent ready to devour its prey against a blood-red background with streaks of darker hues, a metamorphosis of blood turning into dried remnants. The baby, with its full body, reaches up while the mother's mouth, ravenous or perhaps simply ennuied, envelops the baby's head, on the verge of swallowing it. One art critic noted the work refers to a child's curiosity about the 'mother's organ of speech, entering the mouth as a way to enter into language.'[149] The work is called *What Did U Say?*

,

I find the softer, comforting (read: less dystopian) side of *interpretation* in the secret language with my children. It is on our own terms and only we can decipher it. When I say secret language, I consider both the language of childhood (*scabetti* for *spaghetti, elepant* for *elephant, aminal* for *animal*) and our

Polglish.[i] Here, I am not so much an interpreter as simply an interlocutor because interpretation happens for another. Mothers are often interpreters for, and of, their children's language. The interpretation predominantly happens for others, as if they should be lucky enough to know the mother–child private language or, at the very least, try to do the work mothers do. 'What did she say?' someone asks if they didn't understand my daughter. I often see a look of despair spread across my daughter's face as if it is her fault someone doesn't understand her, won't *really* listen to her. It is not *you*, I assure her as I interpret while moving the conversation along swiftly.

These encounters remind me of a part-time job I had at university. I was a standardized patient (sometimes called a simulated or sample patient, or medical actor). (If you grew up watching *Seinfeld*, as my partner did, you might, as he does, use Kramer, who was a standardized patient with gonorrhoea in one episode, as the point of reference.) The reality of the job is there is no improvisation, and each case comes with a detailed write-up and bio for the actor to follow. You must never break character. One of my most memorable cases was a daughter whose mother was admitted to the hospital awaiting a diagnosis. The mother did not speak English and her daughter became the interpreter. The case was not about diagnosing the mother, but to teach medical students how to interact with patients who did not speak the societal language, when a professional interpreter was not present and instead the interpretation was done by a family member. The main point of the case I remember is the medical students were to always address the patient and never the interpreter[ii], or me,

---

[i] Also known as Poglish or Ponglish for Polish and English, like Spanglish.

[ii] My use of 'interpreter' here is not in the professional sense because all patients should have access to medical interpreters who are trained in medical language and systems. Interpreters are highly skilled and trained and not simply someone who speaks the same language as the patient. In the UK, the National Health Service has the legal obligation to provide interpreters and translators. Interpreters work with spoken or signed language; translators work with the written word.

the daughter. I was working with another standardized patient, an actor in her fifties, and although we both spoke French, we could not use it in case one of the medical students also knew French. We made up a nonsensical vernacular no one, not even the two of us, could understand and used it back-and-forth during the exams. Many of the medical students performed by the book, talking to my actor mother in English, never looking away from her face while waiting patiently for me to interpret. Others acted as if she did not exist, her words incoherent and therefore her body invisible.

Only now do I see the parallels in this medical case not only with the invisible mother, but with how immigrant children are often family interpreters. Also known as *language brokering*, children and youth from immigrant families translate and interpret materials or meetings for their parents if the parents feel they lack proficiency or fluency in the societal language. For the children, it may affect well-being and cause anxiety[150] and for the mothers it can be a case of losing parental respect, breaking the mother–child hierarchy. Parent–child roles are reversed and, although it isn't always a negative experience, when there is parental disempowerment paired with a child's unpleasant or uncomfortable encounter of language brokering, the entire family's well-being is at risk.[151]

,

A month after he turned two, my son said his name for the first time and by then, he could say more than a dozen words, split up between two languages. One day, while we were talking about the colour orange in Polish, he began to correct me, saying that it was not *pomarańczowe* but *orange*. I explained that yes, in English it is *orange* but in Polish it is *pomarańczowe* and asked him why he was so certain I was making a mistake. At the time, his keyworker at nursery spoke Polish and the management and staff were supportive of children speaking different languages at home but also during the day at nursery. I eventually realized my son was convinced *orange* was *orange* because when he said the word in Polish at nursery and was around staff who did not speak Polish, they assumed he could not pronounce the word yet and corrected him in English. That week, I wrote two lists of words for the nursery staff: one with all the Polish words he knew (with pronunciations in brackets) and the other with the English ones.

Jajko (yayko) – egg
Koń – horse
mleko – milk
lalka – doll
ryba – fish
Krowa (krova) – cow
(*Cheese, turtle, toast, coffee (kokee), walk, blue, apple, water, moose, puppy, pool*)

Like most multilingual children, my son did not know everything in both languages, it was a mix of the two, across both languages. Sometimes, he would code mix or shift, a common experience for bilingual children where they use multiple languages in the same utterance. There are times now when I cannot remember a word in a certain language and my children remind me. They too are interpreters, our roles reversed. I keep a lengthy document (currently, seventeen pages) on my desktop with the funny, interesting, adorable things both my children say and have said over the years. *Lolo* was once *ice cream*; *instructions* were *constructions*; *earmuffs* were *winter earphones*; *consequences* were *consonations*. When I once asked what *moon* was in Polish, my son replied, unsure, *moon-a*. *Dance* was once the combination of *dance* in English and *tańcz* in Polish: *dańcz*. When my son began to read, my funny document expanded with his written-to-spoken word pronunciations.

There is a common occurrence online and in comment sections of posts where caregivers, predominantly mothers, share funny things their children or they themselves said in childhood. Often these threads have hundreds of comments, all sopping with nostalgic sentiment. The mothers say they never want the adorable saying or phrase to stop and if, or rather *when* because children always learn in their own time, it does, they will miss it *so much*. The saying becomes part of the family vernacular or *familect*, something the parents, children, extended family sometimes use long after the child is grown.[152] These utterances are peepholes into a childhood, a linguistic memory.

There are also family languages used by adults too, a back-and-forth that only certain members know. I once read about a mother and daughter both adults, communicating with one another. The mother was suffering from dementia and the daughter would know if her mother was *there*, as in her old self, the effects of the dementia on a wished-for pause, by the way the two said goodbye on the phone and whether it was *their* familial and familiar greeting. My mother and I also have our own form of goodbye, one that my children sometimes use with me or her, an intergenerational *familect*. There was a recent social media thread, ahead of American Thanksgiving when many families are visiting one another, grown children returning 'home' to their mothers, about the funny things moms said growing up. Many of the replies were from people whose mothers had died, and after sharing a funny word or phrase, the post ended with, 'I miss you, mom.' The mothers were no longer alive but the funny words and sayings – the *familects*, or rather *motherlects* – lived on.

In multilingual families, as often noted in studies of family language policy[153], similarly to what occurs in monolingual families, a multilingual familect or multilingual family repertoire may be part of a family's language practice that makes use of various languages. Family members may create family – biological, chosen, extended – through multilingual familects or multilingual family repertoires in everyday use.[154] I consider my own immediate family in the way my monolingual partner supports our bilingualism by using Polish terms here or there to emphasize something, what one linguist calls 'adopting my voice' in order to demonstrate a united parental stance.[155] The four of us, my partner and our children, use Polish words, and sometimes even made-up words and phrases, to enforce our family's identity, our own personal language practices and repertoires, and our connections to one another. My partner has, throughout our parenting years, and long before when it was just the two of us, been on-again and sometimes off-again the language-learning Duolingo app to learn Polish. I extend this idea of the multilingual familect here to the sound of the Duolingo 'dong ding'. Whenever I hear it, it means he is on his phone, learning Polish and in turn showing our children a united parental front in our family's multilingualism.

Proper is as Proper Does

I adore reading the threads and posts of the funny and cute things people's children say during their early language acquisition years. There is often overlap and many of the 'made-up' words are similar, if not the same – a perfect example of how similarly developing children follow comparable trajectories when acquiring language. In English, most children will begin with *elepant* because *ph* is a phoneme learnt later. And when I say 'learnt later' it means you usually do not have to correct children, they will learn on their own, and in time. And yet I have noticed these funny, cute, endearing words and phrases, all part of childhood language development, are often labelled *mispronunciations*, or sometimes *errors* and *mistakes* rather than simply *early pronunciations*. Children understand speech sounds before they can produce them and there is a pattern, a phonological process, in how they learn speech sounds or signs. Deaf babies acquire language the same way babies acquire spoken language if they have access to a full signing language. If deaf babies do not have access to a sign language, it is language deprivation.[156] One of the most famous examples of the phonological process in spoken language is the *fis phenomenon*, discovered by Jean Berko and Roger Brown. An adult asks a child what they are playing with. The child replies *fis*. When the adult enquires about the *fis* the child repeatedly tries to explain to the adult that it is a *fis*, producing the *fis* but meaning *fish* and not what the adult, who is mimicking the child, is saying. It is only when the adult says *fish* and no longer copies the child's *fis*, does the child agree.

,

Phrases that make me sad when I hear someone say them to a child:

> *'Where is your volume button?'*
> *'Volume off.'*
> *'That is not how you say it!'*
> *'Big girls/big boys use their words.'*
> *'Big girls/boys don't speak like that.'*
> But especially, *speak properly.*

,

In one breath, caregivers say they never want their children to stop saying things a certain way because it is another symbol of a fleeting childhood, while at the same time there can be a trepidation, a feeling of responsibility when it comes to the idea of mispronunciation, especially for multilingual families. A family member once made fun of the way I (mis)pronounced some words in Polish. We were at a family event, and he kept on referring to the way I said something, implying that I was saying it in a very infantile way. In my twenties, I was confident enough not to let it affect me or my Polish, but that was not always the case. Some years earlier as a teenager, I overheard a family friend making fun of the way I read a Polish book to his children because of the way I (mis)pronounced something while reading. He didn't know I overheard him, and I never mentioned it, but I thought about it for a long time and remember feeling a burning embarrassment when I left the family's house that evening. I felt my biliteracy was something to be ashamed of because I did not pronounce a word in the same way he did. What do we hope to gain when we correct someone's pronunciation or grammar? This question is especially poignant if the language user or speaker has been understood and communication has been achieved. Is it a personal satisfaction or, in fact, the belittling of someone else who may leave the conversation feeling defeated and embarrassed? Consider it judgmental gatekeeping where someone has the power to determine the worthiness of someone's else's speech and language use.[157] Why and for what? (Some people appreciate being corrected and may perhaps even desire it. In classroom settings, this is expected to a degree, but I am predominantly referring here to everyday conversations.) But let me go back to the idea of *properly*.

While writing this chapter, a friend coincidentally asked me to go see George Bernard Shaw's play *Pygmalion* at the Old Vic Theatre in London. Written in 1913, the play is about Eliza Doolittle, a flower seller in Covent Garden who, one rainy evening, encounters phonetics professor Henry Higgins. Higgins, along with Colonel Pickering, decide to transform Eliza from Cockney flower girl into a high-society London duchess complete with a posh or 'proper' accent. The two men not only change Eliza's English language variety from Cockney, associated with a lower socio-economic status, to an RP accent, they also change her appearance, clothing, the way she presents herself, and eventually the way she exists in the world. At the end of the play, Eliza realizes to the full extent that by changing the way she speaks and carries herself, she has completely altered her sense of identity and belonging, and in a way her freedom. (*My Fair Lady* with Audrey Hepburn was based on the play.)

In *Communicating Gender*, Suzanne Romaine notes how as much as *Pygmalion* is about the British class system, it is also about gender. Romaine references linguist Julia Penelope's work about how, in the term 'mother tongue' for example, it is how men have held up the ideal state of purity not only for language, but for women. The connection between 'proper English' and 'proper women' (or lady) is not a historical accident:[158]

'It's one of the crucial connections inherent in the logic of patriarchal thinking. Just as men have asserted that their descriptions and idealizations of women are accurate, so they have made their descriptions of English seem plausible, even valid. If a language isn't pure, it is described as "bastardized" one that has been "debased" or "corrupted". Just as men claim that women need protection from their predation, so they claim to "protect" English from the predations of their "inferiors" – the poor non-native speakers of English, and women.'[159]

'Correctness in speech has been associated with both femininity and upper social status,' adds Romaine. And this too has influences on multilingualism and especially language shift. Romaine offers the example of how languages such as Welsh, Gaelic, Sámi and Breton were not passed down from mother to child, especially in rural areas, because English, Norwegian, Finnish, German and French became associated with modernity and higher social class. 'Those aspiring to be ladies had to escape both literally and figuratively from their status as rural peasants by leaving the land and their language behind.'[160] In the case of Breton, some women, involved in the Breton militant movement, learnt and used Breton as an act of liberation from French oppression, demonstrating how the same language can be both a symbol of oppression and liberation depending on the beliefs of those using it.[161] For the language shift from Sámi to Finnish in Finland, the driving force for Sámi women was the concern for their children and a pressure to assimilate. Schools regularly sent messages home for families to speak Finnish in the home, not Sámi, and the language was forbidden in schools.[162] Mothers had to make an impossible choice about maintaining the Sámi language: resisting oppression, and protecting their heritage, or protecting their children from discrimination and hoping for a better future for them. The mothers were required to be 'guardians of non-majority language maintenance,' but also 'innovators toward language shift'.[163]

۹

In 2017, a few months after my daughter was born, and the first time I left her for a few hours, I went to a lecture by Deborah Cameron, professor of language and communication, titled 'Language and the problem of women's authority'. It was a pivotal moment for me as a woman, linguist, mother, and especially mother to a daughter, hearing Cameron speak about how women are told they lack authority around the way they communicate, when the real problem is the public silencing, overt misogyny, and implicit sexist bias. I remember Cameron noting the many examples of articles, the same ones that would appear regularly in my inbox, on how women apologize too often, or how they are told they need to use language that is more 'empowered' and 'empowering'. Cameron often writes on the topic of the 'deficit model', the prevalent idea in society that women are not achieving their full potential because of their 'weak and unauthoritative style of speaking'. Some examples are too many 'sorry' or 'just' or 'ummm' but also vocal fry (a way of speaking at a low pitch with a characteristically creaky sound) and uptalk (a rising intonation at the end of a sentence).[164] As was made clear in the lecture, and as Cameron reiterates time and time again in her writing, women are not the problem, and these types of messages are not 'empowering': '. . . The e-word – so often the canary in the coalmine of language-policing bullshit,' she writes.[165]

In *The Myth of Mars and Venus: Do Men and Women Really Speak Different Languages*, Cameron makes a connection between the infamous book about men being from Mars and women being from Venus and the myth it spurred about the two sexes speaking 'different languages', to how women are considered to have a 'natural vocation to care' because they have a 'gift for cooperative, rapport-seeking, empathetic communication.'[166] The snowball effect of these types of myths starts early, when young girls are said to have 'better' language skills (I have heard this about my daughter), women are said to be better language learners, and they use language more 'correctly' and more 'politely' than men.[167] Cameron references Robin Lakoff's *Language and Woman's Place*, noting how after thirty years (Cameron's book was written in 2007 so add another decade-and-a-half), although some of Lakoff's claims about how women use language have been abandoned, her general argument about the connection between language-use, gender and power is still relevant. I remember reading a 1975 copy of Lakoff's book when I first began studying linguistics. 'Linguistic imbalances are worthy of study because they bring into sharper focus real-world imbalances and inequities,' begins the book's conclusion. 'They are clues that some external situation needs changing, rather than items that one *should* seek to change directly,' writes Lakoff. And then I noticed the book's dedication: 'For Andy,' it said, who after a quick online search I discovered was Lakoff's son, 'whose generation will, I hope, have transcended these issues by the time it can read this book.'

9

Phrases that make me angry when I hear or think of someone saying this to, or about, a woman:

'She talks too much.'
'You're just too emotional.'
'Use strong/powerful/empowering words (in your email).'
'You apologize too much.'
'Stop saying ummmm.'
'You sound like a "valley girl".'
'Women and girls are just better at languages.'
'You need to teach your child to speak properly.'

9

Polish for Foreigners

'I will have to trade in my Polish for Spanish,' my son taunts
me. My children and I have started learning Spanish together
through weekly online classes. My young daughter lost interest
quickly, so most classes it's just my son and I, me looking at
him when I don't know a word, him giving me a look, *I don't
know either*. We are a language-learning team and for an hour
every week, I am his equal. I do not monitor or teach as I do
with Polish. I too am a language student, grasping for words
and making conjugation mistakes constantly. Although I have
some beginner Spanish knowledge, sometimes I play down
my experience, wanting to look vulnerable in front of him.
Look how fun and rewarding it is to learn a language! My
children, until recently, did a weekly one-hour online class with
a Polish teacher in Poland. I hid in the other room, pretending
I was not listening. Unlike the Spanish classes for my daughter,
participation in Polish classes was non-negotiable for both of my
children. Before most classes, I would hear, 'Why do we need to
take Polish classes, we already know Polish.' I couldn't disagree
but I tried to explain, as it is their heritage and home language,
they need to keep hearing and learning new concepts and words
in the language from someone besides me. Truthfully, the classes
were more for me than they were for them. I am a *good mother*;

my children are taking Polish classes. At the same time, it helped alleviate some of the mental load of multilingual mothering. It was a small, hour-long, relief to have someone else, besides me, teaching my children Polish and, most importantly, correcting some of their mistakes, something I try to avoid in fear they will recoil even further from me and the language. I discovered the classes through friends in Canada, also children of Polish immigrants. The company specializes in teaching only Polish, at all levels, with instructors all around the world. As I logged into our account before my children's class one day, I noticed for the first time, the company's url: 'Polish-for-foreigners'.

The familiar is also, and perhaps always, foreign.

PART 3
Bodies & Borders

Sociolinguistics: *the study of language in relation to society*

Bodies of Care

Limbless and headless, sewn together with heavy stitching, the cream-coloured felt sculpture was smaller than I imagined. Between the torso's perky breasts, placed at an angle on the body's abdomen, was a small felt windowless house. My children observed it with short-lived curiosity before running off to see the colossal steel spider, a maternal figure, looming in the corner. We were at the Louise Bourgeois retrospective, *The Woven Child*, at the Hayward Gallery in London. A child of French tapestry restorers, the artist's textile work from the last two decades of her life was the focus of the show. Bourgeois, in her eighties and nineties when producing the work, had returned to her roots.

Created in 2001, the small felt sculpture I searched out was also a homecoming for Bourgeois, an ode to a series she began in the mid-1940s, at a time she was also raising three young sons. Titled *Femme Maison* (woman house/house woman), the early paintings in the series are of a female body where the head and upper torso of the woman are replaced by a house. The woman stands tall and confident, but the weight of a home is pressing down on her, obscuring half her body, representing both comfort and also entrapment. The series continues in other mediums, like marble and felt, but the house women in those pieces are no longer upright; they are now lying down, defeated, or exhausted, sometimes connected to the house by only a thread – a precarious balance between the body and the home.

In *Directions to Myself,* a memoir about the last years of her son's childhood before he began his teenage years, Heidi Julavits compares the pregnant body to a building hosting tenants. After the birth of the baby, the body is no longer the building, and the mother begins to inhabit the child with their ideas and their language. A mother is the embodiment of a home long after the tenants have been evicted. Since my children's birth, I have populated their thoughts and words *with* and *in* Polish, often as an adversary, sometimes as an ally, to the English I knew they would acquire with or without me. But they too have inhabited me in all the ways children often do, but especially in the way they have unearthed a language I had no idea was buried so deeply. Like Bourgeois's *Femme Maison,* at least the horizontal version, I sometimes feel myself splitting from the sheer force and weight of the idea, *my* idea, of a linguistic home for my children, but also for myself. It is a precarious balance: the languages, the (linguistic) home, my own identity as a woman, as a mother, as a multilingual, and how I am to make sense of it all for myself, and for my children, at least while they are still young. In motherhood, my body is my children's home and refuge, but in language I feel as if I am also their entrapment, especially for one of my children who could effortlessly live his life in English as opposed to the strain I notice he feels, and is sometimes felt between us, when Polish is pressed upon him. For him, and often myself, when I insist on Polish, I am both a comfort and an irritation. The emotionality of raising multilingual children is visceral: I feel a physical pressure, my body and voice closing in on me, after the tenth time I ask my children to answer me in Polish. It is the meeting of force and powerlessness.

The definition of *foreign* in the context of language refers to something *unfamiliar* or *unknown*, but foreign also means *distant, irrelevant, remote*. Language, any language used for communication, is never irrelevant. How is it possible for a language to be labelled *foreign* in a country where a considerable part of the population uses that language daily, as is the case with Spanish in the United

States? One is only foreign in the presence of another, another that, or who, considers itself familiar. Familiarity is subjective and immeasurable. And yet I often feel as if I am wandering in and with a *foreign body*: something is trapped inside of me that should not be there. Or, perhaps, it does in fact belong and I incessantly must prove it. *Foreign bodies* in their medical definition are ingested or inhaled and are common in young children who put small objects in their ears, noses, and mouths. Foreign bodies like these can, in extreme cases, migrate to the heart. I hope the foreign body of my familiar language is consumed by my children, devoured, drawn in, inhaled, and eventually migrates to their hearts.

’

In a study about how parents' linguistic identity shapes the way their family uses language(s), the authors share the story of Eun Mi, who became a mother in Korea but moved to Australia when her child was fifteen months old. Mi continued to use her first language, Korean, with her child, but as her child got older, Mi, who no longer had other Korean mothers nearby to learn from, found she now lacked a 'mothering language'. Certain 'parenting terms', like teaching the child to say 'excuse me' in English before they leave the table, or the common English-language disciplining tactic, 'I am going to count to three', did not sound *right* for Mi in Korean. Mi did not necessarily feel uncomfortable as a Korean speaker in Australia, but she did as a Korean-speaking *mother* in Australia.[168] For Mi, the mother body was split, not only by its languages, but in the way it was meant to mother in each vernacular and likely in vastly different parenting cultures.

Although our experiences with language and culture are different, I think of Mi's story when I am questioning my identity as a mother in each of my mothering languages. Although it happens less frequently now that my children are older, I remember the way my body felt when I first tried to mother in Polish in public. In one way, it was simple with a baby and toddler as our conversations were uncomplicated and a few words would suffice to communicate something about sharing, or being careful, or saying thank you. But the moments, ones I would feel deep in my muscles and bones, when I felt anger or frustration, often coupled with exhaustion, surprised me the most. My body took over, blood rushed to my head, my heart pounded, and my muscles seized so intensely they would ache for hours after. In those moments, I remember being lost for words in any language. It still happens on occasion, in a different way, when I have hit a breaking point and my customary calmness, at least for the most part, turns into a low-simmering fury. My body tenses, I fight back the urge to raise my voice but inevitably in these moments, it happens and out comes . . . English. Always English. As my heart rate steadies and I try to reason with one of my children or explain my reaction more calmly, Polish enters the conversation again.

,

In a study at the University of California Berkeley, students between the ages of eighteen and twenty-two taking classes in one of fourteen different languages were asked what learning, writing, and speaking an additional 'foreign language' felt like. All the statements were, in some way, about the physicality of the body: appearances, sounds, tastes, forms, physical manifestations of emotions.[169] Students used actions and emotions – kissing someone for the first time, riding a rollercoaster, breaking in a new pair of shoes, getting hit by a truck – as comparisons to how it felt to learn a new language. As a new mother, attempting to communicate with my baby in a language that was both mine and also unfamiliar in its maternal speak and everyday vernacular felt eerily like the experience of learning a new language in the classroom. There were ecstatic highs, ultimate lows, uncomfortable monotonous moments, and a feeling like I was doing it all on the brink of demise. Polish is not foreign or new to me, and yet, because it is my non-dominant language, there are moments when I feel I am 'scaling a wall' like the students in the classroom learning a new language. From the early moments of my mothering, when I had to learn parts of a dump truck in Polish, my baby son's obsession at the time, to more recent discussions with my kids about multifaceted topics like gender identity, war and what 'migrant' and 'refugee' mean, I move between languages. I search for the right words, in either language (sometimes neither) and I become the embodiment of both a language learner and a language teacher. I am at the top of the rollercoaster about to begin screaming as we descend, and pacing long distances in a pair of shoes that rub my heels raw.

Bodies of Belonging

Languages are not separate from bodies and the people who produce them. But language is multimodal: vocal and visual and may draw on any combination of communicative and sensory modes including sight, sound, body movement, facial expressions, prosody, gesture, sign. If a body uses language in a way that is not considered to fit into a societal expectation, or what is erroneously considered 'the norm', that body and that person is often othered for the way they use language. There are a multitude of ways language is used against people by those who will not accept that there is no one, or 'right', way to use language, or that there are different ways one may use the body for language, or for language to come from the body. Language is used to oppress sex and gender when pronouns are forced on trans and non-binary bodies. Language marks social class in cases where bilingualism is praised in some children but deemed a hindrance for others. Both multilingual and multimodal children, those who may use multiple sensory and communicative modes to communicate, are tested in ways that do not accommodate their multiple languages or modalities.[170] Mothers of neurodivergent children, for example, may be told if they stopped using the home language in favour of *only* the societal language, the child will meet neurotypical development milestones *faster*. The prevailing myth that bilingualism causes speech and learning delays in children is amplified exponentially when an emergent bilingual child is neurodivergent or labelled as having a disability. The deficit-based rhetoric stems from underestimating the children and their families, misunderstanding the research, and the notion of 'it will be *easier* for the child to learn *only* one language', insinuating that two languages will lead to additional developmental challenges.[171] Not only does heritage and home language maintenance and bilingualism not cause or contribute to disability or significant delay, bilingual instruction can be equally, and sometimes more, effective than using *only* the second, predominantly societal language.[172]

We need a more generous and extensive attitude that goes beyond what we consider language to be, and a closer look at what our own attitudes about languaging, how we *do, be* and *make meaning* in language, write Jon Henner and Octavian Robinson. Ultimately, no one is 'bad at language' and no form of language is 'bad', nor should any language or languaging be described as disordered, atypical, or defective. Henner and Robinson unpack deficit rhetoric about languaging, especially because of embodied differences (differences, and often also assumptions of differences, between mental or physical states), through the lens of disability, '. . . how perceptions of embodied deficits, cause people to make assumptions about languaging, and to also focus on how people prioritize speech at the expense of everything else.'[173] Henner and Robinson's research and writing introduced me to the concept of *linguistic care work*,[174] the mutual understanding, patience and working collectively, so that all languages in a conversation are understood. Linguistic care work is also about belonging, access, support, resources, recognizing everyone's importance and role, and creating inclusive and ideal settings for languages and languaging to occur. But linguistic care work takes time and effort and a willingness not only to strive by whatever means for understanding, but to undo longstanding and harmful attitudes around what *languaging* and communication is.[175] Henner and Robinson's work brings into focus the 'bodymind', how the body and mind are interconnected and how language is an embodied action. On the topic of linguistic and developmental benchmarks and children, they write:

'Any failure to meet benchmarks on time reinforces deficit views of the language produced by disabled children. The normal timeline is determined by ideals and averages as imagined by academics, medical professionals, and educators. This does not take into account how different bodyminds take time to process and acquire language. Then when those children fail to meet those temporal linguistic benchmarks, they are labelled with disordered language.'[176]

If a child's language is deemed to be 'disordered' mothers are also *othered*, especially if they themselves cannot conform to the idea of what is 'acceptable' in that environment, including not being fluent in the societal language. Mothers of emergent bilinguals, children who are learning a language in addition to their home language, and those also labelled as dis/abled by the education system, are 'victims of the same deficit-based lens with which their children are viewed', writes María Cioè-Peña.[177] The Latina mothers in Cioè-Peña's study are considered the problem, especially by schools where they often feel they cannot support their children academically because of a language barrier. The language barrier is considered the mother's issue and her failing, rather than a systemic one; they are the ones 'hindering effective communication', as opposed to the institution, which is in fact neglecting the needs of the mothers *and* their children.[178] Emergent bilingual children who have multiple, intersecting identities are often further oppressed and it is not uncommon for their heritage and home languages to be overlooked or discriminated against in favour of the dominant language.[179] Ideas around 'disordered languaging' are rooted in racism and, in particular, anti-blackness.[180]

Just as language is interdependent and co-constructed and may be defined as 'disordered' by an interlocutor or listener, so too can a white listener or reader define and impose a perception of deficiency on a racialized body. The work of Nelson Flores and Jonathan Rosa examines how racialized bodies are considered linguistically deficient through a *raciolinguistic perspective*.[181] Raciolinguistic ideologies impose or reproduce notions of standardized ways of knowing, doing, being, communicating based on linguistic systems of whiteness. The linguistic practices of racialized people are systematically stigmatized irrespective of whether these practices correspond to what are considered, 'standardized' forms of language.[182] The question that echoes once again: who is *allowed* to be bilingual, or which bodies are *permitted* to use their own way of languaging without societal repercussion, language policing and discrimination?

Raciolinguistic ideologies are at the root of the word-gap rhetoric I discussed with Megan Figueroa in the previous part. When caregivers, especially mothers, are blamed for not providing significant linguistic input to racialized children, the onus is taken off structural factors like institutionalized racism and standard language ideology perpetuated by systems of oppression and institutions, and the burden is placed on the individuals and families instead.[183] This in turn becomes a case of well-meaning organizations and people proposing language-based reforms (programs to get 'poor' children reading or talking 'more', for example) and ignoring vast social injustices that are the real problem.

Another example of a raciolinguistic ideology is the notion of 'language loss' children were said to incur after the school closures in places like the U.S., UK and Canada, due to the COVID-19 pandemic, specifically in cases where the children came from homes where a language other than English was used.[184] The belief that there was a 'loss' of language portrays the home, community, language and literacy practices of habitually marginalized children like immigrants, and children of immigrants, as deficient or non-existent.[185] And it also plays into oppressive assumptions that there is only one way to learn and use language, and that is in the classroom, when for many children, remote learning was a positive and rewarding experience. Around the question of access to technology, or the lack of, for predominantly minoritized students, as was also often suggested during the pandemic, it is another systemic problem and not an individual one. In a study on raciolinguistic ideologies and remote learning, Clara Bauler writes:

> 'Reducing . . . students' realities and identities to a matter of access to better technology and face-to-face classes can be a harmful discourse that renders traditionally marginalized students deficient unless they adhere to norms of language use of white monolingual elites.'[186]

I remember during the years of the reoccurring pandemic-related lockdowns reading article after article about the educational losses children faced, and how those losses would only accumulate.[187] The articles painted a bleak deficit-based picture, as if children would never again hear or use English, and hinted at a highly unlikely scenario where the societal language would forever be lost. There were many unknowns and a lot of fear at the time, so panic and dramatizing were perhaps to be expected. And yet the lack of acknowledgement of what students may have gained, in language, learning, albeit in a different way, and where possible being with family, always bothered me. As my children did not attend daily mainstream school at the time of the lockdowns, and my partner and I had the immense privilege of being able to work from home, the shift to 'home-schooling' was not as abrupt for us as it was for many families. But when my son was very young, a few years before the pandemic, something similar occurred with how our home/heritage language was dismissed in favour of the societal school language. At the time, I approached my four-year-old son's headteacher at school about the possibility of a more hybrid schedule for him, for the purpose of, in addition to other reasons, increasing his minoritized language input while he was still young. In response, the head scoffed, telling me there were many multilingual families at the school who managed using their home language just fine with the regular academic schedule. The message was, we were the problem if we could not maintain the heritage language like all the other families, many of whom coincidentally had two parents speaking the minoritized language at home and not just one, and in-person attendance was the priority above all.

Notions around 'language loss' during the pandemic and memories of mothers giving up outside-of-the-home work to be with their children make me think once again of Bourgeois's *Femme Maison*. Survey after survey, and endless anecdotal evidence, showed mothers took on the brunt of the work at home during the pandemic, including the remote schooling of their children. Women were disproportionately affected by job losses during the pandemic, especially women of colour, and forced out of work due to caregiving responsibilities.[188] Mothers were the bodies that moved from, and between, the school language to the heritage language(s), attempting to balance, to communicate, to educate, and to exist, during a time of unprecedented world events and so much fear. The mother bodies in the home were equated with a perceived language loss, rather than seeing the heritage language of the home, as transmitted by the mothers, as a source of immense comfort and familiarity to children during a time of fear and worry. The mother was invisible in her care and comfort, her heritage language a perceived constraint to her children's education and well-being, while the home constrained, and at times, stifled, her own existence.

Home Bodies & Spaces of (Re)Production

One of my children's favourite activities is designing and drawing their dream homes. It is an activity they often do together, side-by-side on a large piece bf paper. Sometimes they will sketch out their own, smaller versions, the younger sibling taking inspiration from the older one in the way he draws the floors, one by one, each its own separate little life. A stick figure of me is usually somewhere in the house, predominantly doing something with water. In one drawing, I am taking a shower, in another, sitting in the imagined roof-top pool, and in yet another, swimming. In my daughter's most recent dream house, I was in line for candy, because of course there is a 'sweet shop'[i] in her dream house. In *The Poetics of Space*, a book that explores how we inhabit a space, how daydreaming and imagination fill a space with meaning and, in turn, how certain spaces evoke memories and emotions, Gaston Bachelard writes:

'Sometimes the house of the future is better built, lighter and larger than all the houses of the past, so that the

---

[i] I mistakenly referred to it in my Canadian English as a 'candy store' and was promptly corrected by my daughter because in British English, candy is 'sweets' and 'stores' are predominantly 'shops'.

image of the dream house is opposed to that of the childhood home . . . Maybe it is a good thing for us to keep a few dreams of a house that we shall live in later, always later, so much later, in fact, that we shall not have time to achieve it. For a house that was final, one that stood in symmetrical relation to the house we were born in, would lead to thoughts – serious, sad thoughts – and not to dreams. It is better to live in a state of impermanence than in one of finality.'[189]

Inhabiting a language is not unlike inhabiting a home, somewhere between a house of the future and a house of the past. When the heritage language is the language of the home, the house and the language are inextricably linked and there is always a state of impermanence. Bachelard's words on architecture echo how mothers and children inhabit one another, not in the literal sense of a childhood home, but in the way their co-existence is both ephemeral and, through language, also everlasting. When I feel frustrated or guilty about the present, the now of our heritage language existence and sometimes, in my view, its lacking, I try to remind myself of the house of the future. Perhaps there will not be enough time to achieve what is to come *later* but there is always hope and the reminder that everything is temporary.

9

The relationship between space and language is prominent in linguistics research: what we do with language in a specific place is our interpretation of that place; how our physical environments are interactive and language use is a 'multifaceted interplay between humans and the world'[190]; how the family is a space, specifically a 'space along the private–public continuum of arenas of social life'.[191] Adding a literal twist on language and space in the context of gender, Suzanne Romaine writes, 'Language has helped to gender the way we think about space; men's space is public, in the workplace, whereas women's place is private and in the home. This difference is encoded discursively in expressions such as *working mother, businessman, housewife,* and so on, making it easier to accept as 'natural' the exclusion of women from public life.'[192]

It is a gendered notion of *home* (also *homemaker* and *stay-at-home mom* or SAHM) and links with the gendered caregiving role of a mother that plays a pivotal part in how we consider a heritage (a.k.a. home) language often less-than or inferior to the public, societal, language outside of the home. *Home language,* synonymous with *heritage language* or even *mother tongue,* refers to the domain of the home. As already noted, languages are used in different domains: work, school, with friends, with family members. There may be multiple languages in the home but the *home language,* singular, is the space where those interactions and negotiations occur in one or multiple languages.

Although ever-changing as children grow up and leave the familial home, *home language* is a nod to the present, while *heritage language* represents the past. The former term signifies some proficiency in the language, even if it is imposed by the parents, while *heritage language* is affiliative.[193] *Heritage language,* too, can carry certain connotations that make it seem outdated, the parents' or grandparents' language and not belonging to the new generation. But languages *in* and *of* the home risk being trapped in the domestic space. Too often I have heard stories, and, as noted earlier, experienced them myself, of the educational or medical professionals a family encounters praising multilingualism or the 'language of the home', *if* it does not affect the school language, *as long as* the speech development in a societal language of the child is not hindered (or rather, perceived to be), or *as long as* they are scoring well enough on standardized tests. The negotiations between the private space of the home and the public life of a language continuously surface and push down on the family. Ideas around the home and domestic space are related to notions of unassuming confinement (*housewife, homemaker, homely*). When languages are not supported outside the home, they are at risk of being undervalued in society. When the message is: multilingualism is great if it does not interfere with the outside world – school, work, the playground – it means society does not value your home/heritage language.

Even the choices parents make when they use their language with and in front of their children, inside and outside of the home, send messages about the value of that language to the kids. And those messages are attached to the bodies that produce the languages. In her extensive work with multilingual families, Eowyn Crisfield found that in families where the mother uses the non-societal minoritized language with the children, and the father uses a majority, societal language, the family has the most difficult situation for raising children with both languages. She writes:

'This intersection of gender and language status is even more problematic when the family has traditional roles as well, with the mother staying at home with the children and the father working outside the home. This dynamic often sends the children the message that the mother's language is less important or useful (and therefore of lower status) than the father's language.'[194]

(This is interestingly a paradox when considering, again, the term 'mother tongue', especially in the gendered primary caregiver definition, in that when a 'mother tongue' is valued in the home, the other language, and perhaps the other caregiver if there are two parents, may be 'undervalued' – but *only* inside the home.[195])

When children are young, it may be advantageous to have the parent who uses the heritage language with the children as much as possible. Sometimes, this set-up is even used as a family language maintenance strategy. The idea is to get as much of the heritage language input and exposure in as possible before the child begins school or nursery, often in the majority/societal language. In countries like the UK, where parental leave is – as it should be everywhere – sometimes up to a year, mothers are still predominantly the ones who spend the majority of that time with the children.[196] When, or if, mothers want to go back to outside-of-the home work, there may be nervousness and fear about maintaining the heritage language, sentiments shared often by mothers on multilingual parenting forums. I've read countless posts of anxious moms asking for advice on how to maintain a heritage language once a child starts daycare or school in a majority language. For many of the mothers, it is not possible to find a nursery or preschool in the heritage language, the cost of a childminder or nanny is extremely high already so finding someone who uses a target language is another hurdle, and even if they have the choice to leave the work force, and many don't, it is another individual sacrifice.

When children begin attending an educational institution regularly in a societal language, the dynamic begins to shift from using predominantly the heritage language in the home with the primary caregiver, to the peer-group and school language. What may occur is that the mother's language, one associated with the home, becomes the less important language, while the father's language, if considered the language of the 'public space', is deemed superior, especially if the parents communicate with one another in the societal language, as is the case with me and my partner.[197] Crisfield notes the importance of discussing with children why the languages each parent uses, and the language everyone else uses, are important rather than letting children make assumptions. Schools and educational institutions are not always helpful and often hinder the use of a heritage language by perpetuating the dichotomous separation of academic language and non-academic language (a.k.a. 'formal'/'informal') but also home language and school language.[ii]

Just as people adapt to their linguistic and social surroundings, home as a space adapts to its inhabitants. Where the home, a private sphere, is an enclave of a heritage language, the public sphere, where the societal language dominates, may swiftly take over. But the reverse is nearly impossible, especially without an army of support – a heritage language of the home is already

---

[ii] I note this dichotomy in various parts of the book because it is one of the biggest issues with how languages of the home, heritage and minoritized languages or varieties are considered, resulting in detrimental effects not only for families but for societies at large.

at a disadvantage before it begins to push against the dominant societal language and is, at times, even considered an obstacle. 'A *foreign* language is potentially a problem as soon as it is heard outside the home; such boundary-crossing may be perceived as a threat, because it steps outside the invisibility of private space,' writes Helma Lutz in *The New Maids: Transnational Women and the Care Economy.* The home is the invisible space where both the work of caregiving and languaging take place. If mothers are the perceived agents of language loss or held responsible solely for heritage language maintenance and development, the home is the space, the mother the body, that will be held accountable where language loss, language shift and language attrition may occur. Rarely are outside sources, often working against the mother and the home, acknowledged as affecting factors. It is an unjust oversimplification because our private and public spaces unceasingly intersect.

,

On a road trip to Wales, I pointed out to my children how all the road signs we saw along the way were in both English and Welsh. Following the passing of the 2011 Welsh Language Measure, an act to ensure Welsh has equal status with English, all signs and public information must now be shown in both languages. Languages die because of a multitude of forces – colonialism, imperialism, neocolonialism, xenophobia – pushing down on them incessantly. The revitalization of Welsh was about outside forces uplifting the language that had been suppressed for so long, pushed further and further into domestic spaces until there too the language often disappeared. With a commitment to its revitalization, Welsh became mandatory in schools. Parents who did not know the language, or who were sometimes punished for speaking it as children, began to (re)learn the language alongside their children. There was an outward demonstration and support for strengthening the language.[198] Just like one mother is never solely responsible for a language dying, nor can one mother be exclusively tasked with maintaining or revitalizing a language.

But that has never stopped anyone from putting the blame on families, and especially mothers. In 2016, David Cameron, then the UK's Prime Minister, announced his £20 million funding plan to ensure, 'Muslim women learn English to prevent radicalisation', implying that someone's proficiency in English, or lack of, could contribute to their risk of engaging with extremist groups. The year before, the government made a £45 million cut to English classes. Cameron's plan was presented in the guise of female empowerment, a way to tackle 'prejudice and bigotry', but the rhetoric around it soon turned to mothers, especially mothers of young Muslim men. The message was, if mothers could just speak English fluently, their sons would not be radicalized, implying that a parent's level of English is directly related to levels of potential extremism. If mothers could not show their proficiency in English after a period, they would be at risk of deportation. There was not only no regard for how these same mothers were raising their sons with morals, empathy, and consideration for others, albeit in a different language than English, but also mothers were being blamed for the actions of their children, often young adults or teenagers. The mothers Cameron singled out in the plan embodied everything from their children's language skills and decisions around engaging with extremism, to the radicalization of youth in the UK and generalized fears about extremism in the public sphere. The message was clear: blame the mothers and, if they do not appease the country's fears by learning English and then being tested on their language proficiency, throw them out! What was never considered was the emotional toll of a new language on the psychological connections between mothers and their children and how, in fact, a language of the home creates a protective enclave for many children and strengthens the caregiver–child relationship. Sometimes, a new language, the societal language, is what comes between children and caregivers, especially if the language is used in hostile ways, to discriminate against, to antagonize and to insult mothers, women, and entire groups of people.

،

Irene Gedalof writes about the 'reproductive sphere', the embodied work of mothering including childbirth and childcare, but also the work of reproducing cultures and structures of belonging, like 'culturally specific histories and traditions', predominantly performed by women and mothers. Gedalof does not discuss language as part of the re-making of heritage and cultural identity, but language too plays a vital part in a sense of cultural belonging and is often part of the reproductive sphere for migrant and immigrant mothers. Gedalof argues that the idea of 'juggling between two worlds' is insufficient because there is an 'entanglement of repetitions and change involved in the work of mothering', and for migrant women and mothers that work also involves the reproduction of a 'home' while finding their own belonging and connectedness.[199] In the context of migration and making a home, she writes:

'It might be the work of displaying objects that bear meanings of the past in new spatial settings, and not presuming that we know what meanings of place are produced through that placement. It can include the work of making food from 'home' with slightly different ingredients, grown in different climates or with just that gap of time between production and consumption that bends their taste or presentation, served in different rooms, on different dishes.'[200]

Is this then a *reproduction* or *sameness*, something *new* and, in turn, going beyond the private sphere? Either way, the juggling of two worlds strikes me as something linked to migrant and immigrant women and language, because they too manage the linguistic ties to a different home while also ensuring the new home (language) is represented and strengthened. The in-between is the embodied mother, and she too is balancing, or attempting to create her own belongingness, linguistically and culturally. Here, the work on migration and motherhood, and mother's work as citizenship practices is not unlike the work of heritage language maintenance.[201] The hidden work of language transmission and maintenance is emotional capital, as outlined in feminist work around mothering as citizenship practice and the often-invisible care work that goes into remaking homes after migration. Mothers, through their monotonous practices of caregiving, also remake a place and, alongside, transform identities of belonging. In this way, they are central to both the home and the public sphere for the entire family following migration.[202] Emotional capital, like the emotional labour and mental load of heritage language maintenance, is invisible because it manifests in the home. But it is equally valuable as human capital outside of the home. The care around language, culture, and notions of belonging, directly impacts on the public sphere. One does not exist without the other.

Where Ya Longs To?[i]

In the same year as the Boston Marathon bombing, Angelina Jolie's bilateral prophylactic mastectomies, Pope Francis's election, and New York reporting the highest number of homeless children since the Great Depression, the most popular story on *The New York Times* website was the dialect quiz, *How Y'all, Youse and You Guys Talk*.[203] After answering twenty-five questions on pronunciation (*crayon*, for example), lexical choices (*soda* versus *pop* for a carbonated beverage) and if *Mary, merry* and *marry* sound the same, a map appears revealing where you are from in the U.S. Although I have never lived in the States, when I completed the quiz, parts of Kansas, Iowa and Illinois matched my answers. The popularity of the dialect quiz is a fascinating example of people's love of quizzes, or more likely their desire and perhaps

---

[i] I was going to call this section 'From Away' or 'Come-from-Away' after the expression used in Newfoundland, Canada to signify a traveller or someone not from that area and the title of the popular musical. But when I began looking up 'Newfinese', a dialect of Newfoundland, I came across 'where ya/y' longs to', meaning 'where are you from?' but also 'where do you belong?' There is something poetic about the play on the words 'longs to', as if you can, in fact, long for somewhere to belong. Even the idea that where we come from is a place we belong is powerful.

need to feel they belong, or *come from* somewhere. Geography is, after all, the first line of not only identification but differentiation (or separation).[204]

While hanging out with American friends in London, who say the quiz is eerily accurate, we discussed our answers. The four of us – one Canadian, one Polish-Canadian, and two Americans, all living in the UK for more than a decade – shared how our local linguistic practices or our respective hometown dialects differed or aligned. Even my husband and I, growing up only one province away from one another in Canada, have lexical variations. No one beyond Saskatchewan, my home province, calls a hooded sweatshirt a 'bunnyhug'. As Canadians in London, it is comical how many times my partner and I say 'toque' (sometimes spelled 'tuque' meaning a beanie/knitted hat) to our children in the winter months. (Power in repetition!) It is a word we consider so very Canadian, complete with our nostalgia and romanticization of Canadian winters. (After so long living away in a much warmer, albeit wetter climate, I would last a couple of days tops in a Canadian winter despite always hearing from London friends during the winter months, 'You must be used to this cold.') *Toque* is a term we probably illogically want our London-born and raised children to use, even though in England, you have to always follow up with, 'Oh, that means beanie or knitted hat in Canada.'

Standing in our friends' kitchen discussing who calls *runners*, *tennis shoes*, based on where we grew up, made me think of something Alastair Pennycook notes in *Language as a Local Practice*: 'The locality of language practices is not then a stage backcloth against which language is used, but is a space that is imagined and created. The landscape is not a canvas or a context but an integrative and invented environment.'[205] Language is motion rather than structure, something we *do* as opposed to simply *use*. Dialect quizzes are popular because they offer an identity, a place of belonging, but they are also reminders of movement, change and how we all use language in different ways. When the question of *tennis shoes* (a.k.a *runners*, *sneakers*, *trainers*) being used for every other sport except tennis came up in the conversation with our

American friends, I had to stop myself from tendering judgment. Who am I, an outsider of a speech and discourse community that uses *tennis shoe*, to judge or decide why this term was *appropriate* or not? I wear *runners*, and I do not run.

Small judgments like these have wider implications, and although it is not *really* about tennis shoes or runners, it is about the we way we *include* and *exclude*. Language, of course, has the power to do both. When I took the British–Irish dialect quiz, published a few years after the American version, also in *The New York Times*, instead of maps appearing to let me know where I was likely from, I got, 'Definitely not from around here are you?' As an English colleague who had taken the British–Irish quiz when it first came out noted, and something I had not considered was, that perhaps the creators of this version of the quiz had missed the mark when it came to considering how in the UK, language and accent are often more defined by class than place. This is also related to the idea of covert and overt prestige a variety of English or accent has in the UK, which was noted in Part 2, when exclusion and inclusion can occur simultaneously, depending on group membership and location.

,

A few years ago, on our way to Cornwall, we stopped to get groceries in a small town. As the owner of the vehicle parked beside us approached with his groceries, my children ran up to pet his dog. After a few dog-related questions, the awkward silence between cars was punctured by the dog owner asking where we were from. I knew if we answered 'London', he would look at us suspiciously, unsatisfied with my answer. 'Where are you *really* from?' he'd likely respond, having heard both our Canadian-English accents and me speaking Polish to the children. After more than a decade in London, I am accustomed to this song and dance and have perfected my routine: 'We are Canadian but have lived in London for twelve years,' I begin. 'Both children were born here, but I am also Polish, and we speak Polish at home.' Like so many others before, I owed him nothing and yet, here I was, affirming we belonged somewhere, anywhere, but also *here*. And what I got in return is something I will never forget. The man we had met only minutes earlier, turned to my son and said, 'So, you're Canadian but you have never lived in Canada.' Our languages, cultures, accents, and nationalities did not align for this man; we were wanderers claiming false identities. He wanted to place us, but our response was unsatisfactory and, more than anything, he decided he would question our belonging. My answer, detailed and perfected, may have avoided the follow-up question of where we were *really* from but for him, it was still incomplete.

If you are Polish, how is your English *so good*, someone often asks. When I speak Polish, if the sentence is short enough and I have all the words I need, they ask me where I am from in Poland. As explored in Part 1, I am fervently against the discriminatory practice of labelling certain language users as *native speakers* of a language who are defined as being *better* or *more qualified/important* than someone who has learnt a language later in life. And yet I experience an immeasurable thrill, with a tinge of shame nevertheless, when someone mistakes me for having grown up in Poland, and they do not bring attention to my Canadian twang others have pointed out, despite also knowing the onus is on the listener and their perception of how I sound. Being white, we were asked where we were from because of the way we sound, but for many people of colour, the question 'Where are you from?' or 'Where are you *really* from?' is asked before they utter a single word.

Afua Hirsch, who grew up in south-west London with a British father and Ghanaian mother, calls it 'The Question'. It is a 'persistent reminder of that sense of not belonging', she writes in *Brit(ish)*.[206] Although Hirsch has lived in five different countries as an adult, nowhere has she been asked The Question more than where she grew up, in Britain. As Hirsch writes, this othering and questioning can also happen because of a first or last name, or in her case, a combination of a Ghanaian first name and a German–Jewish last name.

For my Canadian friend Sekyiwa Wi-Afedzi, it usually does begin with her name. Born and raised in Guelph, Ontario, Sekyiwa's mom is second-generation Canadian Scottish, and her late father was from Ghana. Her parents met while teaching in Ghana and spent time there before moving to Canada in the 1970s, where both Sekyiwa, named after her paternal grandmother, and her younger sister were born. Growing up in a predominantly white Eastern Canadian neighbourhood, Sekyiwa could count on one hand how many children looked like her, and of course, no one had the same name. 'People get nervous,' she tells me about instances when someone sees the spelling of her name and they need to pronounce it. 'If there's time, there are always questions . . . But where are you from? I'm like, "fucking Guelph Ontario" – ask me what you really want to ask me,' she says. During her MBA program, a well-meaning professor suggested Sekyiwa change her name, not from a place of malice, she says, but because, as a Black woman with a name that was 'distinctly not European', she was already at a professional disadvantage. (Studies have shown that job applicants with a name that suggests membership in a non-dominant ethnic group are less likely to receive a response or be called for an interview; language intersects with many forms of privilege and disadvantage.[207]) At that moment, she had a visceral reaction to this profound injustice. 'I spent too many years babysitting people's feelings about my name; I'm not going to apologize for my name anymore, and that's like something I had to come into,' she says. 'One of the things with my name, which was something that was hard for me to reckon with, was it has to do with also being a young Black girl in a community that nobody really looks like you. It was always the question of how much space am I taking up, you know, with my hair and my loudness and my name and our bodies.' Sekyiwa, who knows some Fante, is also fluent in French. Her partner is of Métis heritage and the Vancouver-based couple is creating and nurturing a linguistic and cultural community that brings together all their identities and languages for their five-year-old son.

)

As I began writing this chapter, the Illegal Migration Act, or, as Amnesty International rightfully christened it, the UK's cruel immigration bill, became law. Under the act, people arriving in small boat crossings cannot claim asylum or protection, even if their situation back home is life-threatening or dangerous. NGOs and human rights groups have, rightly in my view, called it an 'asylum ban'. Under the law, people will be detained and sent to, as is proposed at the time I write, Rwanda. The ban not only prevents people from escaping war and persecution and seeking refuge in the UK, but also does not offer provision for safe alternative routes for refugees. These are people who have come to the UK by boat, risking their lives to escape from persecution, imprisonment, often death. They have left their homes and families, jobs, lives because they had no other choice. 'By refusing to abide by a wall, map, property line, border, identity document, or legal regime, mobile people upset the state's schemes of exclusion, control, and violence. They do this simply by moving,' writes Reece Jones in *Violent Borders: Refugees and the Right to Move.*[208] Creating the so-called borders and the consequences for crossing them does not deter migration but it does make it more dangerous, and most of society continues to be ambivalent about the horrors inflicted by borders on bodies, especially brown and Black bodies. As Jones outlines, borders are ways to create inequalities, to favour certain people, while excluding others and restricting their access. 'Borders and lines on maps are not a representation of preexisting difference between peoples and places; they create those differences.'[209]

My mother recently told me a story about the time I was around ten, learning Poland's history at my weekly Thursday evening Polish classes with all the other immigrant children where I grew up. We had to memorize the dates of the three partitions of Poland (the Polish–Lithuanian Commonwealth at the time): 1772, 1793 and 1795 when Russia, Prussia and Austria progressively erased Poland from the world map until finally, in 1795, it was gone completely. Poland did not reappear on a map of Europe until 1918. I was apparently finding it difficult to memorize the dates and years of all the historical events that occurred in Poland, including its partitions. At one point, my mom tells me I said something about how it would have been easier (for memorization, lest anyone thinks I am flippant about Poland's partitions!) if there was only one year, one time the country was erased completely as opposed to the shifting borders and multiple erosions (and more years to memorize for a quiz). I thought about this naively innocent childhood comment recently as I considered the shifting of borders, the erasure of lands and people, linguistic and cultural genocides happening all over the world. Slow and steady erasure and erosion happens because the oppressors and colonizers hope the world will eventually turn a blind eye. A century later, immigrant children, if any remain, memorize dates.

,

In *Linguistic Diversity and Social Justice*, Ingrid Piller explores the 'territorial principle' where the imagined monolingual standard language is born out of the association between language and place. Using the example of a 'language map', Piller demonstrates how these types of maps establish links between language and place and, in turn, normalize the association, particularly the language of a nation-state. Even in countries that have legal rights for more than one language, it is predominantly done so based on this territorial principle.

> 'Political and media debates about the relationship between language and place enjoy a particularly wide reach and are highly influential in shaping the common-sense understanding that a nation should only have one language and that linguistic diversity is detrimental to social harmony and national unity. Even states that do not have an official language (or languages) codified in their constitution in the way that France and Belgium do usually operate on the territorial principle, elevating one language and its standard variety above all others.'[210]

The most poignant example I come across often is that of the U.S., which does not have an official language, and yet the belief that

English is the language of America is part of a national identity, especially in response to immigration. The belief of one nation, one language is linked to the oppression and discrimination against immigrant languages, where any language other than the one considered 'the nation's language' ('official' even when it in fact is not 'official') is seen, at best, as a problem and often as a threat. 'A standard language ideology which proposes that an idealized nation-state has one perfect, homogenous language, becomes the means by which discourse is seized, and provides rationalization for limiting access to discourse,' writes Rosina Lippi-Green.[211] Nationalism, or the one nation, one language ideology, is echoed in heritage language maintenance, where being from *there* means you should use the language from *there*, not unlike the idea of, 'Here, we speak English.' This connection between a nation and a heritage language may create allegiances, inspire language learning or maintenance, and strengthen ties, but it may also enforce borders and othering. (I explore the idea of pride in linguistic and cultural identity and how that may lead to its own form of judgment and intolerance further on in the next part.)

⸮

I remember waking up the morning after the Brexit vote like so many others: bewildered, shocked, numb. Every so often, a photo of my then-toddler son pops up as a memory on my phone. It is the day of the Brexit vote, he is sitting in his buggy smiling, a big blue 'I'm In' sticker adorns his T-shirt. His mother is behind the camera, naively thinking the next day will be the same as any other, the UK will remain in the European Union and the referendum will become a distant memory.

Two of the three promises outlined by the Vote Leave campaign in favour of Brexit had to do with migration and immigration, playing on the fears and xenophobia of those who wanted to have a sense of control over the UK's borders and *their home*.[212] The Leave campaigners promised cuts in immigration, to 'bring it under control' and stated boldly, if erroneously, that if Turkey was to join the European Union, it would mean five million more migrants could enter the UK by 2030. A few days after the Brexit referendum and a confirmed Leave win, news reports began to appear around an increase in hate crimes, especially in areas that were in favour of Brexit. The largest number of EU citizens living in Britain are Poles and many of the reported attacks were against them, calling them cruel and inhumane names, and often telling them to 'go back home'. In a study on Polish-speaking migrants in the UK post-Brexit, the authors found that the public attitude toward Polish speakers had 'changed significantly' following the vote, with a 'general lack of security' and disappointment being reported by most. Experiences of violence and prejudice were encountered particularly among those in socio-economically underprivileged positions.[213]

As I was leaving our flat a day or two after the Brexit vote, my partner apprehensively and gently suggested perhaps I shouldn't speak Polish out loud in public to our young son until things calmed down. I understood his fears, and even felt some myself, but I also, with my entire being, wanted to do the opposite. This idea of 'Here, we speak English!' is nothing new, it happens every day, with or without Brexit, especially for racialized and visibly minoritized people. But the Leave win gave people a newfound sense of permission to enforce borders, linguistic and geographic, they considered under their own control, often solely because of the colour of their skin and the country where they were born. Rhetoric around immigration being bad, or out of control, or the cause of everyone's hardships is also nothing new in the UK and many other countries around the world. A fear of *foreign bodies* results in a fear of *foreign language*.

Bodies as Borders

The relationship between language and space can be one of both alienation and intimacy. In *In Other Words*, Jhumpa Lahiri writes that when you reside in a country where the language you consider yours is deemed *foreign*, as Bengali in America is for her, there forever exists a sense of estrangement: 'You speak a secret, unknown language, lacking any correspondence to the environment. An absence that creates a distance within you,' writes Lahiri.[214] The Polish writer Olga Tokarczuk, on the other hand, considers how lost people who only have English as a 'private language' must feel, considering they have nothing to fall back on or 'turn to in moments of doubt' and 'may be understood by anyone at any moment, whenever they open their mouths'.[215] The monolinguals whose language aligns with their space, immersed in English with no possibility of escape, are to be pitied, writes Tokarczuk. Reading these two interpretations side-by-side – of language aligning with space, or not, estrangement, and either the privilege or the curse of possessing a *secret language* – is an exquisite dichotomy. It reminds me of a postcard I have framed, nestled among books in our living room. It is by the South African artist William Kentridge that reads: 'Her absence filled the world.' The absence of a language fills a space, for better or for worse, just like (a) space may actuate a language.

When I am in doubt of my son's ability to fluently converse in Polish, I just need to put us in a situation where he is uncomfortable speaking English with me and needs our *private language*. Once, when I was speaking to a friend in English, he came up to us and, in Polish, asked pleadingly when we could finally go home and if I could please stop chatting with my friend. I told him we would be going very soon and reminded him that the friend I was conversing with also spoke Polish, so she understood. Growing up in a small Canadian prairie city, immersed in the Polish immigrant community, all the Poles knew each other in the city. Except at community events, Polish was in most day-to-day situations a private language, unless you ran into someone from the community at the grocery store. But in the UK, Polish is the most-spoken language after English and Welsh and you hear it everywhere.[216] 'She's speaking Polish, Mama!' one of my children proclaims at least a few times a week as a woman on her phone walks by. But when I know no one around us knows Polish, it is one of my greatest parenting joys when, for example at a birthday party, I can gently nudge my child to say thank you or let them know to stay away from the kid who is spitting in juice cups or licking random cupcakes, without offending anyone.

The idea of insult is also a prominent one among multilingual parents in a different way. One of the concerns I often hear from multilingual mothers is the worry of seeming rude in the playground (it's always the damn playground!) when speaking a heritage language to their children in front of families who do not understand. I've noticed some mothers, if there are other parents or children around, will switch to the societal language. Others will continue with their heritage language but perhaps translate if it concerns another child. There is no wrong or right way to handle multilingualism in the playground (or any other parenting environment). But it is not rude to communicate with your child in your heritage language around others who do not understand. It is not intentionally excluding anyone (unless you are, of course, but those are rare circumstances, like kids licking random cupcakes) and people need to be respectful and mindful of how language transmission works in a non-societal language. It is not *just* about that hour in the playground maximizing heritage language exposure, but about how we consider the importance of a language, how we use it in society, value it and show our children its importance. I recently met the mom of one of my daughter's new friends and she did something remarkable when she heard my daughter and I speaking Polish with one another. She turned to her children and emphasized our use of a language other than English and asked her children if they could identify the language. At first, the interaction seemed odd and awkward, as if her children were being quizzed and we were meant to stay silent until someone got the correct answer. But the back-and-forth ended up being a tender discussion about multilingualism among five- and six-year-olds. My daughter proudly announced she speaks Polish, while the other two children shared that they are learning French.

> ,

On a recent visit to my parents' home, I was short with my son for not wanting to speak with my mother more, to sit with her at the table and converse with her in Polish. I encouraged him unrelentingly to go talk to my father about football in Polish. He refused, I persisted. It was partly about maximizing their connection because of the infrequency of our visits, but it was also to relieve me of some of the responsibility of being predominantly the only speaker of Polish in my children's lives. I wanted to let go of the burden, just for a few days and desperately needed everyone to perform a role, to play their part, including me, who wanted to show my parents what a good immigrant child I am, passing on the work they had invested to ensure I was multilingual. (Ideologies around multilingualism being a 'gift' run deep and, clearly, across generations!) Also I just wanted a break from the mental and emotional load. The infrequent sound of English coming out of my parents' mouths when speaking to my children or to me feels like I've brushed against a thorny bush, a slow-spreading discomfort moves across my body.[217] As a child, and especially as a teenager, it sometimes felt the opposite, particularly in certain environments where I preferred my parents speak English to me instead of Polish so I didn't seem different compared to my peers being raised in monolingual English homes.

On that visit, I asked my mom how many of her friends, the same women I remember from growing up in the Polish community, had grandchildren who spoke Polish with them. She told me that, as far as she knew, not many. Most of her friends communicated with their grandchildren in English. The fact my mother's friends' adult children, the people I grew up with and remember from the Polish community, didn't pass on Polish to their children did not surprise me and not for a moment did I blame, judge, or think less of them. Many have Canadian, monolingual English-speaking partners and, after being socialized in English all their lives, felt more comfortable parenting and living in English. It happens all the time with second-generation immigrants, and I understand wholeheartedly. Plus, in most of the families, our parents had each other after immigration, a home with two speakers of a heritage language, where most of us, their children, only have ourselves if we have partners who do not know Polish. I also understood how and why the grandparents did and do not insist on Polish. They too want a linguistic and emotional connection with their grandchildren and want to respect the wishes of their own children in how they raise their kids. Some of these parents were also not as diligent as my parents were in using Polish with their own children growing up, so in some cases, the adult children may have felt they did not have the fluency to raise children in Polish. In an interview before she died, Hungarian writer and author of *The Illiterate* Ágota Kristóf, who fled Hungary in her early twenties, raised her children in Switzerland and who wrote in French, said she never tried to pass on Hungarian to her children. With her grandson, she taught him a few words in Hungarian but was worried, if she went further, speaking a language he did not know, he would feel estranged from her.[218]

But the part of this story that made me feel a deep melancholy and envy had to do with the space between grandparent and grandchild, the proximity these families had with one another. I could not help but think about the opportunity of intergenerational language transmission when one lives in the same city, or at least in the same time zone as a grandparent who can facilitate some of that language work. But I also know life is not that seamless, language does not always flow from body to body, uninterrupted by external forces and the sheer strength of a societal language that permeates every opening in life.

Language is not an object passed down from generation to generation, it is a process between and among generations, a cooperation and collaboration.[219] Generational language interaction is a meeting of repertoires, not simply language passed on or not. We need to consider it as users of languages of different generations – biologically connected but also socially – likely with varying linguistic repertoires coming together.[220] In multilingual families, linguistic borders between generations are never straightforward nor simple. Even in monolingual families, language change shifts and reorganizes linguistic borders so that each new generation is unlike the one before. The way my children teach me Polish words from the cartoons they watch is generational language moving up, instead of down. They remind me of Polish words when I can't remember how to say something, and I remind them of the English translations when they too are lost for the English word when telling their father a story.

Plus, there are many reasons why intergenerational language transmission comes to a halt or is interrupted. Sometimes children only come to know the reason(s) when they are older, even if they might not understand and still feel the need to lay blame on a parent for a language that was not passed on. In *Essential Labor: Mothering as Social Change*, Angela Garbes says she only realized when she was a teenager, and was 'pushing the issue', why her parents, each fluent in two or more languages, chose to raise Garbes and her brothers only in English: 'My father admitted their decision wasn't based on my unwillingness to learn Tagalog, as he had once claimed, but instead his refusal to subject his children to the discrimination he endured because of his accent,' writes Garbes, who, like so many others who feel they have lost a childhood language, need to find a reason and, in turn, find meaning in the loss. 'I sometimes feel they did me a disservice by not passing the language on to me. Whatever anger I feel, though is abated by my own guilt over never having mastered Tagalog. Of speaking better Spanish, which I learned in high school, than our native tongue.'

Word by Word

When I lament not being close in proximity to the people in my family who could help me transmit and maintain Polish with my children, my privilege of having easily accessible resources in Polish – books, games, magazines, TV and movies, many online learning tools and calls with people who know the language – is never lost on me. For Sienna Gould, of the Pinaymootang First Nation in Manitoba, the meeting of intergenerational repertoires takes on an entirely new meaning as she navigates learning her family's Indigenous language as fast as she can before all the elderly fluent speakers in her community die and, with them, a language is lost. Gould's parents' generation was forced to attend Canada's residential schools, where horrific abuse and atrocities occurred. Children were stolen from their family homes, forced to change their names, their identities, their culture, and customs, and were punished, often physically, for speaking their Indigenous language, sometimes the only language they knew.

The last of Canada's 139 residential schools closed in the late 1990s, a date I still cannot believe to be true. The children who survived,[i] grew up and became mothers and fathers but could

---

[i] According to the Truth and Reconciliation Commission on Canada's Indian residential schools, the schools were an integral part of 'a

not parent in the language(s) that were stolen from them. There was, and continues to be, intergenerational trauma because of the unimaginable atrocities the children and their families faced. If my children lose their Polish or when I need to draw on more support, we have access to language classes, to a place where they can visit and be immersed in the language, and to many other speakers of the same language. The opportunities, if they exist at all, are much scarcer for Indigenous people to (re)learn a language because they do not necessarily exist, and there are so few fluent or proficient speakers left of so many different Indigenous languages. There is nowhere to return or go to be immersed in their heritage language, and often not many elders remain to pass on oral traditions.

As a child, Gould heard her paternal grandmother use Anishinaabemowin and felt an immediate connection with the language. She started asking questions and her grandmother began slowly to teach her the language. Gould's maternal grandmother, on the other hand, felt the language was useless and didn't want her grandchildren to learn it, likely a sentiment born of centuries of hearing the erroneous message that her language wasn't valuable. Gould's grandparents and some of her parents' generation spoke the language in secret during the days when the residential schools were operating, and that is the only reason the language survived in her family, she tells me.

Gould began learning numbers in Anishinaabemowin followed by the vocabulary of everyday life for her people, discussing the weather and nature, for example. But more than learning vocabulary, she was unravelling history, she says. 'I really have to fight for what I want for my children, because if I don't then it'll be lost with me,' says Gould, who is the

---

conscious policy of cultural genocide' affecting more than 150,000 Indigenous children and their families. It is estimated that at least 6,000 children were killed and died during their time at a residential school, but that number is likely much higher. So many Indigenous did not make it out alive, did *not* survive.

mother of a toddler son and a baby daughter. Not only are there so few speakers of Gould's Indigenous language left in her band, but there is also a lot of push-back against the younger generation embracing cultural traditions – the deep scars and trauma that remain after decades of being punished and tortured for following cultural and traditional practices. Some elders continue to hide their Indigenous names, Gould tells me, but she refuses to continue the cycle of loss and fear. 'This generation is realizing we don't need to hide no more . . . when we are strong with the language, with the mother tongue, it'll make us strong people too.'

Gould's incredible optimism has stayed with me long after our conversation and when I think of her, and our conversation, I am saddened, embarrassed, in awe, and most of all empowered and incredibly moved. When I shared my story of sometimes struggling to pass on Polish to my children, Gould, who has no language resources to draw on except the elders in her community, and a sense of running out of time before the elders pass away, who has endured unfathomable intergenerational trauma and cultural genocide because of colonialism, racism and the profound brutalities of Canada's residential school system, tells me to keep going, to take small steps. Even just ten words a day is something, she reminds me.

In 2019, the Indigenous Languages Act was passed, and UNESCO declared the next decade (2022–2032) the International Decade of Indigenous Languages, aiming to promote the urgent need to preserve Indigenous languages.[221] Some good news is that there are many initiatives under way to help revitalize and preserve Indigenous language, including summer language and cultural camps, language nest daycares and immersion camps. But funding is scarce and there is not enough of it to cover all the proposed language projects.[222] The 2021 Canadian census showed that the number of Indigenous language speakers who learnt their language as a second language has increased since the previous census in 2016. Certain Indigenous languages such as Haisla, Halkomelem, Heiltsuk and Michif saw a large proportional growth of speakers since 2016.[223] However, for the first time since 1991, there was a decline in how many Indigenous people in Canada reported they could speak an Indigenous language well enough to hold a conversation, and Indigenous language acquisition as a first language, in the home, continues to decline.

Beyond the Borders

'Why do I have to speak Polish?' my son asks. 'Because it is important,' is the only thing I think to say. I frantically change the subject, not leaving him the space to question further because I am petrified he will ask, 'But what if it is not important to me?' For a child to become multilingual, a term that encompasses a variety of definitions because no two multilinguals are the same, they require, as already noted, exposure, input and a sense of need for the target language. (There are also many moments when my son is vocal about how he wants to use Polish and considers it an important part of his life!) When my children respond to me in English after I've used Polish, or start a conversation in English, not uncommon occurrences, and predictable for our situation, we have a frequent back-and-forth: I say, 'I don't understand what you are saying!' They repeat the same thing in Polish. I of course *do* understand what they are saying, and my children of course know I understand, but it is the cue I give them when they are supposed to say the same thing but in Polish.

It is a version of the 'minimal grasp' strategy, a well-known approach, used by parents of young children especially who may still believe their parents really do not understand the other language. Identified by Elizabeth Lanza in her work on American–Norwegian families, it is one of five parental strategies.[224] But for me, the name is deceiving: I am *maximally grasping*, greedily, at the hope that my children, after I tell them for the hundredth time I don't understand, won't tell me to fuck right off.

I feel the same way about the parenting strategies for raising multilingual children, especially 'one parent, one language' (OPOL). If you spend time on multilingual parenting forums, OPOL is like a code word to get into a not-so-secret but sort-of top nightclub. The acronym is thrown around incessantly among parents in chat and support groups, and is predominantly considered a frontrunner in multilingual caregiving, even though research has shown it is not necessarily the *best* strategy, let alone the only one. For OPOL families, each caregiver uses one language with the child exclusively, or as much as possible. Sometimes, the caregivers each use a different minoritized language, and there could be a third language outside the home. But other times, the moniker is misleading, in that OPOL is said to be used even in situations where one of the parents uses the societal, majority language and the other uses the minoritized one. In these cases, it is *one* parent against not only the other caregiver, but also all of society including school, peer group and outside-of-the-home life. Outnumbered, the heritage language may, again, be pushed further into the domestic space in these situations, and the *one* caregiver responsible for the language will face a perpetual uphill battle. Some families have parents who each use a heritage language with their children but then use a societal language with one another. In these instances, there are three languages at play in the home, but the children know the parents understand and use the majority language as well, so can easily slip into it. OPOL often translates into one parent inevitably being left out of a language, whether it bothers them or not. The 'one' places the onus on one person, on a sole provider of a language that needs much more than one caregiver using it with the children to thrive. I am the *one parent* who must constantly insist, sometimes beg, my children to respond in the heritage language. Being the *one* can be frustrating and often lonely.

As I wrote the previous sentence, notions of loneliness began to surface in many other facets of multilingual childrearing. Being the one parent responsible for a heritage language may be lonely, but the caregiver who is the only one not using the heritage language in a family may also feel isolated. Aloneness can also manifest as resentment, as I note in the next part of the book with examples of couples where one caregiver requests or demands that a language the children do not know is not used in the home or when they are present. Feeling as if one does not *truly* belong to a linguistic or cultural community is another form of isolation. These sentiments are complex, emotional and different for every family and person, but more reason to cease placing the onus of heritage language maintenance solely on individuals in a family.

In her study on language input environments and language development in multilingual children, Annick De Houwer notes if both parents speak the same heritage language at home, often referred to as the 'minority language at home' or 'non-dominant home language', the 'success' of transmitting that heritage language is higher than if one parent also speaks the majority language.[225] (I put 'success' in' as the study was based on how the parents described their children's multilingualism.) Even so, when a minoritized-language parent, like me, used both the heritage language and the majority language, the reported rate of 'success' fell nearly 40%. The definition of what was 'bilingual' likely differed from family to family in the study, but I use this as an example of how vastly different it can be for a two-caregiver family where both parents use the same heritage language in the home versus only one parent.

Another popular strategy offered to desperate parents wanting and needing to know how they are supposed to go about raising multilingual children, is the 'time and place' strategy. The idea is to use a language consistently at either a specific time (every morning between 9a.m. and noon) or place (in the car, at playgroup on a Wednesday afternoon, at bath time). In some families, this isn't necessarily done by only the mother, but moms still often oversee and facilitate the time and place: visits with grandparents, language immersion school programs, constant monitoring. For families using this strategy, it is incredible to me they stick to one language at breakfast, for example, or before

3p.m., before moving on to the next language, as if there is a clean break, a line that separates this and that, language and life. How do you measure what is *enough* time, *enough* language? When I think of 'time and place' I am reminded of a video clip I recently saw online. An American woman living in Italy, married to an Italian man, sits in her car on the verge of tears. She recounts how she uses English with her young daughter while her husband, the paternal grandparents nearby and the rest of the community all use Italian. She is the daughter's only English input and, predictably, the daughter favours Italian. The mother tells the camera she feels she needs to give up work and her career to be with her daughter at home, so the child is exposed to more English day-to-day.

Strategies can be helpful, they can be useful and comforting and they work for many families, especially when children are young. But life gets busier, things get more complicated, the strategies are thrown around carelessly and parents feel like failures when 'fool-proof' strategies stop working, forgetting or never realizing there are no guarantees. When children get older, maybe they don't tell you to fuck right off, but they imply it, complete with an eyeroll or two, when you remind them to use their minoritized language. It is not lost on me that the (my!) use of strategies and my attempts at getting my children to use one language over another is a form of language policing.[i] I am an ardent advocate of encouraging the use of full linguistic repertoires and practices, where languages are not considered *separate, additive, discouraged*. And yet, in our family, I am the one who separates, who discourages the use of (only) English and who pleads to *add on* ('Please say it again in Polish!'). (For any

---

[i] I monitor myself closely when it comes to how much (not often), or what I choose to correct when my children make mistakes in their minoritized language. I fear 'active language policing' like this will only tip the scales and, rather than help the cause, create more tension and reluctance for my children to use the language. But I do ask, insist, plead and, yes, incentivize and, despite my best intentions, I know these are all forms of language policing.

parents raising multilingual children reading this wondering, yes, I use bribes or, as a friend reminded me recently, 'incentives'.) Sometimes, however, I wonder, am I all that different from the monolingual parent who asks, or *instructs*, their child to, 'use their words!'? Perhaps asking or *insisting* my children use one language over another is simply another form of a request for linguistic compliance.

The concept of 'child agency' in heritage language maintenance and transmission is not new in linguistics research, and several researchers are exploring ways in which children participate, construct, and often lead the use of multiple languages within the family.[226] Putting the focus on the child is another way to examine how families, in their entirety and their singularity, are constructed through multilingual practices. But like everything to do with language, family, and multilingualism, it is multifaced and complex. I don't always get it right, and I avoid answering why I consider the use of Polish in our family 'important', but other times I offer a somewhat convincing reason why my children *should* (as opposed to *must*) use Polish. Sometimes it turns into a mini monologue and my children get bored, shrug their shoulders, and say, 'OK.'

9

As I was writing one morning, while in a café in the woods near one of my children's forest schools, I struck up a conversation with a look-alike mother and adult daughter. Sometimes the universe endows me with linguistic treasure if I pay attention (a.k.a. eavesdrop on conversations in cafés). I was facing their table, the two engrossed in a conversation over cake, coffee, and juice. One of them was either arriving or departing after the meet-up as a large red suitcase stood beside them. The older woman tenderly touched the younger woman's arm throughout the lively and continuous conversation, a dialogue that flowed from Dutch to English, effortlessly, seamlessly, fluidly. A sentence in Dutch was punctured by English, 'the bare minimum' before continuing in Dutch. The words and sentences from both languages softly bumped into one another, like soap bubbles floating in the air, sometimes bouncing around, brushing against each other or something else, until one popped without fanfare or great interruption. Before they left, I stopped them to say how incredible it was the way they used both of their languages. The mother had just arrived from Amsterdam that morning to visit her daughter who is living in London, they told me. When the daughter was a child, the mother only spoke to her and her brother in Dutch and their father, who is American, only spoke English, yes, following OPOL. They lived for a while in the U.S., so English got a boost, but moved back to Holland when the children were ten and seven, and Dutch was then the societal language. Although the mother told me she was strict when the children were young, keeping the languages separate, now knowing they are fluent in both languages as adults, their languages move across and almost beyond the two. The mother does not notice when one language becomes the other, she told me, as her daughter nodded in agreement. It was *translanguaging* in the wild.

Coined by Cen Williams in Welsh, *trawsieithu*, and translated into English by Colin Baker, *translanguaging* as a pedagogical practice has gained popularity in the past decade. It is an approach to multilingualism that is centred on the multiple discursive practices of multilinguals and, as opposed to considering language from an outside perspective (separate languages, for example), it considers languages from *within* or *beyond* named languages.[227] Translanguaging is about a person's full linguistic repertoire, using any and all of their languages when needed or desired, and is also multimodal: considering gestures, movements, anything to facilitate meaning-making in communication. Ofelia García, one of translanguaging's seminal advocates and an early researcher on the topic, who has written numerous articles on the subject, writes:

'Named languages exist as social entities and are important for identity, for nationhood, for citizenship, for learning, for participation in society. But the artificial boundaries that have been drawn around named languages in nation-states and their schools often leave out the very diverse language practices of people and speakers within national borders and the walls of schools. It is the boundaries that have been constructed. The language of people, of speakers, goes beyond those boundaries.'[228]

Translanguaging is different than code-switching or code-borrowing, when a multilingual moves between languages, because it does not consider languages as separate. It is about *doing* language or language practices, as opposed to simply *using* multiple languages at once. It is about challenging the borders of different means of communication, linguistic and non-linguistic, and embracing linguistic diversity rather than viewing it as a barrier. The practice is studied and considered predominantly in classrooms where instructors encourage their students to draw on their full linguistic repertoires in myriad ways. Although translanguaging cannot eliminate racism, classism, colonialism, and notions around language standardization alone, it works to unsettle hierarchies, by 'pushing limits and breaking boundaries'[229], and perceived dichotomies, including ideas around *first* and *second* language, 'native' and 'non-native', 'mother tongue', and one mode of language over another. Language barriers in everyday situations, especially in medical settings where key information can mean life or death, remain a crucial issue, and translanguaging should not take away from the focus on ensuring people have access to translation and interpretation. But it brings awareness to the importance of various linguistic repertoires. People are complex and singular in the way they use language; it is intertwined with their identity and history, and they deserve to have access to whatever they need to communicate with the world around them.

As an educational practice[230], an ideology and a transformative social action, I am an ardent advocate of translanguaging, but I get into trouble with myself when I consider how hard it is for me to accept it in the way I use language with my children. With young children who are still under my (linguistic) care, and with already minimal exposure to Polish, or at least far less than English, I am torn about how to implement, or rather accept and use, translanguaging. (It is not lost on me that we already practise translanguaging in many ways.) Studies have shown that even when parents are supportive of the idea of translanguaging, it is challenging to accept in the home when there is already so little input of a non-societal language. Researchers have noted how children learning two languages, with the aim of being active bilinguals in both, need to have as much time as possible in a minoritized language when the majority language looms at large. But this is not the reality for many families, including my own.

In one study on how parents felt about 'mixing'[231] languages in the home, parents called language separation a 'necessary evil' to ensure maximum input in the minority language, given the overwhelming dominance of English in their sociolinguistic environment.[232] It is the ultimate irony: the flexibility of bilingualism is exactly why I want my children to have access to multiple languages. And yet, if I do not put in the work now, if I do not create the space for heritage language input and exposure, if I do not (as it sometimes feels) give in and give my whole self, the flexibility may never transpire. Of course, it is not as dire as I tell myself it is at 3a.m., but these are valid feelings that need to be addressed, aired out, shared among multilingual mothers and parents. There is fear and there is frustration and that too is reality. As I write this, and for the past few years, I am brainstorming around ways to expose my children to more Polish, beyond me, that work for our family, in the hope it will allow me to feel more confident in our translanguaging. Although theoretical guidance is vital, considering the myths around bilingualism that continue to prevail, parents also need practical support so we can let go of the fear and embrace practices of translanguaging everywhere. 'This is a *pilna sprawa*,' says my daughter in half English and half Polish (*pilna sprawa*: important thing). My children and I talk about what it means to use our full linguistic repertoires and I encourage them to draw on multiple sources to communicate, with a little nudge to at least say the same thing in Polish. I am working on letting go and allowing my children to be empowered and to know they have their own linguistic agency and repertoires, but it is an ongoing endeavour.

,

For the first six months of his life, my son insisted on being carried everywhere. I remember my new mom friends from our prenatal (antenatal!) class rolling up (literally) to coffee meetups with their newborns sleeping peacefully in strollers. My son was strapped to me, enveloped by a thick fabric layer to support his tiny body and delicate head, his body heat radiating from him to me, and mine to him, even during the hottest days of the London summer heatwave that year. It was wonderful but also exhausting, especially during the scorching weather. As much as I miss it today, and despite how I already knew back then how much I would miss it (such is the paradox of mothering), there were days I craved a break from my body being everything to another being, including a place to sleep. When I wasn't shushing, I was swaying – a rhythmic side-to-side, step-to-step motion. My partner and I took turns walking around the neighbourhood for every nap as the only way our son would sleep was on one of us. Eventually, at around six months, my baby decided to give the stroller a chance, but the side-to-side turned back-and-forth motion remained obligatory during stroller naptime. When I carried one of my children in the baby carrier, if they were not sleeping and facing me, I would make faces, noises, kiss their soft cheeks and have one-sided conversations with them. They would coo, sometimes giggle, and often babble. There were also silences when I would be getting us somewhere in a hurry. When I pause and close my eyes, I still feel a little body next to mine, the weight of a baby against my chest, legs eventually getting longer and longer at the side of my body, often the feet pressing against the palms of my hands, and a small bald head with a hint of fuzz under my chin. These were also the moments when I was still unsure of my language. I was getting used to using

Polish every day – in public, with an interlocutor who could not reply. There was so much newness about the experience, emotional but also physical.

In *Translanguaging and the Body*, Adrian Blackledge and Angela Creese note the spatial dimension of translanguaging, but especially its corporeal factor.[233] The authors examine ethnographically how people communicate multilingually and multimodally at a butcher's stall in Birmingham, and how translanguaging occurs through 'the deployment of wide-ranging semiotic repertoires', or 'how *the body* is put to work in the process of communication':

'The way people walk, stand, and sit, the way they tilt their head, the gaze of their eyes, the shrug of their shoulders, the movement of their hands and fingers, their smile or frown, all are part of the semiotic repertoire. The integrated nature of the semiotic repertoire is fundamental. Embodied communicative practice is not in any way separate from linguistic communicative practice. They are integral to each other to the extent that they are one and the same.'[234]

Blackledge and Creese reference Pierre Bourdieu's 'ways of being and doing' (a.k.a. 'habitus') and the notion of the 'historical body' to illustrate how whenever someone enters into social action, they bring their own biographies, or life experiences, purposes, goals, unconscious ways of behaving.[235] The 'historical body' is about placing bodily memories in the individual body or how 'a lifetime of personal habits come to feel so natural that one's body carries out actions seemingly without being told'.[236]

Perhaps far removed from the way the authors consider a historical body, or even translanguaging and the body, I think of those early days with my children when I would carry or push them: our spatial dimension and embodied communicative practice. I still remember what it feels like to snap the baby carrier on, to balance the baby on the chest, to pull the shoulder straps tight. My fingers still curl in as if I am gripping a stroller handlebar. I think of all the moments my body continued to sway and move, like the bodies of so many other mothers you see on sidewalks, streets, on the tube, rocking back and forth, side to side even when there is no baby strapped to them or no stroller to push. The body memory of mother–child communication and the history of maternal habits.

PART 4

Love, Literally & Language, Emotionally

Semantics: *the study of reference, meaning, or truth*

'It is just semantics.' Except, it never is

'Kocham Cię'

The first time I told my then boyfriend, now husband I loved him, it was in Polish. I wrote *Kocham Cię* in a card and gave it to him after a dinner out with friends. Although he has, in our nearly twenty years together, endearingly learnt a significant amount of beginner Polish, it was not a language he knew back then, save for a few swear words Polish friends taught him before we met. I was reasonably confident my boyfriend loved me back, but the first time vocalizing the sentiment can come with unexpected results. Not only was writing the phrase easier than saying it for the first time, doing it in Polish was an added armour. The distance I felt toward my first but non-dominant language was a protective detachment. While my decision to say *I love you* in a non-dominant language (for me) and an unknown one (for my boyfriend) was strategic, for many multilingual couples, communicating devotion becomes a precarious effort of either linguistic frustration or ultimate desire.

In *French Lessons: A Memoir*, American author Alice Kaplan writes about André, the object of her affection for both his body and also his French. Long after the encounter is over, Kaplan reflects on what the young man meant for her physically, emotionally, and linguistically: 'I wanted to breathe in French with André, I wanted to sweat French sweat. It was the rhythm and pulse of his French I wanted, the body of it, and he refused me, he told me I could never get that,' writes Kaplan. Earlier in the chapter, and the relationship, Kaplan writes André a letter during an 'erotic trance', telling him how there is power in not being able to communicate in the same language and how instead she must rely on other senses: 'The taste of your body pursues me . . . like an essence.' More than André's body, Kaplan desired his language to physically fill the space she felt between her dominant English and the French she was learning.

In *When in French: Love in a Second Language*, American Lauren Collins recounts falling in love with her now husband, Olivier, a Frenchman. The couple begin their relationship in English, Collins's first and dominant language, Olivier's third. Newlywed and living in a new country, arguably in a different relationship stage than Kaplan and André, Collins recounts moments of communication-related frustration. And yet, when their respective languages impede a comprehensible common vernacular, an electrifying corporality surfaces, at least for this reader, when Olivier tells Collins, 'Talking to you in English is like touching you with gloves.'

The familiar love-in-multiple-languages story is enthralling because not only does it offer a glimpse of how other couples live and love, but the idea of not sharing a language with a partner can be both inconceivable and intensely alluring.[237] In a contribution to the genre, *The Atlantic* interviewed couples who had fallen in love despite their language barrier, including a duo who used translation apps to communicate.[238] At the end of the story, one half of the couple tells the interviewer she cannot wait to have children so her and her partner can teach them their languages. I had both appreciation for this woman's enthusiasm to raise multilingual children, and commiseration that she, who, according to her own narrative, already struggles to communicate with her partner, would so casually mention childrearing as if mothering does not complicate romantic love in one language, let alone two.

Beyond the diminishing romantic lost-in-translation sensuality, at least at first, multilingual co-parenting may sometimes even turn hostile. I have spoken with mothers whose partners were, at best, indifferent to their co-parent's wish to raise multilingual children and, at worst, adverse to the idea, sometimes even insulting the heritage language or prohibiting the other parent from using it. It is not uncommon to see mothers asking for advice on multilingual parenting forums about partners being unreceptive or dismissive of multilingual parenting, and the mother's use of a language the partner does not know. When the mothers attempt to get to the bottom of these ill feelings, they are often met with their partner's insecurities and notions of feeling left out. This is a challenging topic to navigate and to research, as it highlights hostility between co-parents and multilingualism being a burden rather than a 'gift' – all complicated personal narratives and experiences. One mother I spoke with for my academic research, who told me her partner consistently expressed negative comments about her heritage language, sometimes in front of their children, was no longer married to him, so felt comfortable enough sharing her experience with me.

In *Linguistic Intermarriage in Australia: Between Pride and Shame*, Hannah Irving Torsh writes how for linguistically intermarried couples, typical caregiving negotiations – which parent is putting the kids to bed tonight – can be thwarted by the disagreement of what language will be used. Gendered family roles are a major factor in how family members experience language in the family, with tensions between language, power, gender, and identity often at the centre of their experience. The intersection of gender and the perceived lower status of the minoritized language creates a double disadvantage:

'They are disadvantaged both as mothers who are engaged in the unpaid work of raising children and as multilingual speakers who are expected to teach their children their first language in a majority language environment with little personal or institutional support. Moreover, gendered parenting roles and native speakerism make invisible the language transmission of bilingual mothers, compared with bilingual fathers. Bilingual mothers are often described in the research as feeling guilty and distressed.'[239]

Torsh emphasizes what I have already shared: even when the mother is the user of the majority language, she may still be held, and hold herself, responsible for raising multilingual children, even if she is not proficient in the heritage language.[240] Unlike for Kaplan and André, the rhythm and pulse of multilingual parenting is far less erotic and much more exhausting.

Most days, my partner and I use *I love you* or *kocham cię* interchangeably, in person and over texts, and despite his beginner Polish, he uses both phrases with our children. For us, neither one nor the other is more powerful or more emotional. Although I grew up in a home filled with love, my parents never said *kocham cię* regularly in the same way my partner and I do with each other and our children. (Most of the Polish immigrant children of my generation I know had the same experience, where the sentiment, although felt, was rarely verbalized.) Known as 'affective linguistic conditioning', this is when words and phrases acquire 'affective connotations and personal meanings' through 'emotionally-charged' memories and experiences.[241] These can be positive or negative associations and vary from person to person. Although the Polish love phrase does not necessarily have a childhood connection linked to an emotional memory for me, it does have a maternal one, as does the English version, mostly abbreviated for us to 'love you'. But for many mothers, the idea of uttering affectionate terms in any other language than their first, especially if that language remains their dominant one, is unfathomable.

As part of a large-scale study on language and emotions, Jean-Marc Dewaele examined multilinguals' perceived emotional weight of the phrase *I love you* in their different languages.[242] Nearly half of the participants considered *I love you* to have greater emotional weight in their first language (L1), just under a third judged it to have similar weight in both languages, and a quarter felt it had more weight in a language learnt later in life, referred to as LX in the study. But like love itself, the results were not as simple or obvious as one language or the other. Participants noted *I love you* loses its emotional resonance if it is used too often (frequent use in the media, for example). But in places where the phrase is rarely used, like Finland, it retains a powerful emotional resonance. In cultures where verbal love expressions are uncommon, places like Japan and China, respondents reported using the English phrase instead.[243] One respondent felt the concept of love 'prevailed', regardless of which language he used to express it. These sentiments were specific to the participants of the study and many factors affect how someone feels about *I love you* in a specific language beyond simply the language itself. In some cultures and languages, love is communicated without words, which recalls the many stories I have heard about children of immigrants realizing later in life that a plate of cut-up fruit from their parents was, in fact, an *I love you*.

The way someone proclaims and feels love in each of their languages also depends on where and how a language was learnt or acquired. If you consider a language learnt in a classroom setting, perhaps in adulthood, and even in childhood, as French immersion was for me, it is not acquired and learnt in the same way as a language learnt in a naturalistic setting like the home. Although I am fluent in French, a language I learnt as a child from the age of seven and was immersed in every day in the classroom through to the age of nearly eighteen, I do not feel an emotional connection to the language. (Yes, it was 'immersion' but being immersed in a language in a classroom is vastly different than everyday-life immersion.) French is not *embodied* for me, as Aneta Pavlenko explains in *Emotions and Multilingualism*, and learning the language did not involve my limbic system or sensory modalities, even though I learnt it as a child.[244] (Embodied versus disembodied does not necessarily mean primary/secondary or first/subsequent language.)

As a teenager, I joked around with classmates about swear words in French, specifically a Québécois swear word that, for us, was nothing more than three syllables, but means *holy fuck*, something I would hesitate, depending on the company I was keeping, to say out loud in English.[245] Swear or taboo words also have little emotional resonance for me in Polish, my non-dominant language. I was taught as a child which words were not acceptable to say, but those lessons felt more like a teacher–student interaction, rather than something I embodied around other speakers or peers. Like *I love you*, research on how multilinguals feel about using swear words shows that the first language, particularly if it remains a dominant one, has the strongest emotional force when swearing.[246] If a child learns more than one language simultaneously, or a second language in childhood, multiple languages may be emotionally embodied. For me, immigration and socialization meant English developed an emotionally embodied perception, despite it being my third language. (Oddly, and I have no idea why as I have never learnt the language, my most used swear word is *schiesse, shit* in German.)

Emotional resonance of a language can be explored and is often studied in psychotherapy and autobiographical writing, the latter arguably a form of therapy. In psychotherapy, a patient may choose to use one language over another to discuss traumatic or painful events or memories. A language that has less emotional resonance, perhaps a language learnt later in life or one not associated with a distressing event, may be easier to use in discussing trauma and pain. While a first language may be the only one that can elicit memories or be used to discuss feelings that have never been acknowledged in the past.[247]

For writers who escaped political oppression, or wartime trauma, who may want to evade painful memories, or simply feel they need a new linguistic landscape, a language learnt later in life, perhaps after immigration or exile, can be a linguistic or creative salvation. Think here of translingual writers, like Vladimir Nabokov, Milan Kundera, Eva Hoffman, Kyoko Mori, Nancy Huston, and Jhumpa Lahiri. In *Translating Myself and Others*, Lahiri, who grew up in the United States speaking English and Bengali, wrote about her experience of writing in Italian instead of English. The author chose not to translate *In altre parole (In Other Words)* from Italian to English herself (she wrote the book in Italian), because she felt moving between the languages would take away from her Italian voice and she would rely on, but also be constrained by, her dominant English. As a writer of fiction about immigration, multilingualism and belonging, and as a multilingual child of immigrants, Lahiri has, in fact, been translating all her life, whether in her Bengali–English childhood, or in her books, where the characters who live in her mind speak Bengali and she translates on the page.[248] Just as one experiences affective linguistic conditioning in a first language, that same person may undergo *affective socialization*[249] in a language learnt later in life or, in my case, also an affective (re)socialization after I became a mother.[i]

,

In *Emotions and Multilingualism*, Aneta Pavlenko distinguishes between the languages *of* emotions and languages *and* emotions. Languages *of* emotions are how emotions are performed and expressed on different levels: vocal, semantic, conceptual and discourse levels. Languages *and* emotions explore why multilinguals may have different perceptions of, and reactions to, their different languages. So, how they feel emotionally about their different languages and, in turn, how they express emotions in each of those languages. But it is only when Pavlenko shares her poignant personal experience with Russian and English in the book that I pause, read the passage three more times, and consider how singular every person's experience with language and emotions truly is.

'For me, Russian has no neutral words – each one channels voices, each one inspires feelings. Yet it is also the language that attempted to constrain and obliterate me as a Jew, to tie me down as a woman, to render me voiceless, a mute

---

[i] In case it is not clear yet, it is a myth that multilinguals always express and experience their emotions in their first language. Of course, this may be the case but not always and so many different factors are at play beyond language. Some multilinguals may even feel *more* emotional in a language learnt later in life or choose to use it for emotional expression.

slave to a hated regime. To abandon Russian means to embrace freedom. I can talk and write without hearing echoes of things I should not be saying. I can be me. English is a language that offered me that freedom, and yet it is also my second language, whose words – in the unforgettable terms of another fellow bilingual, Julia Kristeva – make us strangers to ourselves.'[250]

Toward the end of the book, the author describes the despair and grief she feels watching her mother die: 'The English words do capture what I am feeling, and so does their Russian equivalent *gore*, as do many other words of the world's languages, but at that moment, I am beyond language.'[251]

و

When I am angry with my children, English bursts out of my body like an electric charge and I catch myself saying something involuntarily I regret a few minutes later. My disciplining in Polish is much more considered and calm in that I must think before I choose my words because it is my weaker language. When my equilibrium tips and I am no longer able to brush things off calmly, my monologues in front of my children about kindness, respect and appreciation begin in even-toned Polish and, with the rise of my heart rate and the gradual loss of composure, English begins to invade. I turn from the mythical maternal figure offering comfort and guidance to a woman crushed by motherhood and language. I surrender.

My verbal affection is typically offered in Polish, and I hope my soft-spoken utterances envelop my children in a protective layer for many years to come. It does not feel unnatural or uncomfortable to verbalize affection in English, but it also does not feel as effortless, especially after nearly ten years of parenting predominantly in Polish. In a moment of parental defeat, if one of my children has carelessly upset someone or gone against my wishes, I say I am *disappointed*. And in the same breath, when my child is sad or gets hurt, I say, *żal mi ciebie* (translation: *I feel a deep sadness for you* but profounder and, for me, more affectionate than the detached and often offensive *I feel sorry for you*). My daughter, unprompted, has begun to say the same Polish phrase back to me when she sees me upset or hurt, the same phrase my mother spoke to me, the one I still implore her to say when I feel the weight of the world. When I tell my daughter she is *cudna* or my son that he is *cudny*, the meaning is far more ethereal than the English translation, 'wonderful'. When I utter the sentiment before bed, I want my children to know that for me, they are otherworldly, imagined and yet, to my daily astonishment, there, in front of me in the flesh. My affection is beyond language as I hold my child's hand while they fall asleep, breathe them in, stroke the bridge of their nose or tuck their hair behind their ear. Polish has no neutral words for me, not because it is my first language, learnt in childhood, but because it is the language I relearnt and, often, translate for myself as a mother. It has allowed me to be a person I never imagined, a maternal figure I never desired nor expected but one that whispers Polish diminutives into her children's delicate ears. English is always close by when I need to assert authority, or rather some semblance of it when childhood chaos ensues, and to remind myself I am also me, before and beyond motherhood. Even so, my children and my mothering has changed my languages – all my languages – forever in ways that, yes, are outside language but also between, across and entrenched deeply.

Bilinguals may switch languages for a variety of reasons: to show they *really* mean something (not unlike using someone's full name for emphasis), for affection, to connect with someone who uses the same language, or even to distance themselves from a strong emotion as a form of protection, as I did in the early days of my relationship with my partner. The advice I often come across for bilingual parents from trusted professionals is to ensure they, the parents, speak the language they are most comfortable in with their children. This is sound advice, especially because it counters any erroneous suggestions parents receive to stop speaking a heritage language in the home. (Please never give or take this advice!) Families should not force a language they are not comfortable in, especially if this decision is a result of someone else's opinion. However, emotions and language are immeasurably more nuanced and sometimes a non-dominant language may play a part in the parent–child emotional connection or, as in my case, a caregiver may feel the pull to draw on different languages at different times.

Family language planning, or which and how languages will be used, and by whom in the family, is never a bad idea. But language plans can be altered, revised and, in the end, not unlike birth plans, are often out of one's control, especially the language *of/and* emotions. A language may seem *unnatural, false,* or *fake* at first, but may shift over time, as Polish has done for me during motherhood. Looking back at some of the early baby videos with my first child, I hear my piercing voice, first in English and then, as if a jolt awakens me, an apprehensive Polish surfaces. It took a long time to return to my first, now non-dominant language, to feel at ease in its world and make it my own. Polish did not come *naturally* at first with my children, and only now do I consider the connection to another falsehood new mothers are fed, the one about the maternal instinct.[252] When I had children, I began another socialization, this one not only into motherhood but also *back to* Polish. When I am mothering, I am both the agent socializing my children in Polish and also the subject being socialized by my children and my partner, in both languages.[253] It is a complex back-and-forth between identities and languages, but it is not an either/or.

The phenomenon of considering a first language the language of emotional connection for parenting is not one that exists in every language and culture. This association does exist in European languages, what Aneta Pavlenko calls the ideology and romantic discourse of first language primacy.[254] This ideology is also linked with another one: the mother–child emotional attachment. When a language is said to feel *right* or *wrong* in the context of emotion but also, in parenting, how much of that is led by a feeling of *what should be?* Many mothers do not ruminate on their language choice because they do not have one or must go on with life and caregiving. But too often, our relationships with our children are governed by ideals and ideas of what mothering should be, or how we should speak or communicate. Just as a mother may consider using anything but her first language with her child for emotional communication unfathomable, the notion of first language primacy can also contribute to the guilt felt by mothers attempting to raise multilingual children in a language learnt later in life. It is not always one or the other, and yet we are also damned if we do, damned if we don't.

There is a quote in Rachel Cusk's *A Life's Work: On Becoming a Mother* that I consider often in the context of caregiving but also language. Cusk writes how after the birth of a child, a woman's understanding of what it means to exist is completely changed. When the mother is with her children, she is not herself. When she is without them, she too is not herself, so it is a continuous struggle, the child living within 'the jurisdiction of her consciousness'. I do not have singular personalities and I am not a different person in any of my languages, but I often feel I am, also, never fully myself, especially when mothering in multiple languages. 'The experience of motherhood loses nearly everything in its translation to the outside world,' writes Cusk. I am an in-between, an amalgam, a boundary of something I can never truly be part of, and yet, perhaps that is what it means to be forever changed by motherhood.

('A Bit Shitty' But I Still Love You)

When Facetiming with my parents in Canada, my children's favourite thing to do is to paste poop emojis all over the screen: the smiling poop, the crying poop, the frowning poop. My mother, with her infinite patience reserved for her grandchildren, takes it in her stride, laughing at yet another 💩. My children's messages to me, using their father's phone, also strongly feature poop emojis, as well as animals, digital touch messages, photos of football players and dogs. There are also many 👍, 🐕 🐶 ♥ and often an *I love you*, *I miss you*, 😘 *kocham cie, you are the best* typed out amid emojis. I usually send 🐶 ♥ back and throw in a 🐴 or 🐶, more photos of dogs or footballers, a 👍 and then, I type *co robisz?* (*What are you doing?*) and *kocham cię*. (I reserve my most-used emoji 😩, a reflection of how I often feel about the world, for my partner.)

When emojis made their worldwide debut around 2010 (Japan adopted them more than a decade earlier), article after article rhapsodized about whether this was the new language of the youth: would it soon take over? The consensus among

174

linguists was emojis were not a language, predominantly because languages have grammatical rules and emojis mean different things to different people. But emojis play a fundamental role in online communication as paralinguistic elements, the non-lexical elements of communication, used in the same way as gestures in face-to-face communication.[255]

In *Because Internet: Understanding the New Rules of Language*, Gretchen McCulloch devotes a chapter to emoji and other internet gestures, examining how the appeal of the emoji is in its function as a digital embodiment, representing our gestures and our physical space. 'Sometimes, you don't actually have anything informative to say to the other person, and all you're looking to communicate is subtext: "I see this", "I'm listening", or "I am still here and I still want to be talking with you",' writes McCulloch.[256] The emojis that do not correspond to gestures are culture-specific emblems and do not necessarily mean or represent the same thing across cultures. Much to my delight, McCulloch notes the smiling poop emoji. It means, according to the software engineers, that someone doesn't like something, but softly; or, as McCulloch adds, 'a bit shitty'. It makes sense why my young daughter sends me dozens – *a bit shitty* times twelve – from her father's phone when she knows I won't be home for bedtime.

In multilingual contexts, emojis reinforce ideas, emotions, actions, and objects, sometimes also adding cultural context, encouraging engagement and multimodality of language, simplifying communication, and fostering emotional connection. Non-verbal modalities, or means of expression, such as emojis used between parents and children, can also be independent of language choice in emotion work with the caveat that they do not replace the role of language in maintaining parent–child connections and intergenerational intimacy. The use of emojis and other digital practices are forms of kinship 'interwoven within the everyday', maintaining closeness among friends and family and informing care work, not only at a distance but across generations.[257] The use of emojis has been studied in intergenerational communication: children, parents and grandparents communicating with one another using a variety of paralinguistic elements, including emojis but also emoticons and stickers, co-presenting intimacy and care in a playful manner, often across vast geographic separation.[258] I think back to my annoyingly difficult teenage self, self-important and impervious to the passing of time, having uneasy conversations with my own grandparents on the rotary phone, us calling from Canada, them in Poland. Face-to-face, there was no awkwardness (this was long before FaceTime) and I adored spending time with them in person. But the phone calls amplified our geographic distance rather than bringing us closer together. (In the 1980s, telephone calls overseas were also incredibly expensive.) I was habitually handed the telephone unexpectedly, told to talk to my grandparents. I wonder if sending my grandmothers a few 🙂 💜 occasionally would have felt more authentic than trying to discuss the weather on a phone call, complete with a ubiquitous three-second delay.

In '妈妈, *I miss you* 🙂': *Emotional multilingual practices in transnational families*', the authors examine how emotions as everyday practice are communicated, and how emotionality is conveyed through language choice and embodied in the family life of six families from two transnational communities, Chinese and Polish. Looking at daily WhatsApp/WeChat texts and digital-mediated family talk recorded by the families themselves, the researchers found five key features in online or offline family talks regarding expression of emotionality: emojis, terms of endearment, diminutives, declarations of love and situated emotive language use. For four of the six families, emojis played a vital role in communication. Girls in the families were more likely to use 🙂 💜 than the boys because of the differing ages of the children (one girl was younger) but also because of the cultural differences between the Polish and Chinese families. (The boys who did not use 🙂 💜 were between nine and eleven years old, an age when boys may begin to exert their independence from the family and become more peer focused.) Echoing previous research on how different cultures embrace different beliefs and values around emotional expression, the Chinese families differed from the Polish families in their expressions of affection and love.[259]

Digital communication, especially across languages and generations, is a vital part of meaning-making and identity assertion for young people. Although I often ask my children to stop posting 💩 when talking to their grandparents, maybe the exchange is what they need to make it meaningful, or at least fun. After all, language is not only for expressing experiences, but experiences are created through language.[260] As I mother (in Polish), I create (Polish) experiences for my children; as my children express their experiences to other friends and family, they also create experiences with those people, even if it means, for now, some 💩.

How Do You Know Me &
How Do I Know Myself?

It is remarkable to have people in your life who know you in all your languages, especially when they are not biological family. Two friends from my childhood occupy this role in my life. One of them is a Polish immigrant to Canada and a French immersion school kid, like me; the other friend, the daughter of a German immigrant, who, although she is not Polish, spent considerable time with me and my family growing up. I travelled to Poland with each of them when we were younger, even though for one friend the country has no cultural or linguistic roots. Both women know me as a trilingual and I do not mean in separate languages, although there is some crossover, but as multilingually whole. Although we mostly speak English with one another, my Polish friend and I regularly throw in some Polish when we need a private language, but also to describe a childhood memory or something that is *too* Polish to discuss in English.

The other friend and I, if reminiscing about our youth, might add some French to the conversation. (If you were a French immersion kid all the way through to high school in the small city where I grew up, you share a singular educational experience with a small group of people.) I am the same person in all three languages with each woman because they have both known me nearly my entire life. And yet the only reason I feel whole around them is because they know me as someone fractured by language, culture, immigration and a transnational experience. It is endearing and unlike anything else I've experienced in female friendship, when two grown women, who were both cut off from an adult-level Polish by immigration to Canada as children, discuss having *herbatka* or *kawka* together (translation: *little tea* and *little coffee* but both the tea and the coffee are, in fact, regular size). As they inevitably do when I am with my children, Polish diminutives tiptoe into our conversations with this friend. For a moment, we become those little girls again, giggling at Polish church, learning traditional Polish dances and songs, and memorizing the dates of Poland's partitions – caught in a nostalgia of what was both lost and saved.

In *Nord Perdu,* Canadian transplant to France, Nancy Huston, who writes often in French, a language she learnt later in life, remarks how when you leave a place, eventually friends from *there* are replaced by friends from *here.* It is unfeasible to continue some correspondence with people you do not share your daily existence with, she writes. The same sentiment may apply to friendships that were *there* before motherhood, and friendships that are *here* after, especially if only one friend is a new mother. And yet the before and after, the *here* and *there* may have a unifying influence. You may not share your daily existence with someone *there* any longer, but those people from *there,* if they continue to know you *here,* are in some way a life fragmented, bodies and souls split by time and place, becoming whole.

,

Someone once asked me in which language I dream. At first, I said English, but I am no longer so sure. In a bid to find out, in the mornings, I jot down what I remember from my dreams the night before. But there is never a spoken language, not really. Or I don't remember what I've said after waking up. The dreams I remember most are ones where I am mostly alone, trying to remember a phone number to reach a loved one, but I can't get the number right time and time again. Or I am trying to find a room, a classroom or, once, a shower, but never make it. Something always gets in the way, or I get lost, ending up where I began, entering the same numbers repeatedly on the telephone. I had a dream recently where I was trying to usher my children out of a dangerous situation. There was no one else around, only us three and we had to leave immediately. I don't remember saying a word, only using my arms to lead them to safety. There are faces in my dreams, sometimes staring at me with blank expressions, but never voices. The gestures, often panicked, are always my own.

Questions around dreaming in one or more language(s) are often paired with considerations about thinking in a language, and inner speech. A common sentiment I've heard numerous times is that if you begin to dream or think in a language, especially one new to you, it signifies you are beginning to 'truly' acquire and know that language. But thinking and dreaming may both be independent of language. The reason people believe we think in one language has more to do with planning to speak, or 'silent self-talk'[261], which is beyond thinking. In inner speech, several factors affect which language a multilingual might use, including the dominant language, when and where the languages were acquired, proficiency and frequency of language use, and even the size of the language user's social network. In one study on multilingualism and dreams, multilinguals were asked to report their dreams and what language choices they made subconsciously when dreaming. The results showed exposure to a language is the main determinant of subconscious activation such as dreaming. The topic and interlocutors in a dream also play a part in which language the dream occurs, as do the positive or negative attitudes toward a language.[262]

The idea one must dream or think in a language to claim it as yours, or to 'truly' know it, is another attempt to define who is and who isn't a 'true multilingual'. And, in case I have not been clear enough yet, this is a subjective and indefinable designation. Not far behind is the common misconception that bilinguals or multilinguals have split or double personalities. Multilinguals may *feel* differently in different languages, or act in a different way, as perceived by others but also, and perhaps especially, by themselves. They may also communicate *differently*, particularly on a lexical level. But more than a change in personality, it is likely 'a shift in attitudes and behaviours corresponding to a shift in situation or context, independent of language.'[263] In studies on multilinguals 'feeling' differently in their different languages, the connection between proficiency and language is repeatedly highlighted – feeling more 'natural' in a dominant language, for example. How someone perceives themselves as opposed to how others perceive them, and even cultural norms in different languages also come into play.[264]

It is worth repeating not all multilinguals have the immense privilege of considering how they feel and act in their different languages, or of choosing which language to use when, where and with whom. When someone is perceived to act differently in different languages, biculturalism, and not just bilingualism, and the different domains of languages may be involved.[265] A monolingual person who is bicultural and lives their life across two cultures will likely act differently in the different cultures, even if that person is using one language to communicate in both environments. It is far more captivating to think of multilinguals as different people when they use their different languages as opposed to considering biculturalism and other factors. But these thoughts may propagate notions of separation, even hierarchies, that consider multilingualism as something broken. (Think of how languages are considered 'harsh' or 'cold' and how that relates to someone's perceived personality.) Even when languages are likened to fragments of self, and for many multilinguals they may well be, splinters may co-exist amicably. Motherhood cracked me open, left nothing unturned, and shattered what I thought I knew about myself into a thousand pieces. I painstakingly began to put the pieces back together, endlessly rearranging, never complete, if absolute means unchanging but also never in opposition. My linguistic identity, one I presumed was intact, also came apart and that too had to be mended, one precarious bit after another endlessly teetering on the unpredictability of both language and mothering.

Like emotions and language, notions around language and identity are multifaceted and personal. Linguistic identity is socially constructed and studied on various levels, including individual, social (conversations, groups, roles), family, community, and through notions around in-group (belonging) and out-, or sameness and distinction. It is not only about the languages we use but the way we use them and how we consider ourselves as users of those languages, and yes, the stories we tell ourselves, that affect and create identity. 'These links between languages and identity narratives have the power to enhance or weaken speakers' emotional investments in particular languages, steer them away from "languages of the enemy" and toward the languages of power and desire,' writes Aneta Pavlenko in *Emotions and Multilingualism,* who notes ethnic, national, political and gender identities among the many other possible allegiances that often intersect with linguistic identity.[266] In research around raising multilingual children, the degree to which families consider their heritage language as part of their identities varies, but the importance of intergenerational communication and a connection with an ethnocultural identity may encourage some families to transmit and maintain a heritage language.[267]

Despite the common misconception that one language equals one culture, people are made up of collective identities, sometimes accommodating one another, at times struggling to co-exist. Language may be a vital marker of cultural or ethnic identity, but it is far from the only one, even if culture, or at least a cultural memory of language, is within us, a part of our bodies and souls. (Cultural identity may be separate from linguistic identity but often the two are intertwined and may include ethnic identity.) A sense of pride in a cultural or ethnic identity, or as evident by a version of 'Be proud of where you come from', especially reiterated by first-generation immigrant parents, is often an underlying factor for passing on a heritage language. But as authors of one study showed, the pride or 'pride-based ideologies' around passing on a heritage language can also highlight differences with other groups not only in language but also culture, race, and values.[268] Pride may turn into, or highlight, prejudice. This brings up the question of ownership and what it means to 'possess' a language and how feelings around owning a language are parallel to language pride in that they may create a sense of belonging but often at the expense of othering something or someone else.

'Although there is no one-to-one relationship between anyone's language and his or her cultural identity, language is *the* most sensitive indicator of the relationship between an individual and a given social group,' writes Claire Kramsch in *Language and Culture*. She adds that group identity is a cultural perception that we have been conditioned by our own culture to consider, including the racial and ethnic stereotypes that these perceptions impose on certain groups. 'However, if language indexes our relation to the world, it is not itself this relation,' she adds.[269] Kramsch's line echoes as I also consider motherhood in the same way: motherhood is *the* most sensitive indicator of my lived experience, predominantly because I am responsible for other humans but also because the emotion and love I feel toward my children is unlike anything I have ever experienced before. And yet I existed before them and would continue to exist if I had not had my children, not in the same way, but nevertheless I would still hold a place in the world and retain a linguistic identity. Languages unite us but the divisions between them are also part of our human condition, and it is our responsibility to pay attention to the misunderstandings and to work through them, to exist in language but never at the expense of another. The identity created through and by a language is closely linked to identities around mothering and motherhood and, most importantly, a sense of belonging to somewhere and something. This imbalance or uneasiness around identity, language, *and* motherhood, especially in relation to oneself but also to our children and society, is complex and often arduous. As Jean Mills poignantly writes in her work on motherhood and multilingualism: 'In other words, a mother's language choices are related to her notions of mothering.'[270]

Don't Call Me 'Mom'[i]

My daughter recently started a journal all about her likes, dislikes, what she enjoys doing and who she spends time with. While writing about our family one day, she turned to me and asked if she could call me *Mom* instead of the customary *Mama*. 'Why?' I asked while I caught my breath and tried to shake off the unnerved feeling that began to consume me. This is not the first time one of my children has uttered that strange three-letter word. I once overheard my son talking to his English-speaking friend, recounting a story about something where I was the character, 'my mom'. It was unsettling but made sense since he communicates with this friend only in English. Part of me was thankful I wasn't *mummy* or *mommy*, so I let the *mom* slide. (Apologies to the *mummies*, but the moniker is not for me and, as was recently brought to my attention, the longer you call your mum/mom *mummy* and dad *daddy*, apparently the *posher* you

---

[i] Although I am writing about multilingual kinship terms here, I want to mention a campaign in the UK with the same name, although it is 'mum' and not 'mom'. Launched in 2016, 'Don't Call Me Mum' is an initiative to encourage healthcare practitioners and other professionals to work co-productively with parents to ensure children receive the care they require. This begins with learning the caregivers' name(s) rather than referring to them as 'Mum' or 'Dad'.

are.[271]) But with my daughter, I pushed back. I asked her why she wanted to write *Mom* and not *Mama*.[272] She shrugged her shoulders and acquiesced saying, fine, she would write *Mama*. I later realized she had spent the day before with English-speaking friends at forest school who mostly all call their maternal figures *Mom* (or more likely *Mum*). The peer group is a powerful language influencer, even among adults, as I recently learnt when I kept calling my partner *Dad* to my children in front of a few other English-speaking families. Finally, my daughter chimed in, 'His name is *Dada*, not *Dad*.' (It felt uncomfortably childish for me to say *Dada* in front of other adults.)

In '*A Mother's Tongue*', Sandra Kouritzin writes about her own experience of mothering in Japanese, neither her first nor her dominant language. Using Japanese with her children in their early years was a decision she and her partner made so the children could have as much Japanese input and exposure as possible before starting English-language school in Canada. Once children begin school in the language of the community, the heritage language may suffer as a result. The input of the school language increases while the input of the home language often decreases. Plus, peer-group influence and pressure to assimilate and use the language of the group play a vital role. Kouritzin compares her experience, although notes it is also infinitely different, with that of immigrant mothers who are forced or coerced to speak the community language in the guise of encouraging the school language. In both experiences, Kouritzin and the immigrant mothers face complicated and challenging emotions of potential detachment from their children and their own identities. Notwithstanding the reasons behind the choice to mother in a non-dominant language, or one someone considers *foreign*, the decision is a sacrifice the mother makes, and in so doing she often forgoes an emotional connection to one of her languages, to her children, and to the language in which she mothers. And even when the goal, to teach and strengthen a heritage language before the community language takes over in school, as was the case for Kouritzin, is achieved, language and motherhood may be at odds, outwitting each other with every word and phrase.

'English is the language of my heart, the one in which I can easily express love for my children; in which I know instinctively how to coo to a baby; in which I can sing lullabies, tell stories, recite nursery rhymes, talk baby talk. In Japanese, there is an artificiality about my love; I cannot express it naturally or easily. The emotions I feel do not translate well into the Japanese language, and those which I have seen expressed by Japanese mothers do not seem sufficiently intimate when I mouth them ... When my daughter, learning from Japanese cartoons and playmates, calls me *Mama* or *ka-chan* instead of *Mommy*, I feel very far removed from her, as if my identity has been erased.'[273]

Jhumpa Lahiri offers the perspective of the child in her memoir *Translating Myself and Others*. One of her earliest memories of what she calls a 'translation dilemma' was in kindergarten while making cards for Mother's Day. In the cards, all the children were instructed to handwrite the same English message: 'Dear Mom, happy Mother's Day.' 'This part of the project stymied me, given that my mother was not "Mom" but "Ma",' writes Lahiri. 'I was embarrassed to insert the Bengali term I used and knew her by – the one she recognized and responded to. I was also reluctant to resort to the English term, which sounded foreign to me, and would have certainly alienated, even offended her.'

When I asked on social media about how others felt about being called a different version of the mom moniker (*mommy* versus *mama*, for example) especially if the home language was different than the community one and the maternal moniker was something different in the majority language, several mothers responded that because of strained relationships with their own mothers, they had chosen a different language to raise their children in and different names to be called. I know other multilingual mothers living in English-speaking areas passing on a heritage language who are uncomfortable being called *Mom* or *Mommy* when they have always been *Mama*, *Mamãe* or *Mamá*, often what they call their own mother. One Korean American woman told me she grew up calling her mom *Umma* and her father *Appa* but her children call her *Mama* or *Mommy*. The woman's mom, now grandmother, who immigrated to the U.S. in her twenties, used to call her mom *Mother*. Only as an adult did the Korean American woman consider her Korean mother referring to her Korean grandmother as *Mother* instead of *Umma* a consequence of assimilation, either what her grandmother requested or what her mother, then a child, did to feel as if they were fitting into a new country and culture. Another respondent, who grew up in the Dominican Republic, says her parents will forever be *Mami* and *Papi* (a form of *Mommy* and *Daddy*), monikers that did not shift as she got older. This mother of two considers the English *Mommy* to *Mom* shift a symbol of America's obsession with independence and individualism. Another shift may occur in the form of teenage rebellion, as one Polish woman told me. Her older brother began calling their father *Ojciec* (Father) instead of *Tatuś* (Daddy) in Polish and she, along with their younger brother, followed suit. The result was not only a name change but a significant shift in the children's relationship with their father, she says.

In *Memory Speaks: On Losing and Reclaiming Language and Self,* Julie Sedivy writes about the loss of her heritage language after her family immigrated to Canada from Czechoslovakia when Sedivy was a child. 'As my siblings and I distanced ourselves from the Czech language, a space widened between us and our parents ... Even the English names for our parents encouraged dissent: The tender Czech words we'd used – "*Maminka*", "*Tatinek*" – are impossible to pronounce with contempt, but they have no corresponding forms.'[274] Even in monolingual families, there is sometimes a shift from *Mama* or *Mommy* to simply *Mom* when a child gets older. The change can be a heart-breaking assault on identity when the moniker feels unfamiliar, or too formal, like *Mother*. But it is also a marker of time as children grow up and *Mommy* becomes *Mom*, or yes, even the impassive *Mother*!

In multilingual families, kinship terms may play a vital role in family power dialogues and identity formation, often performed in a strategic manner. They can also be used to 'reproduce and contradict social norms'.[275] Exploring kinship terms in multilingual families sheds light not only on how members of a family navigate relationships in multiple languages but also on power dynamics and language socialization:

'Work that family members do to transmit minority languages, use multilingual repertoires, or socialize one another into linguistic practices are all embedded in the activity of being and doing family and focusing on kinterms as discursive, affective markers of these relationships can help to better elucidate when families are 'doing family' and how kinship roles and relationships shape other activities.'[276]

Families come in many distinctive forms and sizes, and kinship looks different for everyone, as do kinship terms. I write about my own experience as a cisgender woman in a heteronormative relationship with a cisgender man whose children call us, predominantly, *Mama* and *Dada*. But there are many different intersections between language and gender in LGBTQ+ multilingual families where the families determine kinship terms that work for them and their children beyond heteronormative monikers.

In *Critical Perspectives on Language and Kinship in Multilingual Families*, Lyn Wright writes about gender, sexuality, and bilingualism in the LGBTQ+-identified family, examining what gendered roles mean beyond the heteronormative father–mother bilingual family. In one Spanish–English bilingual family Wright interviews, the parents go by *Mama* and *Mamo*. As one parent identifies as butch and the other as femme, the former has a masculine ending 'o' in Spanish, and the latter has a feminine ending, 'a'.[277] It would not be possible for this family to do this in English as English does not mark gender for nouns. Another multilingual respondent in Wright's study, who is from Belgium married to a monolingual American man, discusses how in America, masculinity is tied to monolingualism. Wright notes that this is along similar lines to how bilingualism is predominantly women's work, except this power dynamic and struggle is between a certain type of masculinity tied to monolingualism, even though it is between two men.[278] A Norwegian friend of mine, who shares four children with her wife, is *Mama* to their children while her partner is *Mor* (Norwegian for mother). Children of another couple I know, a mother and father, refer to their parents by their first names. When I asked this friend if it has always been this way, she told me it was only when the family moved from Germany to the UK that the children began to use their parents' first names, something she feels was initiated by the initial language barrier for her children, then two, four and six years old.

Melody Makers & Memory Keepers

As my newborn son cried inconsolably after a traumatic birth, my partner and I took turns walking the halls of the maternity ward, rocking him insistently. Bruised and bleeding, barely able to shuffle along, my legs moved sluggishly but my arms rocked fervently while I sang songs about campfires burning and scout leaders telling tales.[i] Mothers are supposed to sing lullabies, I thought. The only Polish songs I knew were the campfire ones from the scout camp I attended every year where immigrant parents sent their children to be immersed in Polish language and culture, with some forest survival skills thrown in for good measure.

Eventually, I started singing another song to both my babies, also one I learnt at camp, not about fires and forests but of patriotism. It was an ode to Poland *and* Canada. I have written about the song, with its proclaimed love for both countries, once before, in a magazine article about young immigrant Canadians and children of immigrants caught between cultures. The lyrics of the song are about not knowing how to show our love for

---

[i] The Polish scout song, '*Płonie ognisko i szumią knieje*'.

a country that has done so much for us and given us many treasures. Sung in two verses, the first one is for Poland, the second for Canada. Both verses end with a melodic *Ja kocham cię* (*I love you*) proclaimed to each country. After a while, instead of Poland and Canada, I decided to dedicate the short verses to each of my children, substituting the countries for first my son's name, followed by my daughter's – patriotic motherhood. The songs I sang to my children in Polish, and later the English nursery rhymes I learnt with them at a baby rhyme-time class at our local library, were sometimes emotional, often odd, but rarely dark. But many lullabies are famously sombre. Federico Garcia Lorca, when studying lullabies, not only referenced their poetic character but their 'depth of sadness' and how they allowed the caregiver, often the mother, to put into words their own fears and worries.[279] Lullabies often also play a part in a cultural practice of preserving language, heritage, and intergenerational relationships. At times, songs are the only remnants of a family language, whether by tragic circumstance, or a common intergenerational loss. One of the most moving introductions I read for a study on the complexity of language attrition was about the recollections of a German–Jewish migrant who came to England by herself in 1939 at only thirteen years old. She later discovered her entire family perished in concentration camps. Afterwards, the German language was a source of immense pain for this woman: 'This repulsion remained with her all her life – with one exception: when she herself became a mother and later a grandmother, she talked and sang to the infants in the language that her own parents had used with her when she was that age,' write the authors.[280]

When I once posted about the power of lullabies online, Sedea Katesdóttir Midjord commented that it is the burden of the daughter to know the mother. The comment intrigued me so much, I got in touch to talk about her experiences as both a daughter and a mother, a multilingual, and about the memories she keeps of her mother, who died when Sedea was only eighteen. And of the burden she carries. Sedea's mother was from the Faroe Islands and her first language was Faroese, the language she first used with Sedea. Once the young girl began school, Danish took over and, as Sedea says, her mother stopped speaking Faroese in the home, likely because her daughter started using the school's and her peer group's language more often. 'The only thing that remained of that language in our relationship was a lullaby she would always sing to me and my siblings, the title is, *Dear Mom, I Want to Sleep*,' says Sedea. 'It's one of the only linguistic links I have with my mother, and it's what I've also passed on to my daughter: the remnants of her grandma's native tongue. I feel a sort of shame sometimes over not being able to give her more than that.' Faroese was a language Sedea's mother reverted to if she was caught by surprise or shocked by something, but otherwise she used Danish with her children. Sedea and her young daughter regularly travel to the Faroe Islands, an emotional and calming experience, she says, because she gets to share the experience of her own childhood in her mother's home with her daughter, who she is raising in Danish and English. For now, experiencing the Faroe Islands with her daughter regularly brings them both closer to the Faroe language, even if they do not use it often. But what Sedea thinks about beyond language, she tells me, is she feels she has the sole responsibility of ensuring her daughter's maternal grandmother exists for her, through memories and, often, through a lullaby.

9

In addition to their emotive quality, children's songs and nursery rhymes are heralded as an effective language-development tool in educational settings. But there is a mismatch between the intuition teachers might feel around using songs for achieving linguistic outcomes in the classroom, and the empirical evidence supporting what is popularly known as 'the Mozart effect', that learning music makes you better at other cognitive tasks (improving spatial awareness) or academic tasks (learning maths or languages).[281] 'It's because of this cultural belief that songs are so powerful, and intuitively, people feel that there is this causal thing,' says Cate Hamilton, author of a study on the 'folk pedagogy' of using songs with young students.[282] 'And the evidence base is really not there . . . if you take the cultural belief out and say, what do we actually know about songs' effects on linguistic development compared to other teaching methods?'

Hamilton, a doctoral candidate at the University of Oxford whose research investigates the effectiveness of using songs with young language learners in formal educational settings, says teachers often feel intuitively that songs and nursery rhymes translate into an effective language teaching practice for young children. But those notions, based on collective belief and anecdotal experience, are not backed by rigorous evidence. (This is not to be confused with how songs can be motivational or used as a memorization tool. Hamilton examines language development through music.) Many primary school Modern Foreign Languages (MFL) teachers are thrown into language instruction unexpectedly, adds Hamilton, so it is no wonder they draw on any available resource they have, including the *Frère Jacques* they learnt as children. But it is also about cultural beliefs, drawn from emotional connection around songs and music.

Hamilton's study found limited evidence to support the use of songs for non-musical learning outcomes, including supporting language development. Her work does not imply songs should *not* be used in the classroom, far from that. Rather, it demonstrates how powerful a cultural belief can be, especially when there is an emotive element, like with music, and particularly songs learnt in childhood. Hamilton's research focus is especially fascinating considering she is also the co-founder of Babel Babies, an organization that runs multisensory and multilingual music and story sessions for young children, where children and parents learn new languages together through songs and play. She is an ardent advocate for exposing children to new languages through music, whether there is a heritage language at home or not. In a way, her research adds the vital element, or reminder, just because something like learning songs in different languages is worth doing, enjoyable and often emotional, does not mean there has to be a form of capital gained from the experience. 'It doesn't mean songs are better for introducing languages than another method . . . And given that it is such a valued tool in teaching, I think that teachers deserve the very best kind of supporting research to be done,' she says.

Hamilton, a mom of three, launched Babel Babies after having her first child and wanting to teach him a language she began learning when she was eleven years old. 'I wanted to introduce him to French, but I felt like a complete middle-class twit speaking French to my baby in Tesco's in Kilmarnock, Scotland,' says Hamilton, who kept being asked by strangers where she was from, to which she replied awkwardly, 'Birmingham.' 'And so, even though I'm bilingual in French through education, I couldn't speak to my baby in French without feeling like I needed an excuse.' Babel Babies gave her that excuse, and she launched the company with another multilingual friend. But beyond French and the German her co-founder was fluent in, the goal was to expose children to as many languages as possible in hopes of inspiring a love of all languages.

Once other parents joined the classes, Hamilton says she often heard caregivers, predominantly mothers, proclaiming they were 'bad at languages' and they did not want their children to inherit this self-perceived predisposition. My conversation with Hamilton brings up many of the questions and ideas I've returned to in this book: who gets to be bilingual and raise bilingual children; the difference between appreciation and appropriation; the fact that no one is truly 'bad at language' and the numerous myths, including that there is a deadline for when children learn subsequent languages. 'It really makes me so angry, and it feeds into this insecurity that parents, especially mums, feel: the guilt of like I must do languages with my kids when I'm already overwhelmed with a new baby, and I've got seventy-five loads of washing and I now have to introduce them to languages. Otherwise, I failed.' But, Hamilton adds, it goes back to us learning from one another, appreciating each other's backgrounds, and acknowledging multilingualism and multiculturalism is everywhere. Many of the parents Hamilton encounters through Babel Babies initially consider language as an educational opportunity, yes, a form of capital. But after a few classes of singing *Itsy Bitsy Spider* in Arabic, they are shocked by how emotional the learning becomes, and the connection they create with their children through music.

,

In *Translating lives: Living with two languages and cultures* Polish–Australian linguist Anna Wierzbicka writes about the Polish term *pamiątka*, one she argues has no English equivalent because of its cultural connotation to Poland's immense loss over the centuries: loss of entire cities and populations during the war; loss of · independence and freedom; loss of existence as Poland was wiped off the world map for 123 years, I add. Wierzbicka equates the word with her own experience as a six-year-old having to flee from Warsaw because of the uprising, leaving everything behind except a few family *pamiątki*. The closest word-for-word translation is *souvenir* but as she argues, *souvenir* has to do with travel and geography and a freedom of movement, while *pamiątka* is history, 'transience of life, loss and destructibility of the past . . . above all, nostalgia and devotion'.[283] (In certain contexts 'heirloom' could work, but it too does not have the same emotional attachment as *pamiątka*; Wierzbicka adds 'memento' or 'keepsake' but argues neither of these terms have implications of great emotional value.) Unlike Wierzbicka, I do not consider words 'untranslatable' as it takes us into dangerous territory of othering: the belief that languages that have one-word or succinct terms for certain feelings or experiences must mean users of these languages are *better, more aware, different*. We all feel similar things, even if in one language it takes multiple words, or sentences, to convey that feeling. It is poetic and romantic to consider *schadenfreude* or *saudade* as experiences and emotions German and Portuguese speakers know *instinctively* or *better* because those languages have lexical terms. (I am including two of the most popular examples but there are many, enough to fill numerous books on 'untranslatable' words.) But speakers of those languages are not the only ones experiencing feelings of longing and nostalgia (*saudade*) or pleasure from someone's misfortune (*schadenfreude*).

Are there cultural differences between language users depending on context? Of course. If someone resides in a place covered in snow and ice for a large part of the year, or somewhere where it rains often, it makes sense they have many ways to describe that weather. But nothing is truly 'untranslatable'. For Wierzbicka, *pamiątka* has a specific emotional connection to the past, drawing on a specific context and time. For me, *pamiątki* (plural) are frivolous objects, material things, symbols – amber jewellery, Polish books, leather slippers, carved wooden boxes called *kasetki* – given to me by Polish family members, for example, to remember my time spent with them in Poland. *Pamiątki* are also concert or theatre ticket stubs, train tickets, museum tickets and other evidence I have been somewhere that mattered to me. Not so much 'souvenirs' but perhaps physical and emotional mementos and keepsakes. For Wierzbicka, who immigrated to Australia as an adult, Polish has a deep emotional resonance, a language in which she experienced war, trauma, and fear:

> 'Arguably, the word *pamiątka* reflects historical experiences of this kind and implies an attitude of treasuring the past and wanting to keep it firmly in one's memory . . . It also seems to suggest an appreciation that the framework of one's life can be destroyed, that the continuity of this framework cannot be taken for granted, and that since the material links between the present and the past are likely to be fragile and limited, they should be an object of special care and devotion (almost veneration, like relics).'[284]

Perhaps a heritage language passed on from mother to child is a *pamiątka*: a fragile framework of continuity, something that requires special care and devotion, untranslatable in its singular experience, but universally comprehensible by mothers as something fleeting in childhood, a permanent proof of existence and care with a generous tinge of nostalgia. After all, mothers are language keepers and memory makers.

PART 5

Departures & Returns

Syntax: *the study of how words and morphemes combine to form larger units, such as phrases and sentences*

Return

'It's *trochę dziwne* (*a little weird*) speaking Polish here,' my son says as we enter our Kraków hotel room. 'We don't have our secret language because *wszyscy* (*everyone*) speaks Polish.' I nod as my body fills with an unfurling amusement and joy at my child's endearing remark about *our* secret language. 'I know, it is both wonderful and weird,' I reply in Polish. We have come to Poland for a few days to see family, to show my children my birth city, and to offer them a few days in a place where, yes, our 'secret language' back in London is not only public but also *ordinary*, *routine* and, most importantly, *needed*. My children trade in their surprise at hearing someone speaking Polish on the street for the appeal of being able to ask the hotel staff for anything and everything – more syrup, more ketchup, why the video game in the hotel lobby isn't working – in Polish. At breakfast, they argue who gets to ask the waiter for more juice – in Polish!

One day, while visiting with a bilingual Polish–English friend in Kraków, my son has had enough but cannot communicate his desire to leave in a language the friend will not understand. He begins to throw out the few sentences he knows in beginner Spanish as a signal for me to wrap up the visit. We both laugh at his attempt to conjure a new secret language in place of the one that has been dissolved temporarily because of his environment.

We haven't been back to Kraków as a family for six years, and the snippets of Ukrainian I hear on the streets because of Russia's invasion of Ukraine two years earlier and the forced migration of Ukrainian people, although expected, add to my daily revelation at how quickly the world changes. Last time we were here, my daughter was only beginning to babble, my son, who then attended a nursery in London surrounded by British-English speakers, was still pronouncing *hot* with the rounded vowel, his tiny lips pursed into a kiss shape when he said the word. *Hot* for him now has a significantly more Canadian-English hum to it.

When we meet with family, my cousins, and my cousin's children, now to my continued astonishment mostly adults, engage my son with talk of football. His passion for the topic breaks down any language inhibitions. Polish, *his Polish*, and some Ponglish leap off his tongue as he talks about his beloved team, his favourite football players, and shares the incredible knowledge he has of the subject. I keep hearing how well my children speak Polish, how I am giving them an incredible gift, how my extended family can get to know them in a way that would not be possible if my children didn't speak Polish. All these sentiments make me happy, proud, and thankful. But only when one of my cousin's makes a comment about how it must be so much work, especially because Polish is my non-dominant language, I exhale and nod in agreement. When I began interviewing mothers about their experiences around raising multilingual children for my academic research, I never imagined a few would begin to weep as we discussed their experiences. Although I think about the subject constantly, and I am acutely aware how complex and exhausting it is, I rarely pause long enough to let go of the weight I carry, of my own experiences, but also of the stories I have heard and the concerns I relentlessly read from many other mothers.

$\mathbf{9}$

As a child visiting Poland with my parents, our days were scheduled around food: where we would be eating dinner every day, which grandmother would be feeding us, what did we want to eat while we were there. I spent a lot of time sitting in my paternal grandmother's tiny kitchen, talking over pickle soup. At my maternal grandmother's we ate *pierogi* with cheese served with *śmietanka* (the diminutive form of *śmietana,* sour cream, because grandmothers use the diminutives with their grandchildren, even when those grandchildren are in their twenties and thirties). But what I remember most about late afternoons at my maternal grandmother's place was making tea with lemon in her equally tiny kitchen while she sat on a stool washing dishes. There were always cups with used teabags on the table, teabags she would reuse throughout the day because, she told me, one teabag could go a long way – remainders and reminders of the economic hardships she endured throughout her life. I was to take a fresh teabag for myself, make my tea, and leave the bag in the other cup for her to use later.

Both of my grandmothers have died, and with them have gone the central meeting places where family gathered, over bowls of *zupa* and plates of *pierogi*. 'If food is central to human life, so is language, and the two intersect at several crucial junctures: We come together to eat and talk; those occasions when silence accompanies food are the remarkable exceptions,' write Alastair Pennycook and Emi Otsuji in *Metrolingualism: Language in the City.* Talking about food also plays a key role in constructing ideas of belonging to a culture and linguistic space because not only is group belonging constructed discursively, but the act of sharing food is also a cultural activity.[285] I tell my children about the Polish food I ate as a child and encourage them, with varying degrees of success, to try *barszcz, naleśniki, kluski.* I had, until a couple of Christmases ago when the pressure finally broke me and I sobbed as I set the table, tried to (re)create a traditional Polish Christmas Eve dinner, *wigilia,* for my family every year. (I am easier on myself around the holidays now since that fateful eve, and we incorporate a few Polish traditions while also creating new ones.)

In Kraków, when my cousin asked where we wanted to eat – family gatherings are mostly held at restaurants now – I requested 'Polish food'. What I meant was I wanted to eat all the things my grandmothers used to make, and the food that has a cultural memory for me, especially being in my birth city, where I spent the first few years of my life. I wanted to expose my children to this culinary language, despite knowing they are not all that keen on Polish staples like soup, perogies or mashed potatoes. My cousin graciously chose a restaurant with *kluska* (*dumpling*) in the name. I ordered perogies for me and the kids, my partner and I ate our children's portion while they filled up on juice and chicken fingers. Not all was lost in the culinary immersion on the trip, as my daughter discovered her love for the *obwarzanek Krakowski*, a braided ring-shaped bread sold in street stalls around Kraków.

The day after my Polish food cravings were satiated, as we walked toward the main square, we noticed a restaurant selling poutine, a distinctly Canadian and specifically Québecois dish of fries, gravy, and cheese curds. As I stepped into the small eatery, a flurry of Canadiana enveloped me: a map of Canada, posters of various Canadian provinces, and a menu with fries, poutine, and different burgers each named after a Canadian city or province. It was an out-of-context culinary, geographical, cultural, and linguistic experience, but especially a humorous reminder that my cultures and my languages always co-exist, despite my attempts to prioritize one over the other. 'Metrolingualism', as coined by Pennycook and Otsuji, how language and the city are involved in interactions between history, people, migration, architecture, linguistic resources, and urban landscapes, highlights the ordinariness of linguistic diversity. Like languages, cities are also in constant change.

As I walked around Kraków, I took photos of graffiti: 'Trans Rights, ♥'. In shop windows, posters hung ahead of the parliamentary election a week earlier remained: pink ones begging women to vote in hopes of getting back the rights their grandmothers and mothers fought for, now consistently eroded by a right-wing government. Another poster had a group of women with their middle fingers placed over their lips – a defiant fuck you to silence – under the typed slogan, *Cicho już byłyśmy* (*We were already silent*) with the date of the election. The last time I visited Poland, the right-wing ruling party in government at the time had yet to do the immeasurable damage, especially to women's rights, reproductive rights, and the rights of marginalized communities, it would carry out in the following five years. But now, change was in the air after the election, with a hopeful promise of a coalition government to restore what had been lost. 'By viewing language use as profoundly bound up with space and activity, metrolingualism also raises questions about how we understand language not only in relation to each other but also in relation to all that is going on in a particular place,' write Pennycook and Otsuji.[286] If *metrolingualism* entails a 'layering of the city' I too create tier after tier of experiences around language and culture for my children, not only in how I care for them, but in how we exist as a family day after day, wherever we are.

,

In *La Lenteur Des Montagnes*, a love letter to her son, outlining the linguistic and cultural differences between mother and child, Ying Chen writes that *source* and *destination* are two equally profound aspects of our existence. Chen prefers *source* over *roots* because the latter has too fixed a quality to be real. What are roots? What does it really mean to 'put down roots'? Or 'go back to one's roots'? How does one go back to their roots without cutting off the rest of their existence, at least for some time, and in turn killing or concealing some part of themselves in favour of another? I think about how I repot plants, their spindly roots poking out of the bottom of a planter, me attempting to shake them out gently without damaging their delicate features. And then I softly place them in a bigger pot, patting the soil around them as if I am tucking my child in before bed. Every time I do this, I am convinced I have killed the plant. Every time, the plant survives and eventually outgrows another pot. *Source* is more promising, as if it is a place to draw upon, at the surface and not buried deep below. A source provides reinforcement of one's multifaceted and multilingual existence without having to suppress anything or anyone. You take what you need and come back again and again. If we consider *destination*, it too conjures ideas of a startling finality. Perhaps if destination is defined as a *purpose*, the definiteness disappears. And yet, does there always have to be a purpose?

,

It is not lost on me that my dreams of never finding certain rooms or the places I am meant to be, the ones I don't remember in any language, could relate to a search for a place, for a home, for something not in exile but also not permanent. There is a shared relationship between language and the home: language forms the home, creates it, while home is rooted in one's language.[287] 'For someone who has a choice of several languages, the language she chooses to express herself at any given time can bear traces of the sounds, shapes, and meanings of the others,' writes Claire Kramsch in *The Multilingual Subject*. 'These unused potential meanings shape her imagination, nourish her intimate memories, and suffuse her understanding of events. They give her the feeling of being both there and not quite there.'[288]

Found in Translation

I first read Eva Hoffman's *Lost in Translation: Life in a New Language* when my children were still babies. I would read one line before being interrupted, as you are, by the needs of small children. And then I would pick the book up again, read another few lines about Hoffman's immigration to Canada from Kraków when she was thirteen years old. Our immigrations were decades apart, and worlds apart considering I was only five when we moved to Canada, a lifetime younger than a new teenager moving abroad involuntarily without knowing the new country's language. I was ten when Hoffman published her book in 1989, shortly before my family and I first returned to Kraków after we left six years earlier. It wasn't until I began studying linguistics however, that I was introduced to Hoffman's work and her name kept reappearing in front of me. Paper after paper, numerous journal articles and academic tomes about language and emotions, identity, learning a new language later in life, and especially about translingual writing and self-translation, referenced Hoffman's memoir.

Divided into three parts, *Paradise, Exile, The New World*, the book begins when thirteen-year-old Hoffman is about to leave Kraków for Vancouver. The memoir is about displacement, detachment, *tęsknota*, a feeling Hoffman returns to several times in the book, but only in Polish, defining it as 'a word that adds to nostalgia the tonalities of sadness and longing'. It is also about the loss of a beloved language to save oneself from the pain of exile, and the discovery of something new through a profound cultural, linguistic and life shift. Hoffman eventually emigrates to the U.S. for university, an emigration from immigration of sorts, that solidifies the gulf between the language of the past (Polish) and the language of the present and, most importantly, future (English). 'But how does one bend toward another culture without falling over, how does one strike an elastic balance between rigidity and self-effacement?' asks Hoffman. I wanted to know if she'd found the answer to this question, and so I did what any journalist would do: I emailed and asked her to meet me for a coffee.

We met in a café near Finchley Road in London in the spring of 2022, shortly after Russia invaded Ukraine. It was a topic Hoffman, now in her seventies, emotively mentioned a few times during our time together and how her Jewish parents, originally from Ukraine, survived the Holocaust by hiding with Ukrainian neighbours. When I first got in touch with Hoffman to meet, she warned me the subjects I was keen on discussing – immigration, language loss, Kraków, multilingualism – were not topics she had thought of in a long time. I recorded our conversation as I was planning to write an article about Hoffman and the enduring allure of her memoir for an American magazine. When I listened to the recording recently, the desperation and trepidation in my voice made me uncomfortable in my own skin. Hearing my own recorded voice during an interview often evokes such unnerving feelings, but this time was different. I was searching for something, yes, research for an article, but more than that, I was hoping to get answers and find solutions to unsolvable dilemmas of what it means to belong culturally and linguistically to *here*, to *there*, to *anywhere*. I was not the only one.

When the book was first published, Hoffman received hundreds of letters, she says, not only from immigrants, but also from Americans who felt a similar alienation in their own country. When I bring up *Lost in Translation*, Hoffman gently rolls her eyes, telling me she is in fact 'sick of it', having talked about the book *enough*. She is funny and we laugh a lot. I tell her not to worry, I didn't bring my copy for her to sign, although that had more to do with forgetting to grab it when I ran out of the house than consciously thinking she may not want to revisit her experience yet again. I tell her about my children and my constant struggles to maintain Polish with them. She tells me it will be their choice if they want to speak Polish in the future or if they stop. Our conversation is mostly in English, peppered with some Polish as it goes on. She tells me she rarely uses Polish anymore, but that it all derives from how fiercely she wanted to transpose herself into English when she emigrated as a child.

I never wrote the magazine article on the allure of Hoffman's biography for no reason other than I realized we are always telling one another stories of language and culture loss every day, in different forms. It is not a unique experience in its common occurrence, and yet it is singular for everyone experiencing it. The reason Hoffman's book is alluring so many years after it was first published, besides the obvious one that it is beautifully and poignantly written, is because its subject continues to be one that confounds us. For those with the immense privilege to ruminate on *home, heritage, language,* and *identity,* we find ourselves searching for words, for writing, for someone to tell us why we feel the way we do: divided, detached, disoriented. Must we choose between detachment or transposition?

What I was looking for the day of our meeting, at least partly, I found in an essay Hoffman wrote in 1998, nine years after *Lost in Translation* was published, and one I only recently read. In *The New Nomads*, Hoffman writes about a trip she took to Kraków in 1994, and the westernization she encountered in the city she left decades earlier. After seeing a shopwindow with a display she calls 'familiar from the days of yore' amid the sea of newness Poland was coming into in the 1990s, Hoffman realizes that *there* was not the same *there* she left behind. In fact, the contrast with *there* and *here* was not as pronounced as it once had been. She would have to change her narrative, she writes.

'At this vanishing of contrasts I confess that I felt not only relief but regret. It was a regret, undoubtedly perverse, for the waning of clarity. But I also felt the loss of the very sense of loss I had experienced on my emigration. For the paroxysm I experienced on leaving Poland was, for all the pain, an index of significance I attached to what I left behind.'[289]

Nothing remains and eventually a language, a place, a culture change. The gap may widen, but it also may become narrower, the *there* and *here* blurred. Perhaps for me, it is the shadow or attached significance of what *may* be lost I am trying to recreate through language and culture with my children. The weight of a conceivable defeat is what makes the burden heavy in its significance – a nonsensical equation because nothing remains, and change does not have to be defined by, or as, loss.

Arrivals[i]

On our last trip to Canada, when I hugged my mother goodbye, I held a bit longer. I felt her soft skin, the folds of her curves, and her warmth envelop me. I wanted badly to stay in that moment while at the same time to pull apart and let go of expectations I had held about her body, her voice, her language, her presence being a conduit for my children's Polish exposure during our visit. The summer before, the first time we had made the trip back to Canada in four years, it was my father's body I could not stop thinking about. At the time, he was ill and had lost a substantial amount of weight. His emaciated face reminded me of the way my grandmother, his mother, appeared shortly before her death. A year later, recovered physically, the sharp bones were once again hidden by flesh, the sunken cheeks filled in and he looked like the man from before. In middle age, physical reminders of life's impermanence, children growing, parents becoming grandparents, sickness, health, life, and death are everywhere.

---

[i] 'As if there were only arrivals [arrivées], and therefore only events without arrival,' writes Jacques Derrida in *Monolingualism of the Other or The Prosthesis of Origin*. 'From these sole 'arrivals,' and from these arrivals alone, desire springs forth.'

In *Real Estate*, Deborah Levy, who emigrated from South Africa to England as a child in the late 1960s, calls her mother's body her 'first landmark', her 'primal satnav', her connection to South Africa and England. After her mother's death, Levy no longer had directions – at least not to the past, its places, and its memories. Both my parents, especially when I was younger, were my connection to Poland and Polish, and the ones who ensured I held my course. Even in my late teenage years and my twenties, I would visit the country with them, as if I could not navigate it on my own. I could, of course, but rarely did. Since the birth of my children, in many ways, they now point me in the direction of both Poland and Canada. Perhaps they are my new (linguistic) landmarks, my 'primal satnavs' or, as my daughter learnt from the Polish version of *Bluey*, my '*nawki*' (short for '*nawigacja*', navigation in the context of satnavs). Just as I want them to be connected to me not only in the present but in the past, and to steer them toward countries and languages that are meaningful for me, they have unexpectedly and unintentionally directed me back to words and places I never knew existed, at least not in this way.

,

Marco Espinoza and Gillian Wigglesworth argue that to diversify the study of family language policy in linguistics, there must be a shift in how norms of 'success' (language maintenance and, especially, active bilingualism) and 'failure' (language shift or loss) are considered or defined, particularly in relation to Indigenous languages.[290] In research, and in a wider societal context, there is an overarching tendency to consider passive bilingualism, incomplete acquisition, language mixing or no acquisition at all as 'failure'. The only definition of 'success' is active bilingualism (when the language is being used, not only understood) or balanced bilingualism (when both or multiple languages are actively being used in a perceived equality, predominantly still with the idea of double monolingualism). It is apparent in the multitude of ways we perceive multilingualism and multiculturalism, beginning with the separation of languages, of cultures, of identities. Perhaps redefining 'success' and 'failure' would not only absolve mothers and caregivers from the colossal sense of guilt associated with the fear of heritage language shift and loss but could loosen our grip on the need to define and compartmentalize everything.

In 1991, Lily Wong Fillmore wrote 'When Learning a Second Language Means Losing the First' in which she explored why so many children were dropping their home languages as they learnt English. What Wong Fillmore concluded is this happens predominantly only in places where linguistic or ethnic diversity is not valued. When diversity makes people uncomfortable, when multilingualism is considered an anomaly or a threat, so too is a language other than English. There are external pressures, forces of assimilation, especially in classrooms, but also internal pressures like the awareness children possess they are *different* the moment they leave their homes or even by turning on the TV. 'Although young children neither know nor care about prestige and status, they do care about belonging and acceptance. They quickly sense that without English they will not be able to participate in the English-speaking world of the school, and so they learn it, and they give up their primary language,' writes Wong Fillmore.[291] More than thirty years since the publication of her paper, so much of what Wong Fillmore writes continues to transpire. Celebrating linguistic diversity, as is more common now at least, is not enough. For many families, depending on their language(s), multilingualism is still considered a threat, and their language(s) deemed valueless. But we all care about belonging and acceptance. Multilingualism is never neutral and often produces social differences, 'conferring to some individuals or groups the profit of distinction while depriving others of symbolic and material resources,' writes Alexandre Duchêne, who adds that acknowledgement of linguistic diversity alone will not advance social progress.[292]

꠵

As I mother, I challenge notions around monolingual mindsets and standardization, assimilation and that any language is more important than another, while observing as my children use their languages in their own ways. I constantly acknowledge my own predetermined judgments of what multilingualism is and isn't. I want my children to be multilingual and use Polish as much as possible, otherwise I would not be writing these words or caregiving in the way I am. But the communication I share with my children is also beyond language: it is an embodiment of multiple vernaculars, linked by translation, by emotion, by gesture and parental love. It is more than words, beyond idioms and separate from the study of language. But we do not mother alone, just as we do not communicate in isolation. Can everything that is lost in the space between words and between language(s) be recovered? No, but new things can be uncovered. A common language is not necessarily a common cause. But when one language tries to dominate another, that is when linguistic and cultural identity is under threat.

My children do not owe me anything in language, but I do owe them, and other multilingual mothers, especially ones who feel they have no choice, to try to disrupt the prevailing misconceptions around raising multilingual children and to put an end to deficit-based rhetoric. There is no threshold of when a language becomes *truly* ours, because all languages should be accessible, valued, uplifted. I never felt more acutely culturally torn, or in between or undefined, as I did after I became a mother. It wasn't just about language and culture; it was a colossal shift of identity. Mothering amplified all the questions I had about myself, about the feelings that perhaps I was not enough in any culture, in any language. But when I think of that initial sense of loss, that feeling of uncertainty, I think of a story my children told me not long ago. At the time, my son was around eight, my daughter was five and they were attending a forest school together. One of the teachers, discussing languages, asked the children if they knew how to say *Hello* in a language other than English. My son, who was taking beginner Spanish classes at the time, told me he said *Hola*. Initially a bit indignant, I asked him why he did not say *Cześć*, the Polish word for *Hi*. To which he responded, 'Why would I, Mama? Polish is not a different language; it is just mine.'

I thought I could end the book there, on this ultimate validation and acknowledgement that perhaps I am doing something *right* or, at least, *enough*. But the more I thought about it, ending on such a note seemed to undermine many of the things I have written here. Instead, I kept returning to the question of possession: who is allowed to say they possess a language and why do we believe we own our language(s). *My* language, we say, or I can't use that language with my children because it is not *our* language, or this language is not *my language of the heart* or why do you use only *your* language when *my* language is *better*? I tread lightly here as this is not an absolution for appropriation, nor do I invalidate the importance of how someone feels in and about a language, especially if it is a minoritized or racialized one. But 'possessing' a language is another way of thinking about divisions and inequality. I don't think my son meant Polish was *his* language while othering Spanish. With his childhood innocence still firmly intact, he was simply considering Polish in the same realm as English, two languages he uses daily, irrespective of his unequal fluency and proficiency in each.

In a poem titled 'Here', Wisława Szymborska writes about life on Earth and how 'ignorance works overtime here, something is always being counted, compared, measured, from which roots and conclusions are then drawn.' And yet, 'illusions are costly only when lost' but, if we take a closer look, 'through the open window comes a breath of air, the walls reveal no terrifying cracks through which nowhere might extinguish you.' Here, there, nowhere. Emigrate from, immigrate to. Departure and destination, or arrivals without departures. One linguistic repertoire and, most of all, a sense of belonging across and beyond language(s). Nothing to fear because it is the illusion of loss we fear most. Multilingualism alone will not change the world, but perhaps mothers will.

Acknowledgements

This book would not have been possible without so many generous people. To my literary agent, Kate Evans, thank you for the leap of faith, unceasing enthusiasm and reminding me that a bit of breathing room is a good thing. Thank you to my wonderful editors Rose Green and Fritha Saunders. Rose, I am forever grateful you took a chance on me and my work, and thank you especially for your endless encouragement, patience, editorial brilliance, and thoughtfulness. Thank you, Fritha, for swiftly taking over and for your calm reassurance. And to the Footnote Press team: Vidisha Biswas, Paris Ferguson, Lucy Richardson, Francesca Eades, and everyone else who worked on this book. I am forever thankful for your care, enthusiasm, and faith, and I am proud to be a part of what you are creating at Footnote. Thank you to Jane Henshall and Charlotte Atyeo for your incredible attention to detail, to Emilie Bailey for the author photo and to Emma Ewbank for the cover of my dreams.

To Megan Figueroa, Diandra Morse, Pooja Kalyan, Sienna Gould, Sedea Katesdóttir Midjord, Sekyiwa Wi-Afedzi and Cate Hamilton, thank you for sharing your time, your candour, your expertise, and your poignant stories with me for these pages. To the incredible scholars, linguists, researchers, artists, and authors I mention, quote and reference in these pages, your work inspires me infinitely and I am always learning from each one of you. Your work, ideas and research push me to be a better writer, academic, linguist but especially, person. Thank you, Clara Vaz Bauler and Rita Sirignano, for reading early parts of this book and for inspiring me in so many ways.

To my dearest Joanna MacKenzie, thank you for answering a million questions about publishing and reading my words time and time again but most of all, for always being there and for being you. I am beyond lucky to know so many incredible women and have such amazing female friendships in so many different parts of the world. There are too many of you to mention here by name but thank you to each one of my marvellous female friends (and a couple of great male ones too). Thank you for being you, for asking me about the book repeatedly, for being so supportive and caring especially in the darkest of times this year, for sending me messages reminding me I can do the hard stuff, and especially for loving me and my children. You all mean the world to me.

To the Hanas family, thank you for your support over the years and asking time and time again how it was all going. To my family in Poland and my immigration family in Canada, thank you for the memories, for always ensuring I had a connection with Poland and Polish, and especially for all the care and love over the years. To my parents for everything you have ever done for me, for always encouraging me to follow any and every path and yes, for the gift of multilingualism. I am forever grateful. Sadly, my father unexpectedly died a couple of months before the book was published. He was an intelligent and complicated man, a caring father, a language teacher who loved words and language, a proud Pole who taught me there is no greater thing in life than travel and experiencing new languages, environments, and cultures. I am heartbroken he is no longer with us, but I hope his memory lives on in the stories I write here, and especially in the Polish I share with my children.

To my children: M, for your steadfast pep talks and your wisdom far beyond your years. You tell me you want to be a writer and although of course this may change and I hope you do whatever makes you happy in life, I hope this book inspires you to always keep writing and *languaging* in many ways. To L, for your amazing love notes and the chocolate that fuelled me during every writing session. Your creativity and enjoyment of life knows no bounds, I hope it always remains this way. Thank you both for your love and patience and not making me feel too guilty for not being around while I wrote. My work is inspired by you, and for you, always. To my partner, C, I am not sure how to begin to thank you for all that you do for me and for our family. Thank you for your unwavering support, encouragement, humour and especially for your love. *Kocham cię.*

Bibliography

Abley, Mark, 'It's like bombing the Louvre', *The Guardian* (January 28, 2008). https://www.theguardian.com/world/2008/jan/28/usa.features11

Aciman, André, *Letters of transit: reflections on exile, identity, language and loss* (New York: New Press, 1999).

Allen, Ansgar and Spencer, Sarah, 'Regimes of motherhood: Social class, the word gap and the optimisation of mothers' talk', *The Sociological Review*, 70.6 (2022): 1181-1198.

Alim, H. S., Rickford, R., and Ball, A. F., (eds), *Raciolinguistics: How language shapes our ideas about race* (Oxford: Oxford University Press, 2016).

Aikio, Marjut, 'Are women innovators in the shift to a second language? A case study of Reindeer Sámi women and men', *International Journal of the Sociology of Language*, 94 (1992): 43-61.

Antonini, Rachele, 'Caught in the middle: Child language brokering as a form of unrecognised language service', *Journal of Multilingual and Multicultural Development*, 37.7 (2016): 710-725.

Bachelard, Gaston, *The Poetics of Space* (Boston, Beacon Press, 1994).

Bahun, Sanja, and Petric, Bojana, (eds), *Thinking home: Interdisciplinary dialogues* (Routledge, 2020).

Baker, Colin, *Foundations of bilingual education and bilingualism*, (Multilingual Matters, 2011).

Baker, Colin, *A parents' and teachers' guide to bilingualism*, Vol. 18 (Multilingual Matters, 2014).

Baker-Bell, April, *Linguistic justice: Black language, literacy, identity, and pedagogy* (New York and Oxon, Routledge, 2020).

Baraitser, Lisa, *Maternal encounters: The ethics of interruption* (London and New York: Routledge, 2009).

Baraitser, Lisa, 'Touching time: maintenance, endurance, care', *Psychosocial Imaginaries: Perspectives on Temporality, Subjectivities and Activism* (London: Palgrave Macmillan UK, 2015): 21-47.

Baraitser, Lisa, *Enduring time* (London: Bloomsbury Publishing, 2017).

Bascaramurty, Dakshana and Alphonso, Caroline, 'How French immersion inadvertently created class and cultural divides at schools across Canada', *The Globe and Mail* (October 16, 2023). https://www.theglobeandmail.com/canada/article-french-immersion-program-schools-divide/

Bauler, Clara V., 'Liberating Languaging through Raciolinguistic Ideologies', *The Ideologies of 'Good' Languaging Working Group*, The Latinx Project, NYU, February 21, 2023 (online seminar).

Bauler, Clara V., 'Have we learned anything? Raciolinguistic ideologies in remote learning public discourses', *Journal of Critical Study of Communication & Disability*, 1.1 (2023): 48-68.

Besemeres, Mary and Wierzbicka, Anna, (eds), *Translating lives: Living with two languages and cultures* (Brisbane: Univ. of Queensland Press, 2007).

Blackledge, Adrian and Creese, Angela, 'Translanguaging and the body', *International Journal of Multilingualism*, 14.3 (2017): 250-268.

Bonfiglio, Thomas Paul, *Mother tongues and nations: The invention of the native speaker* (Berlin: De Gruyter Mouton, 2010).

Bourdieu, Pierre, *Language and symbolic power* (Cambridge: Polity Press, 1991).

Bourdieu, Pierre, *Pascalian meditations* (Cambridge: Polity Press, 2000).

Bulag, Uradyn E, 'Dying for the mother tongue: Why have people in Inner Mongolia recently taken their lives?', *Index on Censorship*, 49.4 (2020): 49-51.

Byers-Heinlein, Krista, Burns, Tracey C., and Werker, Janet F., 'The roots of bilingualism in newborns', *Psychological Science*, 21.3 (2010): 343-348.

Cameron, Deborah, *Language: A feminist guide*. https://debuk. wordpress.com/

Cameron, Deborah, *The myth of Mars and Venus: Do men and women really speak different languages?* (Oxford and New York: Oxford University Press, 2007).

Chan, Jessamine, *School for good mothers* (New York: Penguin Random House, 2021).

Chen, Ying, *La lenteur des montagnes* (Québec: Les Éditions du Boréal, 2014).

Cheatham, Gregory A., and Lim, Sumin, '20 disabilities and home language maintenance: Myths, models of disability, and equity', *Handbook of Home Language Maintenance and Development: Social and Affective Factors*, 18 (2020): 401.

Cioè-Peña, María, *(M)othering labeled children: Bilingualism and disability in the lives of Latinx mothers*, Vol. 131 (Multilingual Matters, 2021).

Clyne, Michael, *Australia's language potential* (Sydney: UNSW Press, 2005).

Collins, Lauren, *When in French: Love in a second language* (London: Fourth Estate 2016).

Cook, Vivian, and Wei, Li, (eds), *The Cambridge handbook of linguistic multi-competence* (Cambridge: Cambridge University Press, 2016).

Cook, Vivian, 'Evidence for multicompetence', *Language Learning*, 42.4 (1992): 557-591.

Crenshaw, Kimberlé, 'Demarginalizing the intersection of race and sex: A black feminist critique of antidiscrimination doctrine, feminist theory and antiracist politics', *University of Chicago Legal Forum*: Vol. 1989, Article 8.

Crisfield, Eowyn, *Bilingual families: A practical language planning guide* (Bristol and Blue Ridge Summit Multilingual Matters, 2021).

Curdt-Christiansen, X., and Iwaniec, J., '妈妈, I miss you: Emotional multilingual practices in transnational families', *International Journal of Bilingualism*, 27.2 (2023): 159-180.

Curdt-Christiansen, X., Lei, W., and Zhu, H., 'Pride, prejudice and pragmatism: family language policies in the UK', *Language Policy* (2023): 391-411.

Cushing, Ian, 'The policy and policing of language in schools' *Language in Society*, *49* (2019): 425-450.

Cushing, Ian, '"Say it like the Queen": the standard language ideology and language policy making in English primary schools', *Language, Culture and Curriculum*, 34.3 (2021): 321-336.

Cushing, Ian, 'Word rich or word poor? Deficit discourses, raciolinguistic ideologies and the resurgence of the "word gap" in England's education policy', *Critical Inquiry in Language Studies* (2022): 1-27.

Cushing, Ian, 'A raciolinguistic perspective from the United Kingdom', *Journal of Sociolinguistics* (2023): 473-477.

Cusk, Rachel, *A life's work: On becoming a mother* (New York: Picador, 2001).

Davies, Karen, *Women, time and the weaving of strands of everyday life* (Aldershot UK: Avebury, 1990).

De Houwer, Annick, 'Parental language input patterns and children's bilingual use', *Applied Psycholinguistics*, 28.3 (2007): 411-424.

De Houwer, Annick, *Bilingual first language acquisition*, Vol. 2 (Bristol: Multilingual Matters, 2009).

De Houwer, Annick, 'Language input environments and language development in bilingual acquisition', *Applied Linguistics Review*, 2.2 (2011): 221-240.

De Houwer, Annick, and Bornstein, Marc H., 'Bilingual mothers' language choice in child-directed speech: Continuity and change', *Journal of Multilingual and Multicultural Development*, 37.7 (2016): 680-693.

De Houwer, Annick, 'Harmonious bilingualism: Well-being for families in bilingual settings', *Handbook of Home Language Maintenance and Development: Social and Affective Factors* (2020): 63-83.

Derrida, Jacques, *Monolingualism of the other: Or, the prosthesis of origin* (Redwood City: Stanford University Press, 1998).

Dewaele, Jean-Marc, 'The emotional force of swearwords and taboo words in the speech of multilinguals', *Journal of Multilingual and Multicultural Development*, 25.2-3 (2004): 204-222.

Dewaele, Jean-Marc, 'The emotional weight of I love you in multilinguals' languages', *Journal of Pragmatics*, 40.10 (2008): 1753-1780.

Dewaele, Jean-Marc, *Emotions in multiple languages* (Basingstoke: Palgrave Macmillan, 2010).

Dewaele, Jean-Marc, 'Why do so many bi-and multilinguals feel different when switching languages?', *International Journal of Multilingualism*, 13.1 (2016): 92-105.

Dewaele, Jean-Marc, Bak, T., and Ortega, Lourdes, 'Why the mythical "native speaker" has mud on its face', in *The Changing Face of the 'Native Speaker': Perspectives from multilingualism and globalization*, Nadja Kerschhofer-Puhalo, Nikolay Slavkov, Sílvia Melo-Pfeifer, (eds), (Berlin: De Gruyter: 2021): 23-43.

Dewaele, Jean-Marc, and Costa, Beverley, 'Multilingual clients' experience of psychotherapy', *Language and Psychoanalysis*, 2.2 (2013): 31-50.

Dewaele, Jean-Marc and Pavlenko, Aneta, Web Questionnaire Bilingualism and Emotions, University of London (2001).

Dewaele, Jean-Marc, and Salomidou, Lora, 'Loving a partner in a foreign language', *Journal of Pragmatics*, 108 (2017): 116-130.

Dey, Claudia. 'Mothers as makers of death', *The Paris Review* (August 14, 2018). https://www.theparisreview.org/blog/2018/08/14/mothers-as-makers-of-death/

Digard, Bérengère Galadriel, Johnson, Ellie, Kašćelan, Draško, and Davis, Rachael, 'Raising bilingual autistic children in the UK: At the intersection between neurological and language diversity', *Frontiers in Psychiatry*, 14 (2023).

Drummond, Rob, *You're all talk: Why we are what we speak* (London: Scribe Publications, 2023).

Duchêne, Alexandre, 'Multilingualism: An insufficient answer to sociolinguistic inequalities', *International Journal of the Sociology of Language*, 2020.263 (2020): 91-97.

Duranti, Alessandro, Ochs, Elinor, and Schieffelin, Bambi B., (eds), *The handbook of language socialization* (New Jersey: John Wiley & Sons, 2014).

Dyck, Isabel, 'Migrant mothers, home and emotional capital – hidden citizenship practices', *Ethnic and Racial Studies*, 41.1 (2018): 98-113.

Ehala, Martin, 'Refining the notion of ethnolinguistic vitality', *International Journal of Multilingualism*, 7.4 (2010): 363-378.

Ellis, Elizabeth Margaret, and Sims, Margaret, "'It's like the root of a tree that I grew up from. . . .": parents' linguistic identity shaping family language policy in isolated circumstances', *Multilingua*, 41.5 (2022): 529-548.

Eisenchlas, Susana A., and Schalley, Andrea C., 'Making sense of "home language" and related concepts', *Handbook of Home Language Maintenance and Development. Social and Affective Factors* (2020): 17-37.

Erel, Umut, and Reynolds, Tracey, 'Introduction: Migrant mothers challenging racialized citizenship', *Ethnic and Racial Studies*, 41.1 (2018): 1-16.

Erel, Umut, 'Reframing migrant mothers as citizens', *Citizenship Studies*, 15.6-7 (2011): 695-709.

Espinoza, Marco, and Wigglesworth, Gillian, 'Beyond success and failure: Intergenerational language transmission from within Indigenous families in Southern Chile', *Diversifying Family Language Policy* (2022): 277-298.

Ferjan Ramirez, Naja, et al., '*Habla conmigo*, daddy! Fathers' language input in North American bilingual Latinx families', *Infancy*, 27.2 (2022): 301-323.

Figueroa, Megan, 'Language development, linguistic input, and linguistic racism' *PsyArXiv*, 4 Sept. 2023. https://doi.org/10.31234/osf.io/gpsfe

Figueroa, Megan, 'Language development, linguistic input, and linguistic racism', *Wiley Interdisciplinary Reviews: Cognitive Science* (2024): e1673.

Figueroa, Megan, 'Decolonizing (psycho)linguistics means dropping the "language gap" rhetoric', In *Decolonizing linguistics*, Anne Charity Hudley, Christine Mallinson, and Mary Bucholtz, (eds), Oxford University Press (in press).

Fishman, Joshua, *Reversing language shift* (Bristol: Multilingual Matters: 1991).

Fillmore, Lily Wong, 'When learning a second language means losing the first', *Early Childhood Research Quarterly*, 6.3 (1991): 323-346.

Flint, Sunshine, 'Why don't my kids have my accent', in *Romper* (March 8, 2023). https://www.romper.com/parenting/why-kids-do-not-have-parents-accent

Flores, Nelson, 'From academic language to language architecture: Challenging raciolinguistic ideologies in research and practice', *Theory into Practice*, 59.1 (2020): 22-31.

Flores, Nelson, 'Let's not forget that translanguaging is a political act', *The Educational Linguist* (July 19, 2014). https://educationallinguist.wordpress.com/2014/07/19/letsnot-forget-that-translanguaging-is-a-political-act/

Flores, Nelson, and Rosa, Jonathan, 'Undoing appropriateness: Raciolinguistic ideologies and language diversity in education', *Harvard Educational Review*, 85.2 (2015): 149-171.

Fuller-Wright, Liz, 'Uncovering the sound of "motherese" baby talk across languages,' Princeton University (October 12, 2017). https://www.princeton.edu/news/2017/10/12/uncovering-sound-motherese-baby-talk-across-languages

Gabryś-Barker, Danuta, 'What the languages of our dreams tell us about our multilinguality', *The Ecosystem of the Foreign Language Learner: Selected Issues* (2015): 3-17.

Garbes, Angela, *Essential labor: Mothering as social change* (New York: Harper Wave, 2022).

García, Ofelia, *Bilingual education in the 21st century: A global perspective* (Malden, MA and Oxford: Wiley/Blackwell, 2009).

García, Ofelia, 'TESOL translanguaged in NYS: Alternative perspectives', *NYS TESOL Journal*, 1.1 (2014): 2-10.

García, Ofelia, 'Translanguaged TESOL in transit', *NYS TESOL Journal*, 10.1 (July 2023).

García, Ofelia and Wei, Li, *Translanguaging: Language, bilingualism and education* (United Kingdom: Palgrave Macmillan, 2014).

García, Ofelia, 'The education of Latinx bilingual children in times of isolation: Unlearning and relearning', *MinneTESOL Journal*, 36.1 (2020). https://minnetesoljournal.org/journal-archive/mtj-2020-1/the-education-of-latinx-bilingual-children-in-times-of-isolation-unlearning-and-relearning/

Gedalof, Irene, 'Birth, belonging and migrant mothers: Narratives of reproduction in feminist migration studies', *Feminist Review*, 93.1 (2009): 81-100.

Gessen, Keith, 'Why did I teach my son to speak Russian?' *The New Yorker* (June 16, 2018). https://www.newyorker.com/culture/personal-history/why-did-i-teach-my-son-to-speak-russian

Greve, Werner, et al., 'Extending the scope of the "cognitive advantage hypothesis": Multilingual individuals show higher flexibility of goal adjustment', *Journal of Multilingual and Multicultural Development* (2021): 1-17.

Gordon, Cynthia, *Making meanings, creating family: Intertextuality and framing in family interaction* (Oxford University Press, United States, 2009).

Grosjean, François, *Life with two languages: An introduction to bilingualism* (Cambridge, Massachusetts: Harvard University Press, 1982).

Grosjean, François, 'Neurolinguists, beware! The bilingual is not two monolinguals in one person', *Brain and Language*, 36.1 (1989): 3-15.

Grosjean, François, 'The bilingual individual', *Interpreting*, 2.1-2 (1997): 163-187.

Grosjean, François, *Bilingual: Life and reality* (Cambridge, Massachusetts: Harvard University Press, 2010).

Grosjean, François, *Life as a bilingual: Knowing and using two or more languages* (Cambridge: Cambridge University Press, 2021).

Hall, Wyatte C., 'What you don't know can hurt you: The risk of language deprivation by impairing sign language development in deaf children', *Maternal and Child Health Journal*, 21.5 (2017): 961-965.

Hamilton, Catherine, and Murphy, Victoria A., 'Folk pedagogy? Investigating how and why UK early years and primary teachers use songs with young learners', *Education* 3-13 (2023): 1-22.

Hardach, Sophie, 'In quarantine, kids pick up parents' mother tongues: For some families, the pandemic has meant a return to their native languages', *The New York Times* (September 10, 2020). https://www.nytimes.com/2020/09/10/parenting/family-second-language-coronavirus.html

Henner, Jon, and Robinson, Octavian, 'Unsettling languages, unruly bodyminds: A Crip linguistics manifesto', *Journal of Critical Study of Communication & Disability*, 1.1 (2023): 7-37.

Hirsch, Afua, *Brit(ish): On race, identity and belonging*, (London, Vintage: 2018).

Hjorth, Larissa, et al., *Digital media practices in households: Kinship through data* (Amsterdam: Amsterdam University Press, 2020).

Hoffman, Eva, *Lost in Translation* (Boston: E.P. Dutton, 1989).

Hoffman, Eva, 'The new nomads', In *Letters of Transit*, edited by André Aciman (New York and London, The New Press: 1999).

hooks, bell, *Teaching to transgress: Education as the practice of freedom* (New York: Routledge, 1994).

Hua, Zhu, and Wei, Li, 'Transnational experience, aspiration and family language policy,' *Journal of Multilingual and Multicultural Development*, 37.7 (2016): 655-666.

Huston, Nancy, *Nord perdu* (France: Actes Sud, 1999).

Illich, Ivan, 'Vernacular values', *Philosophica*, 26 (1980).

Isurin, Ludmila and Wilson, Hope, 'First language attrition in bilingual immigrants: Attitude, identity, and emotion', In: *Handbook on language and emotion* G. Schiewer, J. Altarriba, & B.C. Ng, (eds), (Berlin: De Gruyter, 2023).

Jones, Reece, *Violent borders: Refugees and the right to move* (London and Brooklyn: Verso Books, 2016).

Julavits, Heidi, *Directions to myself* (London: Hogarth Press, 2023).

Kaplan, Alice, *French lessons: A memoir* (Chicago: University of Chicago Press, 1994).

Kimmerer, Robin Wall, *Braiding sweetgrass* (Minneapolis: Milkweed Editions, 2015).

King, Kendall, and Fogle, Lyn, 'Bilingual parenting as good parenting: Parents' perspectives on family language policy for additive bilingualism', *International Journal of Bilingual Education and Bilingualism*, 9.6 (2006): 695-712.

King, Kendall, and Lanza, Elizabeth, 'Ideology, agency, and imagination in multilingual families: An introduction', *International Journal of Bilingualism*, 23.3 (2019): 717-723.

Kristeva, Julia, *Motherhood today*, Colloque Gypsy V (Paris, October 21-22, 2005). http://www.kristeva.fr/motherhood.html

Królak, Emilia, and Rudnicka, Kinga, 'Selected aspects of directives in Polish', *Revista Española de Lingüística Aplicada*, 19 (2006): 129-142.

Kouritzin, Sandra, 'A Mother's Tongue', *TESOL Quarterly*, 34.2 (2000): 311-324.

Kouritzin, Sandra, 'Immigrant mothers redefine access to ESL classes: Contradiction and ambivalence', *Journal of Multilingual and Multicultural Development*, 21.1 (2000): 14-32.

Kozminska, Kinga, and Zhu, Hua, 'The promise and resilience of multilingualism: Language ideologies and practices of Polish-speaking migrants in the UK post the Brexit vote', *Journal of Multilingual and Multicultural Development*, 42.5 (2021): 444-461.

Kramsch, Claire, *Language and culture* (Oxford: Oxford University Press, 1998).

Kramsch, Claire, 'The multilingual experience: Insights from language memoirs', *Transit*, 1.1 (2004).

Kramsch, Claire, *The multilingual subject: What foreign language learners say about their experience and why it matters* (Oxford: Oxford University Press, 2009).

Kuhl, Patricia K., 'Baby talk', *Scientific American*, 313.5 (2015): 64-69.

Lahiri, Jhumpa, *In other words* (New York and London: Bloomsbury Publishing, 2017).

Lahiri, Jhumpa, *Translating myself and others* (Princeton and Oxford: Princeton University Press, 2022).

Lakoff, George, and Mark Johnson, *Metaphors we live by* (Chicago: University of Chicago Press, 2008).

Lakoff, Robin, *Language and woman's place* (New York: Harper Torch Books, 1975).

Lane, Pia, 'From silence to silencing? Contradictions and tensions in language revitalization', *Applied Linguistics*, 44 (5), 2023: 833-847.

Lanza, Elizabeth, 'Multilingualism and the family', In *Handbook of multilingualism and multilingual communication*, Peter Auer, and Li Wei, (eds), 5 (2007): 45-67.

Lanza, Elizabeth, 'The family as a space: Multilingual repertoires, language practices and lived experiences', *Journal of Multilingual and Multicultural Development*, 42.8 (2021): 763-771.

Lanza, Elizabeth, and Lomeu Gomes, Rafael, 'Family language policy: Foundations, theoretical perspectives and critical approaches', *Handbook of home language maintenance and development: Social and affective factors*, 153 (2020): 173.

Lepschy, Giulio, 'Mother tongues and literary languages', *The Modern Language Review* (2001): xxxiii-xlix.

Little, Sabine, 'Whose heritage? What inheritance?: Conceptualising family language identities', *International Journal of Bilingual Education and Bilingualism*, 23.2 (2020): 198-212.

Little, Sabine, 'Children and parents collaborating in home language maintenance', *Raising Multilinguals LIVE* (June 16, 2021). https://www.youtube.com/watch?v=LE1PBCx7lMQ

Lippi-Green, Rosina, *English with an accent: Language ideology and discrimination in the United States* (London and New York, Routledge, 1997; Oxon and New York: Routledge, Taylor & Francis Group, 2012).

Lutz, Helma, 'Gender in the migratory process', *Journal of ethnic and migration studies*, 36.10 (2010): 1647-1663.

Lutz, Helma, *The new maids: Transnational women and the care economy* (Bloomsbury Publishing, 2011).

Madison, Stephanie (Interviewer) and Johnson, Stacey Margarita (Producer), *We teach languages*, Episode 145, Bilingual Learners' Language Practices with Nelson Flores (Audio podcast), (November 1, 2020). https://weteachlang.com/2020/11/01/145-with-nelson-flores/

Mampe, Birgit, et al. 'Newborns' cry melody is shaped by their native language', *Current biology* 19.23 (2009): 1994-1997.

Marlow, Kathryn, 'It was deemed extinct. But now Pentl'ach has been declared a living language thanks to Qualicum researchers' (CBC News, December 2, 2023). https://www.cbc.ca/news/canada/british-columbia/pentl-ach-officially-declared-a-living-language-added-to-b-c-list-of-first-nations-languages-1.7045803

Martinez Jr, Charles R., McClure, Heather H. and Eddy, J. Mark, 'Language brokering contexts and behavioral and emotional adjustment among Latino parents and adolescents', *The Journal of Early Adolescence*, 29.1 (2009): 71-98.

McCulloch, Gretchen, *Because internet: Understanding the new rules of language* (New York: Riverhead Books, 2019).

McNerney, M., 'Multiculturalism: Myth and Reality', Rikka VII, (1980) 27–30, In: 'Immigrant Mothers Redefine Access to

ESL classes: Contradiction and Ambivalence', Kouritzin, S., *Journal of Multilingual and Multicultural Development*, 21(1), 15, (2000).

Meighan, Paul J., 'Colonialingualism: Colonial legacies, imperial mindsets, and inequitable practices in English language education', *Diaspora, Indigenous, and Minority Education*, 17.2 (2023): 146-155.

Meighan, Paul, 'Languages do not "die", they are persecuted: A Scottish Gael's perspective on language "loss"', *Belonging, Identity, Language, Diversity Research Group (BILD)* (December 4, 2022). https://bild-lida.ca/blog/uncategorized/languages-do-not-die-they-are-persecuted-a-scottish-gaels-perspective-on-language-loss-by-dr-paul-meighan-chiblow/

Mills, Jean, 'Mothers and mother tongue: Perspectives on self-construction by mothers of Pakistani heritage', In *Negotiation of identities in multilingual contexts*, Aneta Pavlenko, and Adrian Blackledge, (eds), (Bristol: Multilingualism Matters, 2004): p.161-191.

Mumm, Hanne, et al., 'Maternal cortisol levels in third trimester and early language development: A study of 1093 mother–child pairs from the Odense Child Cohort', *Journal of Neuroendocrinology*, 35.8 (2023): e13314.

Munkhbayar, Undarmaa, 'How to maintain Mongolian in Australia', *Language on the Move* (December 11, 2023). https://www.languageonthemove.com/how-to-maintain-mongolian-in-australia/

Murphy, Lynne, *The prodigal tongue: The love-hate relationship between American and British English* (London: One World Publications, 2018).

Norton, Bonny, *Identity and Language Learning* (Bristol: Multilingual Matters, 2013).

O'Brien, Jane, 'How foetuses learn language', BBC News (May 9, 2013). https://www.bbc.co.uk/news/world-us-canada-22457797

Ochs, Elinor, *Culture and language development: Language acquisition and language socialization in a Samoan village*, 10, (Cambridge: CUP Archive, 1988).

Ochs, Elinor, and Schieffelin, Bambi B., 'The theory of language socialization', In *The handbook of language socialization*, Alessandro Duranti, Elinor Ochs, and Bambi B.Schieffelin, (eds), (2011): 1-21.

Okita, Toshie, *Invisible work: Bilingualism, language choice and childrearing in intermarried families*, 12 (Amsterdam: John Benjamins Publishing, 2002).

Omar, Laila, 'Foreclosed futures and entangled timelines: conceptualization of the "future" among Syrian newcomer mothers in Canada', *Journal of Ethnic and Migration Studies*, 49.5 (2023): 1210-1228.

Orah Mark, Sabrina, 'Rapunzel, draft one thousand', *The Paris Review* (August 6, 2020). https://www.theparisreview.org/blog/2020/08/06/rapunzel-draft-one-thousand/

Pavlenko, Aneta, '"Stop doing that, *ia komu skazala!*": Language choice and emotions in parent–child communication', *Journal of Multilingual and Multicultural Development*, 25.2-3 (2004): 179-203.

Pavlenko, Aneta, *Emotions and multilingualism* (Cambridge: CUP, 2005).

Pavlenko, Aneta, 'Emotion and emotion-laden words in the bilingual lexicon', *Bilingualism: Language and Cognition*, 11.2 (2008): 147-164.

Pavlenko, Aneta, 'Affective processing in bilingual speakers: Disembodied cognition?', *International Journal of Psychology*, 47.6 (2012): 405-428.

Pavlenko, Aneta, *Thinking and Speaking in Two Languages* (Bristol/Buffalo/Toronto: *Multilingualism Matters,* 2011).

Pavlenko, Aneta, *The bilingual mind: And what it tells us about language and thought* (Cambridge: Cambridge University Press, 2014).

Penelope, Julia, *Prescribed passivity: The language of sexism*, published in *A Feminist Ethic for Social Science Research* (The Nebraska Sociological Feminist Collective, Lewiston/Queenston: Edwin Mellen, 1988): 119-138.

Penelope, Julia, *Speaking freely: Unlearning the lies of the father's tongues* (Oxford: Pergamon Press, 1990).

Pennycook, Alastair, *Language as a local practice* (New York: Routledge, 2010).

Pennycook, Alastair, and Emi Otsuji, *Metrolingualism: Language in the city* (New York: Routledge, 2015).

Piepzna-Samarasinha, Leah Lakshmi, *Care work: Dreaming disability justice* (Vancouver: Arsenal Pulp Press, 2018).

Pierce, Lara J., et al., 'Mapping the unconscious maintenance of a lost first language', *Proceedings of the National Academy of Sciences*, 111.48 (2014): 17314-17319.

Piller, Ingrid, 'Private language planning: The best of both worlds', *Estudios de Sociolingüística*, 2.1 (2001): 61-80.

Piller, Ingrid, *Linguistic diversity and social justice: An introduction to applied sociolinguistics* (Oxford: Oxford University Press, 2016).

Piller, Ingrid, and Livia Gerber, 'Family language policy between the bilingual advantage and the monolingual mindset', *International Journal of Bilingual Education and Bilingualism* (2018).

Piller, Ingrid and Pavlenko, Aneta, 'Bilingualism and gender', In *The Handbook of bilingualism*, T. K. Bhatia, and W. C. Ritchie, (eds), 489-511 (Malden, MA: Blackwell, 2004).

Prochnow, Annette, et al., 'Does a "musical" mother tongue influence cry melodies? A comparative study of Swedish and German newborns', *Musicae Scientiae*, 23.2 (2019): 143-156.

Purkarthofer, Judith, 'Intergenerational challenges: Of handing down languages, passing on practices, and bringing multilingual speakers into being', In *Handbook of home language maintenance and development: Social and affective factors*, Andrea C. Schalley, and Susana A. Eisenchlas, (eds), 18 (Berlin: Walter de Gruyter GmbH & Co KG, 2020):130-150.

Pye, Clifton, 'Quiché Mayan speech to children', *Journal of Child Language*, 13.1 (1986): 85-100.

Ramjattan, Vijay A., 'Accent reduction as raciolinguistic pedagogy', *Toward a New Object, Method, and Practice* (2023): 37.

Ramjattan, Vijay A., 'Accent reduction as raciolinguistic pedagogy', In *Thinking with an Accent: Toward a new object, method, and practice*, Pooja Rangan, Akshya Saxena, Ragini Tharoor Srinivasan, and Pavitra Sundar, (eds), (Berkeley: University of California Press, 2023): 37-53.

Rangan, Pooja, Saxena, Akshya, Tharoor Srinivasan, Ragini and Sundar, Pavitra, (eds) *Thinking with an accent: toward a new object, method, and practice* (Berkeley: University of California Press, 2023).

Rich, Adrienne, *Of woman born: Motherhood as experience and institution* (New York: WW Norton & Company, 2021).

Robinson, Octavian, 'Crip linguistics and linguistic care work', *Medium* (September 2, 2022). https://notanangrydeafperson. medium.com/crip-linguistics-and-linguistic-care-work-74ac63c22c2e

Rolland, Louise, Dewaele, Jean-Marc, and Costa, Beverley, 'Multilingualism and psychotherapy: exploring multilingual clients' experiences of language practices in psychotherapy', *International Journal of Multilingualism*, 14.1 (2017): 69-85.

Romaine, Suzanne, *Communicating gender* (London: Psychology Press, 1998).

Romaine, Suzanne, *Bilingualism* (New Jersey: Wiley-Blackwell, 2001).

Rosa, Jonathan, and Flores, Nelson, 'Unsettling race and language: Toward a raciolinguistic perspective', *Language in Society*, 46.5 (2017): 621-647.

Rosa, Jonathan, and Flores, Nelson, 'Hearing language gaps and reproducing social inequality', *Journal of Linguistic Anthropology*, 25.1 (2015): 77-79.

Samata, Susan, 'Language at home: A reclaimed heritage', *Thinking home*, Sanja Bahun, and Bojana Petric, (eds), (Oxfordshire: Routledge, 2020): 207-223.

Samata, Susan, *Cultural memory of language* (London: Bloomsbury, 2014).

Sander-Montant, Andrea, Byers-Heinlein, Krista, and Bissonnette, Rébecca, 'Like mother like child: Differential impact of mothers' and fathers' individual language use on bilingual language exposure', *PsyArXiv* (September 27, 2023).

Schalley, Andrea C., and Eisenchlas, Susana A., (eds), *Handbook of home language maintenance and development: Social and affective factors*, 18 (Berlin: Walter de Gruyter GmbH & Co KG, 2020).

Schieffelin, Bambi B., and Ochs, Elinor, 'Language socialization', *Annual Review of Anthropology*, 15.1 (1986): 163-191.

Schieffelin, Bambi B, *The give and take of everyday life: Language, socialization of Kaluli children*, 9 (Cambridge: CUP Archive, 1990).

Schmid, Monika S., Köpke, Barbara and De Bot, Kees, 'Language attrition as a complex, non-linear development', *International Journal of Bilingualism*, 17.6 (2013): 675-682.

Scollon, Suzie Wong, Scollon Ron, *Nexus analysis: Discourse and the emerging internet* (Oxfordshire: Routledge, 2004).

Sedivy, Julie, *Memory speaks: On losing and reclaiming language and self* (Cambridge, Massachusetts Harvard University Press, 2021).

Setter, Jane, *Your voice speaks volumes: It's not what you say, but how you say it* (Oxford: Oxford University Press, US, 2019).

Serratrice, Ludovica, 'Languages in lockdown: Time to think about multilingualism', *The ESRC International Centre for Language and Communicative Development Blog* (2020).

Sevinç, Yeşim, and Dewaele, Jean-Marc, 'Heritage language anxiety and majority language anxiety among Turkish immigrants in the Netherlands', *International Journal of Bilingualism*, 22.2 (2018): 159-179.

Shen, Yishan, et al., 'Language brokering and immigrant-origin youth's well-being: A meta-analytic review', *American Psychologist*, 77.8 (2022): 921-939.

Smith, Zadie, 'Speaking in tongues', *The New York Review of Books*, 26 (2009): 1-16.

Smith-Christmas, Cassie, 'Child agency and home language maintenance', In *Handbook of home language maintenance and development: Social and affective factors*, 18, Andrea Schalley, and Susana Eisenchlas, (eds), (2020): 218.

Smitherman, Geneva, 'Raciolinguistics, "mis-education", and language arts teaching in the 21st century', *Language Arts Journal of Michigan*, 32.2 (2017): Article 3 (3-12).

Solomon, Olga, 'Rethinking baby talk', In *The handbook of language socialization*, Alessandro Duranti, Elinor Ochs, and Bambi B. Schieffelin, (eds), (New York: John Wiley & Sons, 2012): 121-149.

Søndergaard, Bent, 'Switching between seven codes within one family – A linguistic resource', *Journal of Multilingual & Multicultural Development*, 12.1-2 (1991): 85-92.

Spolsky, Bernard, 'Family language policy – the critical domain', *Journal of Multilingual and Multicultural Development*, 33.1 (2012): 3-11.

Starosta, Anita, 'Everything is accented: Labor and the weight of things unsaid', In *Thinking with an accent: Toward a new object, method, and practice*, P. Rangan, et al., (eds), (California: University of California, 2023): 95-110.

Surrain, Sarah, 'Spanish at home, English at school: How perceptions of bilingualism shape family language policies among Spanish-speaking parents of preschoolers', *International Journal of Bilingual Education and Bilingualism* (2018).

Szymborska, Wisława, 'Here', translated by Clare Cavanagh and Stanisław Barańczak (Boston and New York: Houghton Mifflin Harcourt, 2010).

Thomas, Katie, Kliff, Sarah, and Silver-Greenberg, Jessica, 'Inside the booming business of cutting babies' tongues', *The New York Times* (December 18, 2023). https://www.nytimes.com/2023/12/18/health/tongue-tie-release-breastfeeding.html

Tokarczuk, Olga, *Flights*, translated by Jennifer Croft (London: Fitzcarraldo Editions, 2018).

Torsh, Hanna Irving, *Linguistic intermarriage in Australia: Between pride and shame* (Berlin: Springer Nature, 2019).

Torsh, Hanna Irving, 'Maybe if you talk to her about it: Intensive mothering expectations and heritage language maintenance,' *Multilingua*, 41.5 (2022): 611-628.

Tseng, Amelia, 'Identity in home-language maintenance', *Handbook of home language maintenance and development: social and affective factors*, 18 (2020): 109.

Tseng, Vivian, and Andrew J. Fuligni, 'Parent-Adolescent language use and relationships among immigrant families with East Asian, Filipino, and Latin American backgrounds', *Journal of Marriage and Family*, 62.2 (2000): 465-476.

Van Mensel, Luk, '"*Quiere koffie?*" The multilingual families of transcultural families', *International Journal of Multilingualism*, 15.3 (2018): 233-248.

Wei, Li, and García, Ofelia, 'Not a first language but one repertoire: Translanguaging as a decolonizing project', *RELIC Journal*, 53.2 (2022): 313-324.

Wei, Li, and Lin, Angel M. Y., 'Translanguaging classroom discourse: Pushing limits, breaking boundaries', *Classroom Discourse*, 10.3-4 (2019): 209-215.

Wei, Li, 'Moment analysis and translanguaging space: Discursive construction of identities by multilingual Chinese youth in Britain', *Journal of Pragmatics*, 43, 5 (2011): 1222-1235.

Wei, Li, 'Translanguaging as a practical theory of language', *Applied Linguistics*, 39 (1) (2018): 9–30.

Wermke, Kathleen, Robb, Michael P. and Schluter, Philip J., 'Melody complexity of infants' cry and non-cry vocalisations increases across the first six months', *Scientific Reports*, 11.1 (2021): 4137.

Wierzbicka, Anna. 'Two languages, two cultures, one (?) self: Between Polish and English', In *Translating lives: Living with two languages and cultures*, Mary Besemeres and Anna Wierzbicka, (eds), (2007): 96-113.

Wilson, Sonia, 'To mix or not to mix: Parental attitudes towards translanguaging and language management choices', *International Journal of Bilingualism*, 5.1 (2021): 58-76.

Wright, Lyn, *Critical perspectives on language and kinship in multilingual families* (Bloomsbury Publishing, 2022).

Wright, Lyn L., 'The discursive functions of kinship terms in family conversation', In *Diversifying family language policy*, Lyn Wright, and Christina Higgins, (eds), (London and New York: Bloomsbury Publishing, 2022): 15-32.

Wright, Lyn, and Higgins, Christina (eds), *Diversifying family language policy* (London and New York: Bloomsbury Publishing, 2022).

Yildiz, Yasemin, *Beyond the mother tongue: The postmonolingual condition* (Fordham University Press, 2012).

Yong, Ed, 'The bitter fight over the benefits of bilingualism', *The Atlantic* (February 10, 2016). https://www.theatlantic.com/science/archive/2016/02/the-battle-over-bilingualism/462114/

Zentella, Ana Celia, *Growing up bilingual: Puerto Rican children in New York* (Oxford and Malden: Blackwell, 1998).

Zhao, Sumin, and Flewitt, Rosie, 'Young Chinese immigrant children's language and literacy practices on social media: A translanguaging perspective', *Language and Education*, 34.3 (2020): 267-285.

Notes

INTRODUCTION

[1] A good place to start is Wright, Lyn, and Christina Higgins, eds. *Diversifying family language policy* (Bloomsbury Publishing, 2022). Also, Wright, Lyn, *Critical perspectives on language and kinship in multilingual families* (Bloomsbury Publishing, 2022). Other scholars include, King, Kendall, and Elizabeth Lanza, 'Ideology, agency, and imagination in multilingual families: An introduction, *International Journal of Bilingualism*, 23.3 (2019): p. 717-723 and, Hua, Zhu, and Li Wei, 'Transnational experience, aspiration and family language policy,' *Journal of Multilingual and Multicultural Development*, 37.7 (2016): p. 655-666.

[2] Lanza, Elizabeth, 'The family as a space: Multilingual repertoires, language practices and lived experiences', *Journal of Multilingual and Multicultural Development*, 42.8 (2021): p. 765.

[3] Pennycook, Alastair, *Language as a local practice* (Routledge, 2010): p. 12. Also, this idea languages are separate structures, or what some linguists call additive, influences many myths around bilingualism and multilingualism, especially around the separation of languages: home/ school, for example, or when a child is acquiring multiple languages and parents are erroneously told to only use one language before introducing another.

[4] Piller, Ingrid, *Linguistic diversity and social justice: An introduction to applied sociolinguistics* (Oxford University Press, 2016): p. 19.

[5] See the discussion about the use of 'languaging' in sociolinguistics in García, Ofelia and Li Wei, *Translanguaging: Language, bilingualism and education* (Palgrave Macmillan UK, 2014): p. 9.

[6] For more on American-English and British-English differences, I recommend, Murphy, Lynne, *The Prodigal Tongue: The love-hate relationship between American and British English* (Penguin, 2018). (Yes, I know I am Canadian but close enough and it is a great book!)

[7] There is a beautiful line in Nancy Huston's *Nord Perdu* (Actes Sud, 1999), where she writes that one's first language mothers us, but languages learnt later in life need our mothering and mastering: '*Les mots le disent bien: la première langue, la "maternelle", acquise dès la prime enfance, vous enveloppe et vous fait sienne, alors que pour la deuxième, "l'adoptive", c'est vous qui devez la materner, la maîtriser, vous l'approprier.*' p. 61.

[8] Kristeva, Julia, *Motherhood Today*, Colloque Gypsy V (Paris, 21/22 October, 2005): http://www.kristeva.fr/motherhood.html

[9] In what Lanza (in Lanza, Elizabeth, 'The family as a space: Multilingual repertoires, language practices and lived experiences') calls 'classic Fishmanian sociolinguistics, the family has been considered a private domain that sets parameters for, and thus constrains, how one uses and chooses language with family members,' referring to, Fishman, Joshua, *Reversing language shift* (Multilingual Matters: 1991). The idea of home as a private domain is nothing new but I reference it here in parallel with how the home is also considered a private space in the context of caregiving, parenting and, especially, mothering.

[10] Okita, Toshie, *Invisible work: Bilingualism, language choice and childrearing in intermarried families*, 12 (John Benjamins Publishing, 2002): p.36.

[11] Sander-Montant, Andrea, Krista Byers-Heinlein, and Rébecca Bissonnette, 'Like mother like child: differential impact of mothers' and fathers' individual language use on bilingual language exposure', *PsyArXiv* (September 27, 2023): p. 2.

[12] King, Kendall, and Lyn Fogle, 'Bilingual parenting as good parenting: Parents' perspectives on family language policy for additive bilingualism', *International Journal of Bilingual Education and Bilingualism*, 9.6 (2006): p. 697.

[13] Surrain, Sarah, 'Spanish at home, English at school: How perceptions of bilingualism shape family language policies among Spanish-speaking parents of preschoolers', *International Journal of Bilingual Education and Bilingualism* (2018): p.14.

[14] Piller, Ingrid, and Livia Gerber, 'Family language policy between the bilingual advantage and the monolingual mindset', *International Journal of Bilingual Education and Bilingualism* (2018): p. 632.

[15] Okita, Toshie, *Invisible work: Bilingualism, language choice and childrearing in intermarried families*, 12 (John Benjamins Publishing, 2002): p. 28.

[16] Romaine, Suzanne, *Communicating gender* (Psychology Press, 1998): p. 180.

[17] Kouritzin, Sandra, 'Immigrant mothers redefine access to ESL classes: Contradiction and ambivalence', *Journal of Multilingual and Multicultural Development*, 21.1 (2000): 14-32: p. 15, quoting McNerney, M., 'Multiculturalism: myth and reality', *Rikka VII*, 27–30 (1980).

[18] Tseng, Vivian, and Andrew J. Fuligni, 'Parent–adolescent language use and relationships among immigrant families with East Asian, Filipino, and Latin American backgrounds', *Journal of Marriage and Family*, 62.2 (2000): p. 465-476: In this study, the authors reported that adolescents

who mutually communicated with their parents in their parents' 'native language' reported the highest levels of cohesion and discussion.

[19] Allen, Ansgar and Sarah Spencer, 'Regimes of motherhood: Social class, the word gap and the optimisation of mothers' talk', *The Sociological Review*, 70,6 (2022): p. 1183.

[20] If you'd like to read more about one father's experience, I recommend Gessen, Keith, 'Why did I teach my son to speak Russian?', *The New Yorker* (June 16, 2018). https://www.newyorker.com/culture/personal-history/why-did-i-teach-my-son-to-speak-russian and Gessen's interview with François Grosjean, in Grosjean, François, *Life as a bilingual: Knowing and using two or more languages* (Cambridge University Press, 2021): p. 128-131.

[21] For more information on the studies that both support and refute the 'cognitive advantage', see Greve, Werner, et al., 'Extending the scope of the "cognitive advantage hypothesis": Multilingual individuals show higher flexibility of goal adjustment', *Journal of Multilingual and Multicultural Development* (2021): p. 1-17. Also, 'The bitter fight over the benefits of bilingualism' by Ed Yong, *The Atlantic* (February 10, 2016). https://www.theatlantic.com/science/archive/2016/02/the-battle-over-bilingualism/462114/

[22] Grosjean, François, 'Neurolinguists, beware! The bilingual is not two monolinguals in one person', *Brain and Language*, 36.1 (1989): p. 3-15.

[23] Cook, Vivian J, 'Evidence for multicompetence', *Language Learning*, 42.4 (1992): 557-591. Also, for more of a recent discussion see Cook, Vivian, and Li Wei, (eds.), *The Cambridge handbook of linguistic multi-competence* (Cambridge University Press, 2016).

[24] García, Ofelia and Li Wei, *Translanguaging: Language, bilingualism and education* (United Kingdom, Palgrave Macmillan, 2014): p. 13, citing García, Ofelia, *Bilingual education in the 21st century: A global perspective* (Malden, MA and Oxford: Wiley/Blackwell, 2009).

[25] Lippi-Green, Rosina, *English with an accent: Language ideology and discrimination in the United States* (London and New York, Routledge, 1997; Oxon and New York: Routledge, Taylor & Francis Group, 2012): p. 41.

[26] Munkhbayar, Undarmaa, 'How to Maintain Mongolian in Australia', *Language on the Move* (December 11, 2023). https://www.languageonthemove.com/how-to-maintain-mongolian-in-australia/

[27] Bulag, Uradyn E., 'Dying for the mother tongue: Why have people in Inner Mongolia recently taken their lives?' *Index on Censorship*, 49.4 (2020): p. 49-51.

[28] Piller, Ingrid, *Linguistic diversity and social justice: An introduction to applied sociolinguistics*: p. 3.

[29] Piller, Ingrid, *Linguistic diversity and social justice: An introduction to applied sociolinguistics*: p. 30.

[30] Little, Sabine, 'Children and parents collaborating in home language maintenance', *Raising Multilinguals LIVE* (June 16, 2021). https://www.youtube.com/watch?v=LE1PBCx7lMQ

31 Noam Chomsky's theory of language acquisition, or Universal Grammar, argues that language acquisition is innate, or that we are born with a set of rules about language. The theory was one of the first things we discussed in an introduction to linguistics class. It is often debated, sometimes controversial, and always multilayered and a lot has been written on the topic over the years. Here, I am taking a surface approach to the term by predominantly highlighting the parallel between the idea of innateness in language, and in motherhood, and what that means when we consider the definition of 'innate' and what the consequences for mothers are when the message is about how a maternal instinct, for example, is innate for women and mothers.

32 In Piller, Ingrid, *Linguistic diversity and social justice*, p. 32, the author notes that 'monolingual mindset' was introduced by linguist Michael Clyne to represent the disparity between how widespread multilingualism is in Australia and the 'idealized representation' of Australia as a monolingual, English-speaking nation. For more, see Clyne, Michael, *Australia's Language Potential* (Sydney: UNSW Press, 2005).

AN INTERRUPTION

33 When babies utter 'mama' for the first time, it doesn't mean the mother, at least not initially. Mama is the pairing of the most basic phonological sequence with the first intended referent. In 1960, Roman Jakobson wrote a paper titled 'Why Mama and Papa?' where he wrote /ma/ and /pa/ represent the 'most ideal' syllables in any language because the pairs are maximally opposed sounds, the complete closure of the lips for the bilabial and then a complete opening for the vowel and then, reduplication or repetition. The /m/, /p/, /b/ followed by /d/ and /g/ are the earliest sounds many babies make.

34 It was not until I read Claudia Dey's essay, 'Mothers as makers of death' in *The Paris Review*, I realized the fear of death is amplified exponentially after you become a mother, and also while giving birth, especially for women of colour in parts of the world where maternal deaths are on the rise. In her essay, Dey quotes another writer I adore, Samantha Hunt, when she tells *The New Yorker*: 'When I became a mom, no one ever said, "Hey, you made a death. You made your children's deaths." Meanwhile, I could think of little else. It's scary to think of mothers as makers of death, but it sure gives them more power and complexity than one usually finds.'

35 In, Penelope, Julia, *Prescribed passivity: The language of sexism*, (1988), feminist linguist Penelope, in reference to the male and man being treated as the default in language, says it relegates women to 'negative semantic space'. I thought about Penelope's reference here in the context of how most fathers, who are predominantly men, would not worry about blank pages in a baby book in the same way I know so many women, and mothers would, and do.

[36] Baraitser, Lisa, *Maternal encounters: The ethics of interruption* (London and New York: Routledge, 2009): p. 68-69.

[37] Penelope, Julia, *Speaking freely: Unlearning the lies of the father's tongues* (Pergamon Press, 1990): p. xxxiii.

[38] Pennycook, Alastair, *Language as a local practice* (Routledge, 2010): p. 36.

[39] Pennycook, Alastair, *Language as a local practice*: p. 13.

[40] In *Making meanings, creating family: Intertextuality and framing in family interaction* (OUP USA, 2009), author Cynthia Gordon examines how and why family members repeat one another's words and what those repetitions mean for the family.

PART 1

[41] While I was finishing a draft of the book, *The New York Times* published an article about how dentists and lactation consultants are pushing for more and more 'tongue-tie releases' on new mothers, often when they are unnecessary and sometimes with devastating consequences: Thomas, Katie, Kliff, Sarah and Silver-Greenberg, Jessica, 'Inside the booming business of cutting babies' tongues' (December 18, 2023). What struck me the most was how much guilt and blame there was put on the mothers. They endured immense pressure to breast- or chest-feed, so much so they agreed for their babies to have the tongue-tie release, despite little evidence it would help with feeding and possibly lead to speech impediments in the future. Then, if the procedure went wrong, the mothers again blamed themselves. One interviewee said she questioned her abilities as a mother after the procedure left her child with debilitating side effects.

[42] Statistics Canada: Definition of 'mother tongue of a person'. https://www23.statcan.gc.ca/imdb/p3Var.pl?Function=DEC&Id=34023

[43] François Grosjeans's Complementarity Principle: 'Bilinguals usually acquire and use their languages for different purposes, in different domains of life, with different people. Different aspects of life require different languages,' proposed in 1985: Grosjean, François, 'The bilingual individual', *Interpreting*, 2.1-2 (1997): p. 163-187. For the children mentioned here, English was the language of school, so it was likely very difficult to describe school-related events in Mandarin for them.

[44] Romaine, Suzanne, *Bilingualism* (Wiley-Blackwell, 2001): p.18. Romaine continues with examples of communities where fathers pass on their language to their children, including in areas of Brazil and Colombia where there are patrilineal societies.

[45] Illich, Ivan, 'Vernacular values', *Philosophica*, 26 (1980): 87.

[46] Mills, Jean, 'Mothers and mother tongue: Perspectives on self-construction by mothers of Pakistani heritage' in *Negotiation of identities in multilingual contexts* (eds.), Pavlenko, Aneta and Blackledge, Adrian, (Multilingualism Matters, 2004): p. 166.

[47] Dewaele, Jean-Marc, T. Bak, and Lourdes Ortega, 'Why the mythical "native speaker" has mud on its face', In *Changing Face of the 'Native Speaker': Perspectives from multilingualism and globalization*, (eds.) Nadja Kerschhofer-Puhalo, Nikolay Slavkov, Sílvia Melo-Pfeifer (De Gruyter: 2021): p. 25.

[48] Ramjattan, Vijay A., 'Accent reduction as raciolinguistic pedagogy,' *Toward a New Object, Method, and Practice* (2023): p. 44.

[49] Kramsch, Claire, *Language and culture* (Oxford University Press, 1998): p. 79–80.

[50] Giulio Lepschy asks this question in, Lepschy, Giulio, 'Mother tongues and literary languages', *The Modern Language Review* (2001): xxxiii-xlix.

[51] Yildiz, Yasemin, *Beyond the mother tongue: The postmonolingual condition* (Fordham University Press, 2012): p. 12.

[52] Yildiz, Yasemin, *Beyond the mother tongue: The postmonolingual condition* p. 205.

[53] Henner, Jon, and Octavian Robinson, 'Unsettling languages, unruly bodyminds: A Crip linguistics manifesto', *Journal of Critical Study of Communication & Disability*, 1.1 (2023): p. 12.

[54] This was brought to my attention on the social media platform X, formerly known as Twitter, by linguist and Professor Adam Schembri whose research focuses on the linguistics of sign languages.

[55] Grosjean, François, *Bilingual: Life and reality* (Harvard University Press, 2010): p. 90.

[56] Lakoff, George, and Mark Johnson, *Metaphors we live by* (University of Chicago Press, 2008): p.3.

[57] According to the Oxford English Corpus (https://languages.oup.com/), a text collected mainly from web pages but also some print texts like novels, journals and newspapers, the most-used noun in the English language is *time*. It is not lost on me that this is something that is predominantly noted in media as clickbait. As Benjamin Zimmer writes in a June 22, 2006 entry on *Language Log* (http://itre.cis.upenn.edu/~myl/languagelog/archives/003274.html) it is important to be somewhat sceptical when it comes to word-frequency lists. And yet, as someone who is obsessed with time, I cannot help but find small comfort in knowing that I am not alone.

[58] Tseng, Vivian, and Andrew J. Fuligni, 'Parent–adolescent language use and relationships among immigrant families with East Asian, Filipino, and Latin American backgrounds', *Journal of Marriage and Family*, 62.2 (2000): p. 465-476.

[59] Sevinç, Yeşim, and Jean-Marc Dewaele, 'Heritage language anxiety and majority language anxiety among Turkish immigrants in the Netherlands', *International Journal of Bilingualism*, 22.2 (2018): p. 159-179.

[60] Tseng, Vivian, and Andrew J. Fuligni, 'Parent–adolescent language use and relationships among immigrant families with East Asian, Filipino, and Latin American backgrounds': p. 466. See also De Houwer, Annick,

'Harmonious bilingualism: Well-being for families in bilingual settings', *Handbook of home language maintenance and development: Social and affective factors* (2020): p. 63-83.

61 Omar, Laila, 'Foreclosed futures and entangled timelines: conceptualization of the "future" among Syrian newcomer mothers in Canada', *Journal of Ethnic and Migration Studies*, 49.5 (2023): p. 1210-1228.

62 Norton, Bonny, *Identity and Language Learning* (Multilingual Matters, 2013): p. 126.

63 Henner, Jon, and Octavian Robinson, 'Unsettling languages, unruly bodyminds: A Crip linguistics manifesto', *Journal of Critical Study of Communication & Disability*, 1.1 (2023): p. 19.

64 Digard, Bérengère Galadriel, Johnson, Ellie, Kašćelan, Draško, Davis, Rachael, 'Raising bilingual autistic children in the UK: At the intersection between neurological and language diversity', *Frontiers in Psychiatry*, 14: 1250199 (2023): p. 2.

65 Digard, Bérengère Galadriel, Johnson, Ellie, Kašćelan, Draško, Davis, Rachael, 'Raising bilingual autistic children in the UK: at the intersection between neurological and language diversity': p. 10.

66 King, Kendall, and Lyn Fogle, 'Bilingual parenting as good parenting: Parents' perspectives on family language policy for additive bilingualism', *International Journal of Bilingual Education and Bilingualism*, 9.6 (2006): p. 695-712.

67 Pavlenko, Aneta, *The bilingual mind: And what it tells us about language and thought* (Cambridge University Press: 2014): p.106.

68 Baraitser, Lisa, *Maternal encounters: The ethics of interruption*: p. 74-75 referencing the work of Davies, Karen, *Women, time and the weaving of strands of everyday life* (Aldershot UK, Avebury, 1990).

69 Davies, Karen, *Women, time and the weaving of strands of everyday life* (Aldershot UK, Avebury, 1990) in Baraitser, Lisa, *Maternal encounters: The ethics of interruption*: p. 74-75.

70 Okita, Toshie, *Invisible work: Bilingualism, language choice and childrearing in intermarried families*: p. 225-227.

71 Baraitser, Lisa, *Enduring time* (Bloomsbury Publishing, 2017): p.49.

72 Foreign Service Institute: Foreign Language Training (https://www.state.gov/foreign-language-training/): Group 1: French, German, Indonesian, Italian, Portuguese, Romanian, Spanish, Swahili; Group 2: Bulgarian, Burmese, Greek, Hindi, Persian, Urdu; Group 3: Amharic, Cambodian, Czech, Finnish, Hebrew, Hungarian, Lao, Polish, Russian, Serbo-Croatian, Thai, Turkish, Vietnamese; Group 4: Arabic, Chinese, Japanese, Korean.

73 Piller, Ingrid, *Linguistic diversity and social justice: An introduction to applied sociolinguistics*: p. 46.

74 Piller, Ingrid, *Linguistic diversity and social justice: An introduction to applied sociolinguistics*: p. 208.

[75] In Pierce, Lara J., et al., 'Mapping the unconscious maintenance of a lost first language', *Proceedings of the National Academy of Sciences*, 111.48 (2014): 17314-17319, the authors examined through MRI how the brains of internationally adopted children from China responded to hearing spoken Chinese. The French-Canadian children, between the ages of 9 and 17, had all been adopted (mean age of adoption: 12.8 months) and since then were not exposed to Chinese. However, the children maintained 'neural representations of their birth language despite functionally losing that language and having no conscious recollection of it'.

[76] Grosjean, François, *Bilingual: Life and reality*: p. 92.

[77] Schmid, Monika S., Barbara Köpke, and Kees De Bot, 'Language attrition as a complex, non-linear development', *International Journal of Bilingualism*, 17.6 (2013): p. 675-682.

[78] Samata, Susan, *Cultural memory of language* (Bloomsbury, 2014): p. 135.

[79] Samata, Susan, *Cultural memory of language*: p. 27.

[80] This is not to say writers should not write about their feelings of disconnect from their parents' languages but what always pains me about these heart-wrenching essays and recordings is the search to not only lay blame but a quick fix, and a notion that this is a deficit, a lacking, a failure on either the grown child's part or the parent's.

[81] Samata, Susan, *Cultural memory of language*: p. 167.

[82] Ehala, Martin, 'Refining the notion of ethnolinguistic vitality', *International Journal of Multilingualism*, 7.4 (2010): p. 363-378.

[83] Abley, Mark, 'It's like bombing the Louvre', *The Guardian* (January 28, 2008). https://www.theguardian.com/world/2008/jan/28/usa.features11

[84] Meighan, Paul, 'Languages do not "die", they are persecuted: A Scottish Gael's perspective on language "loss"', *Belonging, Identity, Language, Diversity Research Group (BILD)*, (December 4, 2022). https://bild-lida.ca/blog/uncategorized/languages-do-not-die-they-are-persecuted-a-scottish-gaels-perspective-on-language-loss-by-dr-paul-meighan-chiblow/

[85] Isurin, Ludmila and Wilson, Hope, 'First language attrition in bilingual immigrants: Attitude, identity, and emotion' In: G. Schiewer, J. Altarriba, & BC. Ng (eds.), *Handbook on Language and Emotion* (Berlin: De Gruyter, 2023).

[86] Marlow, Kathryn, 'It was deemed extinct. But now Pentl'ach has been declared a living language thanks to Qualicum researchers' (CBC News, December 2, 2023). https://www.cbc.ca/news/canada/british-columbia/pentl-ach-officially-declared-a-living-language-added-to-b-c-list-of-first-nations-languages-1.7045803

[87] Lane, Pia, 'From silence to silencing? contradictions and tensions in language revitalization', *Applied Linguistics*, 44 (5), 2023: p. 844.

[88] Lane, Pia, 'From Silence to Silencing? Contradictions and Tensions in Language Revitalization': p. 843.

[89] Orah Mark, Sabrina, 'Rapunzel, draft one thousand', *The Paris Review* (August 6, 2020). https://www.theparisreview.org/blog/2020/08/06/rapunzel-draft-one-thousand/

PART 2

[90] Guttural sounds are often perceived as 'harsh', predominantly by English speakers who are not familiar with sounds produced at the back of the vocal track. When we label a language 'harsh', we also attach that label to the people who use it. Just because we are unfamiliar with certain sounds and do not how to produce them, it does not make a language with those phonemes 'unattractive'. *Guttural:* Latin 'of the throat', place of articulation for guttural sounds is at the back of the oral cavity. Guttural languages include Arabic, Dutch, Welsh, French, Kurdish, Hebrew, Pashto, Urdu, German, and more.

[91] Slattery Claire and Sami, Mandie, 'Caesarean births linked to developmental delays in primary school children, scientists find', Australian Broadcast Company (September 13, 2017). https://www.abc.net.au/news/2017-09-14/caesarean-births-linked-to-developmental-delays-later-in-life/8943838

[92] 'Breastfeeding may give babies a language boost by influencing brain growth', West Virginia University (May 7, 2020). https://wvutoday.wvu.edu/stories/2020/05/07/breastfeeding-may-give-babies-a-language-boost-by-influencing-brain-growth

[93] Mumm, Hanne, et al., 'Maternal cortisol levels in third trimester and early language development: A study of 1093 mother–child pairs from the Odense Child Cohort', *Journal of Neuroendocrinology*, 35.8 (2023): e13314. In this study, researchers from the Odense University Hospital analyzed data on the cortisol levels of 1,093 Danish women during their third trimester of pregnancy and on the speech and language skills of 1,093 Danish children aged 12–37 months, from the Odense Child Cohort. They found that boys exposed to high cortisol levels in the womb could say more words at ages 12–37 months, while girls were better at understanding more words at the age of 12–21 months.

[94] O'Brien, Jane, 'How foetuses learn language', BBC News (May 9, 2013). https://www.bbc.co.uk/news/world-us-canada-22457797

[95] Mampe, Birgit, et al. 'Newborns' cry melody is shaped by their native language', *Current biology*, 19.23 (2009): 1994-1997.

[96] Prochnow, Annette, et al., 'Does a "musical" mother tongue influence cry melodies? A comparative study of Swedish and German newborns', *Musicae Scientiae*, 23.2 (2019): p. 143-156.

[97] Byers-Heinlein, Krista, Tracey C. Burns, and Janet F. Werker, 'The roots of bilingualism in newborns', *Psychological Science*, 21.3 (2010): p. 343-348.

[98] Wermke, Kathleen, Michael P. Robb, and Philip J. Schluter. 'Melody complexity of infants' cry and non-cry vocalisations increases across the first six months', *Scientific Reports*, 11.1 (2021): p. 4137. https://www.uni-wuerzburg.de/en/news-and-events/news/detail/news/aus-der-melodie-waechst-die-sprache/

[99] Kuhl, Patricia, 'The linguistic genius of babies', TED (February 2011). https://www.youtube.com/watch?v=G2XBIkHW954. See also: Kuhl, Patricia K., 'Baby talk', *Scientific American*, 313.5 (2015): p. 64-69.

[100] François Grosjeans's Complementarity Principle is always at play: 'Bilinguals usually acquire and use their languages for different purposes, in different domains of life, with different people. Different aspects of life require different languages.' Also, 'Balanced bilingualism as the expected outcome', in Piller, Ingrid, 'Private language planning: The best of both worlds': p. 76.

[101] King, Kendall, and Lyn Fogle, 'Bilingual parenting as good parenting: Parents' perspectives on family language policy for additive bilingualism': p. 697.

[102] Not long after I wrote that, I came across a paper on 'paternal parentese'. See: Ferjan Ramirez, Naja, et al., '*Habla conmigo*, daddy! Fathers' language input in North American bilingual Latinx families', *Infancy*, 27.2 (2022): p. 301-323.

[103] Fuller-Wright, Liz, 'Uncovering the sound of "motherese" baby talk across languages, Princeton University (October 12, 2017). https://www.princeton.edu/news/2017/10/12/uncovering-sound-motherese-baby-talk-across-languages

[104] Solomon, Olga, 'Rethinking baby talk', In *The handbook of language socialization*, (eds.) Duranti, Alessandro, Ochs, Elinor, and Schieffelin, Bambi B., (John Wiley & Sons, 2012): p. 132.

[105] Ochs, Elinor, and Bambi B. Schieffelin, 'The theory of language socialization', In *The handbook of language socialization*, (eds.), Duranti, Alessandro, Ochs, Elinor, and Schieffelin, Bambi B., (John Wiley & Sons, 2012): p. 3.

[106] Ochs, Elinor, '*Culture and language development: Language acquisition and language socialization in a Samoan village*', 10 (CUP Archive, 1988); Schieffelin, Bambi B., *The give and take of everyday life: Language, socialization of Kaluli children*, 9 (CUP Archive, 1990).

[107] Pye, Clifton, 'Quiché Mayan speech to children', *Journal of Child Language*, 13.1 (1986): p. 85-100.

[108] Burgess, Kaya, 'Chatty mothers boost unborn babies' language skills', *The Times* (November 22, 2023). https://www.thetimes.co.uk/article/chatty-mums-boost-their-unborn-babies-language-skills-wjl2bxbzl

[109] Figueroa, Megan, 'Decolonizing (psycho)linguistics means dropping the "language gap" rhetoric', In Anne H. Charity Hudley, Christine Mallinson, and Mary Bucholtz (eds.), *Decolonizing linguistics*, Oxford University Press (in press).

[110] Figueroa, Megan, 'Decolonizing (psycho)linguistics means dropping the "language gap" rhetoric'.

[111] See for a discussion on raciolinguistic ideologies: Flores, Nelson, and Jonathan Rosa, 'Undoing appropriateness: Raciolinguistic ideologies and language diversity in education', *Harvard Educational Review*, 85.2 (2015): p. 149-171.

[112] I want to make the distinction clear here between language acquisition of a first language in childhood and language transmission or maintenance

of a heritage/minoritized language in the home. There is an element of 'teaching' when it comes to maintaining the minoritized language, especially once children get older, but this is not the same as explicit teaching of a first language a child is predominantly exposed to when acquiring language.

[113] For a more in-depth analysis and references of the many methodological issues of the Hart and Risley study, see: Figueroa, Megan, 'Decolonizing (psycho)linguistics means dropping the "language gap" rhetoric'.

[114] Figueroa, Megan, 'Decolonizing (psycho)linguistics means dropping the "language gap" rhetoric'.

[115] First seen on X, formerly Twitter, and confirmed through personal communication with Figueroa.

[116] Cushing, Ian, 'Word rich or word poor? Deficit discourses, raciolinguistic ideologies and the resurgence of the "word gap" in England's education policy', *Critical Inquiry in Language Studies* (2022): p. 1-27.

[117] Piller, Ingrid, *Linguistic diversity and social justice: An introduction to applied sociolinguistics*. See Chapter 5: Linguistic Diversity in Education, 98-129. For more on home/heritage language maintenance and education, see also the section on 'Formal Education', in Schalley, Andrea C., and Susana A. Eisenchlas, (eds.) *Handbook of home language maintenance and development: Social and affective factors*, 18 (Walter de Gruyter GmbH & Co KG, 2020): p. 425-481; and Lippi-Green, Rosina, *English with an accent: Language ideology and discrimination in the United States*: Chapter 6. For a UK perspective focused on varieties of English, Cushing, Ian, 'The policy and policing of language in schools', *Language in Society*, *49* (2019) p. 425-450.

[118] Curdt-Christiansen, Xiao Lan, Li Wei, and Zhu Hua, 'Pride, prejudice and pragmatism: family language policies in the UK', *Language Policy* (2023): p. 395.

[119] Lippi-Green, Rosina, *English with an accent: Language ideology and discrimination in the United States* (London and New York, Routledge, 1997): p. 64.

[120] Drummond, Rob, *You're all talk: Why we are what we speak* (Scribe Publications, 2023): p. 32.

[121] Lippi-Green, Rosina, *English with an accent: Language ideology and discrimination in the United States*: p. 33.

[122] Baker-Bell, April, *Linguistic justice: Black language, literacy, identity, and pedagogy* (New York and Oxon, Routledge, 2020): p. 2.

[123] Baker-Bell, April, *Linguistic justice: Black language, literacy, identity, and pedagogy*: p. 7.

[124] Piller, Ingrid, 'Private language planning: The best of both worlds': p. 67.

[125] Zentella, Ana Celia, *Growing up bilingual: Puerto Rican children in New York* (Blackwell, 1998): p. 269.

[126] Zentella, Ana Celia, *Growing up bilingual: Puerto Rican children in New York*: p. 212.

[127] Zentella, Ana Celia, *Growing up bilingual: Puerto Rican children in New York*: p. 212.

[128] Gassam Asare, Janice, 'Accent discrimination is still a pervasive issue in the workplace, research finds', *Forbes* (November 18, 2022). https://www.forbes.com/sites/janicegassam/2022/11/18/accent-discrimination-is-still-a-pervasive-issue-in-the-workplace-research-finds/

[129] Levon, Erez, Sharma Devyani and Ilbury, Christian, *Speaking up: Accents and social mobility*, Sutton Trust (2022). https://www.suttontrust.com/wp-content/uploads/2022/11/Accents-and-social-mobility.pdf

[130] GOV.UK, Discrimination: Your rights. https://www.gov.uk/discrimination-your-rights

[131] British Deaf Association: What is BSL? https://bda.org.uk/help-resources/

[132] Rangan, Pooja, Saxena, Akshya, Tharoor Srinivasan, Ragini and Sundar, Pavitra (eds.) *Thinking with an accent: Toward a new object, method, and practice* (University of California Press, 2023): p.3.

[133] Starosta, Anita, 'Everything is accented: Labor and the weight of things unsaid', In Pooja Rangan, et al., (eds) *Thinking with an accent: Toward a new object, method, and practice* (California: University of California, 2023): p. 96.

[134] Lippi-Green, Rosina, *English with an accent: Language ideology and discrimination in the United States*: p. 70.

[135] Lippi-Green, Rosina, *English with an accent: Language ideology and discrimination in the United States*: p. 17.

[136] Flint, Sunshine, 'Why don't my kids have my accent?', In *Romper* (March 8, 2023). https://www.romper.com/parenting/why-kids-do-not-have-parents-accent

[137] Królak, Emilia, and Kinga Rudnicka, 'Selected aspects of directives in Polish', *Revista Española de lingüística aplicada*, 19 (2006): p. 131.

[138] Drummond, Rob, *You're all talk: Why we are what we speak*: p. 57.

[139] Drummond, Rob, *You're all talk: Why we are what we speak*: p. 83.

[140] A concise summary of the differences between a first-language accent, a second-language accent when first-language phonology 'breaks through' a target language, and the difference between dialect and accent can be found in Lippi-Green, Rosina, *English with an accent: Language ideology and discrimination in the United States*: p. 43.

[141] Post by Vijay Ramjattan. https://twitter.com/Vijay_Ramjattan

[142] Lippi-Green, Rosina, *English with an accent: Language ideology and discrimination in the United States*: p. 50.

[143] See Drummond, Rob, *You're all talk: Why we are what we speak*: 158-162, for more of a discussion on this.

[144] Lippi-Green, Rosina, *English with an accent: Language ideology and discrimination in the United States*: p. 71.

[145] Lippi-Green, Rosina, *English with an accent: Language ideology and discrimination in the United States*: p. 73.

[146] Smith, Zadie, 'Speaking in tongues', *The New York Review of Books*, 26 (2009): p. 1-16. For the audio file: https://www.nypl.org/audiovideo/speaking-tongues-zadie-smith

[147] Bascaramurty, Dakshana and Alphonso, Caroline, 'How French immersion inadvertently created class and cultural divides at schools across Canada', *The Globe and Mail* (October 16, 2023). https://www.theglobeandmail.com/canada/article-french-immersion-program-schools-divide/

[148] Madison, Stephanie (Interviewer) and Johnson, Stacey Margarita (Producer), *We Teach Languages:* Episode 145: Bilingual Learners' Language Practices with Nelson Flores (Audio podcast), (November 1, 2020). https://weteachlang.com/2020/11/01/145-with-nelson

[149] Witt, Andrew, 'Camille Henrot', *Artforum*. https://www.artforum.com/print/reviews/202109/camille-henrot-86982

[150] Antonini, Rachele, 'Caught in the middle: Child language brokering as a form of unrecognised language service', *Journal of Multilingual and Multicultural Development*, 37.7 (2016): p.720, and Shen, Yishan, et al. 'Language brokering and immigrant-origin youth's well-being: A meta-analytic review', *American Psychologist*, 77.8 (2022): p. 921.

[151] Martinez Jr, Charles R., Heather H. McClure, and J. Mark Eddy, 'Language brokering contexts and behavioral and emotional adjustment among Latino parents and adolescents', *The Journal of Early Adolescence*, 29.1 (2009): p. 71-98.

[152] Familect is a play on dialect but within the family, a private language, often of funny or made-up words in a home shared by family members, or ways of speaking or using language. According to, Van Mensel, Luk, In '"Quiere koffie?" The multilingual familect of transcultural families', *International Journal of Multilingualism*, 15.3 (2018): p. 235, 'familect' was coined by Søndergaard, Bent. 'Switching between seven codes within one family – A linguistic resource', *Journal of Multilingual & Multicultural Development*, 12.1-2 (1991): p. 85-92.

[153] Language practices in linguistics research are predominantly part of 'family language policy', the tripartite model of FLP, which comprises language ideology, language practice, and language management, by Spolsky, Bernard, 'Family language policy – the critical domain', *Journal of Multilingual and Multicultural Development*, 33.1 (2012): p. 3-11.

[154] Van Mensel, Luk, '"Quiere koffie?" The multilingual familect of transcultural families', cites Gordon, Cynthia, *Making meanings, creating family: Intertextuality and framing in family interaction* (OUP USA, 2009): 'In her book, Gordon (2009) illustrates how family members "use language in patterned, ritualized ways to construct themselves as a social group" (p. 197), showing how families are created – or how linguistic family worlds are constructed – through the use of shared language and language practices.'

[155] Van Mensel, Luk, "'Quiere koffie?'' The multilingual familect of transcultural families', *International Journal of Multilingualism*, 15.3 (2018): p. 240.

[156] Hall, Wyatte C., 'What you don't know can hurt you: The risk of language deprivation by impairing sign language development in deaf children', *Maternal and Child Health Journal*, 21.5 (2017): p. 961-965.

[157] Penelope, Julia, *Speaking freely: Unlearning the lies of the father's tongues*: p. xviii.

[158] Romaine, Suzanne, *Communicating gender*, (Psychology Press, 1998): p. 13. Also, Penelope, Julia, *Speaking freely*: p. 16.

[159] Penelope, Julia, *Speaking freely: Unlearning the lies of the father's tongues* (Pergamon Press, 1990): p.16.

[160] Romaine, Suzanne, *Communicating gender*: p. 181.

[161] Romaine, Suzanne, *Communicating gender*: p. 181.

[162] Romaine, Suzanne, *Communicating gender*: p. 178.

[163] Aikio, Marjut, 'Are women innovators in the shift to a second language? A case study of Reindeer Sámi women and men', *International Journal of the Sociology of Language*, 94 (1992): p. 43-61.

[164] Cameron, Deborah, 'A message to our sponsors', *Language: A feminist guide* (March 8, 2020). https://debuk.wordpress.com/2020/03/08/a-message-to-our-sponsors/

[165] Cameron, Deborah, 'Are women over-emojinal?' *Language: A feminist guide* (September 10, 2017). https://debuk.wordpress.com/2017/09/10/are-women-over-emojinal/

[166] Cameron, Deborah, *The myth of Mars and Venus: Do men and women really speak different languages?* (Oxford and New York: Oxford University Press, 2007): p. 11.

[167] Cameron, Deborah, *The myth of Mars and Venus: Do men and women really speak different languages?* p. 24.

PART 3

[168] Ellis, Elizabeth Margaret, and Sims, Margaret, "'It's like the root of a tree that I grew up from . . .'': parents' linguistic identity shaping family language policy in isolated circumstances', *Multilingua*, 41.5 (2022): p. 539.

[169] Kramsch, Claire, *The multilingual subject: What foreign language learners say about their experience and why it matters* (Oxford: Oxford University Press, 2009): p. 60-66.

[170] Henner, Jon, and Octavian Robinson, 'Unsettling languages, unruly bodyminds: A Crip linguistics manifesto', *Journal of Critical Study of Communication & Disability*, 1.1 (2023): p. 7-37.

[171] Cheatham, Gregory A., and Sumin Lim, '20 disabilities and home language maintenance: Myths, models of disability, and equity', *Handbook of Home Language Maintenance and Development: Social and Affective Factors*, 18 (2020): p. 402.

[172] Cheatham, Gregory A., and Sumin Lim, '20 disabilities and home language maintenance: Myths, models of disability, and equity': p. 402.

[173] Henner, Jon, and Octavian Robinson, 'Unsettling languages, unruly bodyminds: A Crip linguistics manifesto': p. 8.

[174] A departure from traditional care work or caregiving, linguistic care work is considered through a framework developed by disability justice activist and author of *Care Work: Dreaming Disability Justice*, Leah Piepzna-Samarasinha.

[175] Robinson, Octavian, 'Crip linguistics and linguistic care work', *Medium* (September 2, 2022). https://notanangrydeafperson.medium.com/crip-linguistics-and-linguistic-care-work-74ac63c22c2e

[176] Henner, Jon, and Octavian Robinson, 'Unsettling languages, unruly bodyminds: A Crip linguistics manifesto': p. 25.

[177] Cioè-Peña, María, *(M)othering labeled children: Bilingualism and disability in the lives of Latinx mothers*, 131, (Multilingual Matters, 2021): p. 108.

[178] Cioè-Peña, María, *(M)othering labeled children: Bilingualism and disability in the lives of Latinx mothers*: p. 107.

[179] Cheatham, Gregory A., and Sumin Lim, '20 disabilities and home language maintenance: Myths, models of disability, and equity': p. 404.

[180] Henner, Jon, and Octavian Robinson, 'Unsettling languages, unruly bodyminds: A Crip linguistics manifesto': p. 25.

[181] The term *raciolinguistics* is originally attributed to H. Samy Alim (see discussion by Smitherman, Geneva, 'Raciolinguistics, "mis-education," and language arts teaching in the 21st century', *Language Arts Journal of Michigan*, 32.2 (2017): p. 3 on this) but has been developed further and widely by Nelson Flores and Jonathan Rosa. See especially: Flores, Nelson, and Jonathan Rosa, 'Undoing appropriateness: Raciolinguistic ideologies and language diversity in education', *Harvard Educational Review*, 85.2 (2015): 149-171, and Rosa, Jonathan, and Nelson Flores, 'Unsettling race and language: Toward a raciolinguistic perspective', *Language in Society*, 46.5 (2017): p. 621-647. For how sociolinguists in the UK position work as advocating for the home language while not addressing structures of white supremacy and colonial histories of named languages and varieties, all under the guise of social justice, see Cushing, Ian, 'A raciolinguistic perspective from the United Kingdom', *Journal of Sociolinguistics* (2023).

[182] Flores, Nelson, and Jonathan Rosa, 'Undoing appropriateness: Raciolinguistic ideologies and language diversity in education', *Harvard Educational Review*, 85.2 (2015): p. 149-171.

[183] Figueroa, Megan, 'Decolonizing (psycho)linguistics means dropping the "language gap" rhetoric', In Anne H. Charity Hudley, Christine Mallinson, and Mary Bucholtz, (eds), *Decolonizing linguistics*, Oxford University Press (in press).

[184] Bauler, Clara, 'Have we learned anything? Raciolinguistic ideologies in remote learning public discourses', *Journal of Critical Study of Communication & Disability*, 1.1 (2023): p. 48-68.

[185] Bauler, Clara, 'Have we learned anything? Raciolinguistic ideologies in remote learning public discourses': p. 58.

[186] Bauler, Clara, 'Have we learned anything? Raciolinguistic ideologies in remote learning public discourses': p. 58.

[187] Amongst all the articles on language and learning loss, there was only one I read discussing the positive side of children being exposed more to their heritage languages during lockdowns. The article included a number of studies that looked at how families used heritage languages during the pandemic. For more, see: Hardach, Sophie, 'In quarantine, kids pick up parents' mother tongues: For some families, the pandemic has meant a return to their native languages', *The New York Times* (September 10, 2020). https://www.nytimes.com/2020/09/10/parenting/family-second-language-coronavirus.html

[188] Morrone, Megan, 'Women are returning to work, but there's more to the story', BBC Worklife (September 15, 2023). https://www.bbc.com/worklife/article/20230914-women-are-returning-to-work-but-theres-more-to-the-story

[189] Bachelard, Gaston, *The poetics of space* (Boston, Beacon Press, 1994): p. 61.

[190] Pennycook, Alastair, *Language as a local practice* (Routledge, 2010): p. 2.

[191] Lanza, Elizabeth, and Rafael Lomeu Gomes, 'Family language policy: Foundations, theoretical perspectives and critical approaches', *Handbook of Home Language Maintenance and Development: Social and affective factors*, 153 (2020): p. 165.

[192] Romaine, Suzanne, *Communicating Gender*: p. 12.

[193] Eisenchlas, Susana A., and Andrea C. Schalley, 'Making sense of "home language" and related concepts', *Handbook of Home Language Maintenance and Development. Social and Affective Factors* (2020): p. 25-26.

[194] Crisfield, Eowyn, *Bilingual families: A practical language planning guide* (Multilingual Matters, 2021): p. 68-69.

[195] Mills, Jean, 'Mothers and mother tongue: Perspectives on self-construction by mothers of Pakistani heritage', in *Negotiation of identities in multilingual contexts*, Aneta Pavlenko and Adrian Blackledge, (eds), (Multilingualism Matters, 2004): p. 162-163.

[196] Statistics on shared parental leave are hard to come by but a good place to start is with the work of Maternity Action (full disclosure: I volunteered for the organization when my first child was a baby). This post by the director of Maternity Action breaks down some information on shared parental leave in the UK: Bragg, Ros, 'Shared Parental Leave evaluation: What is the take-up of Shared Parental Leave', *Maternity Action* (July 31, 2023). https://maternityaction.org.uk/2023/07/shared-parental-leave-evaluation-what-is-the-take-up-of-shared-parental-leave/?utm_source=rss&utm_medium=rss&utm_campaign=shared-parental-leave-evaluation-what-is-the-take-up-of-shared-parental-leave

[197] In Crisfield, Eowyn, *Bilingual families: A practical language planning guide*, the author notes the families she worked with were predominantly heteronormative with a 'mother' and 'father' but that this may differ in other types of families. For a look at diversifying studies around family language policy, see Lyn Wright, and Christina Higgins, (eds), *Diversifying family language policy* (Bloomsbury Publishing, 2022).

[198] Cymraeg 2050: A Million Welsh Speakers, gov.wales. https://www.gov.wales/sites/default/files/publications/2018-12/cymraeg-2050-welsh-language-strategy.pdf

[199] Gedalof, Irene, 'Birth, belonging and migrant mothers: Narratives of reproduction in feminist migration studies', *Feminist Review*, 93.1 (2009): p. 97.

[200] Gedalof, Irene, 'Birth, belonging and migrant mothers: Narratives of reproduction in feminist migration studies': p. 96.

[201] Erel, Umut, 'Reframing migrant mothers as citizens', *Citizenship Studies*, 15.6-7 (2011): p. 695-709.

[202] Dyck, Isabel, 'Migrant mothers, home and emotional capital – hidden citizenship practices', *Ethnic and Racial Studies*, 41.1 (2018): p. 98-113.

[203] Meyer, Robinson, '*The New York Times'* Most Popular Story of 2013 Was Not an Article', *The Atlantic* (January 17, 2014). https://www.theatlantic.com/technology/archive/2014/01/-em-the-new-york-times-em-most-popular-story-of-2013-was-not-an-article/283167/

[204] Lippi-Green, Rosina, *English with an accent: Language ideology and discrimination in the United States* (London and New York, Routledge, 1997): p. 42.

[205] Pennycook, Alastair, *Language as a local practice* (Routledge, 2010): p. 141.

[206] Hirsch, Afua, *Brit(ish): On race, identity and belonging* (London, Vintage: 2018): p. 32.

[207] Piller, Ingrid, *Linguistic diversity and social justice: An introduction to applied sociolinguistics*: p. 67; and see more in Part 4: 'Linguistic Diversity at Work': p. 63-97.

[208] Jones, Reece, *Violent Borders: Refugees and the Right to Move* (Verso, London, New York, 2016): p. 180.

[209] Jones, Reece, *Violent Borders: Refugees and the Right to Move*: p. 166.

[210] Piller, Ingrid, *Linguistic diversity and social justice: An introduction to applied sociolinguistics* (Oxford University Press, 2016): p. 39.

[211] Lippi-Green, Rosina, *English with an accent: Language ideology and discrimination in the United States*: p. 64.

[212] Travis, Allan, 'The leave campaign made three key promises – are they keeping them?', *The Guardian* (June 27, 2016). https://www.theguardian.com/politics/2016/jun/27/eu-referendum-reality-check-leave-campaign-promises

[213] Kozminska, Kinga, and Zhu, Hua, 'The promise and resilience of multilingualism: language ideologies and practices of Polish-speaking migrants in the UK post the Brexit vote', *Journal of Multilingual and Multicultural Development*, 42.5 (2021): p. 444-461.

[214] Lahiri, Jhumpa, *In Other Words* (London and New York: Bloomsbury, 2016): p. 19.

[215] Tokarczuk, Olga, *Flights*, translated by Jennifer Croft (Fitzcarraldo Editions, 2018): p. 183.

[216] Language, England and Wales: Census 2021. https://www.ons.gov.uk/peoplepopulationandcommunity/culturalidentity/language/bulletins/languageenglandandwales/census2021

[217] I never considered this until recently as being part of what Grosjean, François in *Life as a bilingual: Knowing and using two or more languages* (p. 136) refers to as the person–language bond. This is especially prevalent in young multilingual children who have a preferred language with other multilinguals they know well (for example, their parents or caregivers). When either person deviates from the preferred/predictable language, it can feel unexpected, awkward and even uncomfortable.

[218] Krasinski, Jennifer, 'Agota Kristof and the uses of illiteracy', *The New Yorker* (June 27, 2023). https://www.newyorker.com/books/second-read/agota-kristof-and-the-uses-of-illiteracy

[219] Purkarthofer, Judith, 'Intergenerational challenges: Of handing down languages, passing on practices, and bringing multilingual speakers into being,' In *Handbook of home language maintenance and development: Social and affective factors*, Andrea C. Schalley, and Susana A. Eisenchlas, (eds), 18 (Walter de Gruyter GmbH & Co KG, 2020): p. 130.

[220] Purkarthofer, Judith, 'Intergenerational challenges: Of handing down languages, passing on practices, and bringing multilingual speakers into being': p. 143-144.

[221] UNESCO: Indigenous Languages Decade (2022-2032). https://www.unesco.org/en/decades/indigenous-languages

[222] Provost, Kelly, 'Not enough funding to cover all Indigenous language program requests, group says', *The Saskatoon StarPhoenix* (September 6, 2019). https://www.cbc.ca/news/canada/saskatoon/saskatchewan-indigenous-language-camps-demand-1.5273521

[223] Statistics Canada: Indigenous Languages across Canada (March 29, 2023). https://www12.statcan.gc.ca/census-recensement/2021/as-sa/98-200-X/2021012/98-200-X2021012-eng.cfm

[224] The other strategies identified by Lanza in, Lanza, Elizabeth, 'Multilingualism and the family', In *Handbook of multilingualism and multilingual communication*, Peter Auer, and Li Wei (eds), *Handbook of multilingualism and multilingual communication*, 5 (2007): 45-67 include: 'expressed guess' (parents attempt to reformulate the child's utterance, often with a yes/no in target language), 'adult repetition' (parents repeat the child's utterance in the target language), 'move on' (parents acknowledge understanding while sending the message that it is OK to respond in the other language), and 'adult code-switching' (parents actively incorporate the language the child is using into their own

utterances, often moving between two or more languages within a conversation or even a sentence).

[225] De Houwer, Annick, *Bilingual first language acquisition* (Vol. 2, Multilingual Matters, 2009) and De Houwer, Annick, 'Language input environments and language development in bilingual acquisition', *Applied Linguistics Review*, 2.2 (2011): p. 226: 'Those bilingual families where children ended up speaking just the majority language, Dutch, tended to be families where both parents used the majority language at home, and only one parent used the minority language.'

[226] There is fascinating and important work being done on multilingualism in the family and the child's agency. It is a multifaceted topic specific to every family's experience. Some recent work I recommend: Smith-Christmas, Cassie, 'Child agency and home language maintenance', In *Handbook of home language maintenance and development: Social and affective factors*, 18, Andrea Schalley, and Susana Eisenchlas, (2020): p. 218; and Little, Sabine, 'Whose heritage? What inheritance?: Conceptualising family language identities', *International Journal of Bilingual Education and Bilingualism*, 23.2 (2020): p. 198-212.

[227] García, Ofelia and Wei, Li, '*Translanguaging: Language, bilingualism and education*' (United Kingdom, Palgrave Macmillan, 2014): p. 20.

[228] García, Ofelia, 'Translanguaged TESOL in Transit', *NYS TESOL Journal*, 10(1), (July 2023).

[229] Wei, Li, and Lin, Angel M. Y., 'Translanguaging classroom discourse: Pushing limits, breaking boundaries', *Classroom Discourse*, 10.3-4 (2019): p. 209-215.

[230] Translanguaging within education systems that are 'instruments of the nation-state' is complex and challenging. Many scholars, including Ofelia García, Li Wei and Nelson Flores, are doing a lot of work in this field. For more on translanguaging in education, see García, Ofelia and Wei, Li, 'Translanguaging: Language, bilingualism and education'.

[231] Translanguaging is beyond 'mixing', so the terminology here is a bit deceiving. But this is the only study I could find about using full linguistic repertoires in the home and especially how parents felt about it.

[232] Wilson, Sonia, 'To mix or not to mix: Parental attitudes towards translanguaging and language management choices', *International Journal of Bilingualism*, 25.1 (2021): p. 72.

[233] See also, Wei, Li, 'Moment analysis and translanguaging space: Discursive construction of identities by multilingual Chinese youth in Britain', *Journal of Pragmatics*, 43, 5, (2011): p. 1222-1235.

[234] Blackledge, Adrian and Creese, Angela, 'Translanguaging and the body', *International Journal of Multilingualism*, 14.3 (2017): p. 252.

[235] Blackledge, Adrian and Creese, Angela, 'Translanguaging and the body', *International Journal of Multilingualism*, 14.3 (2017): 250-268; Bourdieu, Pierre, *Pascalian meditations* (Cambridge: Polity Press, 2000): p. 145; and

Scollon, Suzie Wong and Scollon, Ron, *Nexus analysis: Discourse and the emerging internet* (Routledge, 2004): p. 13.

236 Scollon, Suzie Wong, and Scollon, Ron, *Nexus analysis: Discourse and the emerging internet*): p. 13, In Adrian Blackledge, and Angela Creese, 'Translanguaging and the body': p. 253.

PART 4

237 For more on language desire, multilingual couples and love, an intermarriage, see Piller, Ingrid, *Bilingual couples talk: The discursive construction of hybridity* (25), (John Benjamins Publishing, 2002). Also, to note, not all multilingual love is lustful and lovely, of course, as the work of Jean-Marc Dewaele and Lora Salomidou, 'Loving a partner in a foreign language', *Journal of Pragmatics*,108 (2017): 116-130, describes: lost-in-translation moments are still prevalent, but they tend to fade after some time. Also see Stępkowska, Agnieszka, 'Language as a source of problems in bilingual couples', *Language Use, Education, and Professional Contexts* (Cham: Springer International Publishing, 2022): p. 99-113, for the more challenging side of multilingual coupledom.

238 Hill, Faith, 'How to fall in love when you don't speak the same language', *The Atlantic*, May 30, 2023.

239 Torsh, Hanna Irving, *Linguistic intermarriage in Australia: Between pride and shame* (Springer Nature, 2019): p. 28.

240 Torsh, Hanna Irving, *Linguistic intermarriage in Australia: Between pride and shame*: p. 126.

241 Pavlenko, Aneta, *Emotions and multilingualism* (Cambridge: CUP, 2005): p. 155.

242 Dewaele, Jean-Marc, 'The emotional weight of I love you in multilinguals' languages', *Journal of Pragmatics*, 40.10 (2008): p. 1753-1780.

243 Dewaele, Jean-Marc, 'The emotional weight of I love you in multilinguals' languages': p. 1770.

244 Pavlenko, Aneta, *Emotions and multilingualism*: p. 155.

245 See Dewaele, Jean-Marc, 'The emotional force of swearwords and taboo words in the speech of multilinguals', *Journal of Multilingual and Multicultural Development*, 25.2-3 (2004): p. 204-222, for more on the emotion of swears and taboo words.

246 Dewaele, Jean-Marc, 'The emotional force of swearwords and taboo words in the speech of multilinguals', *Journal of Multilingual and Multicultural Development*, 25.2/3 (2004): p. 204-222.

247 For more on multilingualism and psychotherapy, see Rolland, Louise, Dewaele, Jean-Marc and Costa, Beverley, 'Multilingualism and psychotherapy: exploring multilingual clients' experiences of language practices in psychotherapy', *International Journal of Multilingualism*, 14.1 (2017): p. 69-85.

[248] Lahiri, Jhumpa, *Translating myself and others* (Princeton and Oxford, Princeton University Press, 2022) p. 3.

[249] Pavlenko, Aneta, *Emotions and multilingualism*: p. 231.

[250] Pavlenko, Aneta, *Emotions and multilingualism*: p. 22.

[251] Pavlenko, Aneta, *Emotions and multilingualism*: p. 228.

[252] Conaboy, Chelsea, 'Maternal instinct is a myth men created', *The New York Times* (August 26, 2022). https://www.nytimes.com/2022/08/26/opinion/sunday/maternal-instinct-myth.html

[253] Pavlenko, Aneta, '"Stop doing that, ia komu skazala!": Language choice and emotions in parent–child communication', *Journal of Multilingual and Multicultural Development*, 25.2-3 (2004): 179-203: p.183.

[254] Pavlenko, Aneta, '"Stop doing that, ia komu skazala!": Language choice and emotions in parent–child communication': p. 192.

[255] Curdt-Christiansen, Xiao Lan, and Iwaniec, Janina, '"妈妈, I miss you": Emotional multilingual practices in transnational families', *International Journal of Bilingualism*, 27.2 (2023): p. 4.

[256] McCulloch, Gretchen, *Because Internet: Understanding the New Rules of Language* (New York: Riverhead Books, 2019): p. 276.

[257] Hjorth, Larissa, et al., *Digital media practices in households: Kinship through data* (Amsterdam University Press, 2020): p. 19.

[258] Hjorth, Larissa, et al., *Digital media practices in households: Kinship through data*: p. 19.

[259] Curdt-Christiansen, Xiao Lan, and Iwaniec, Janina, '"妈妈, I miss you": Emotional multilingual practices in transnational families'.

[260] Kramsch, Claire, *Language and culture* (Oxford, Oxford University Press, 1998): p. 3.

[261] Grosjean, François, *Life as a bilingual: Knowing and using two or more languages* (Cambridge University Press, 2021): p. 255-256; and Pavlenko, Aneta, *Thinking and speaking in two languages* (Bristol/Buffalo/Toronto, 2011).

[262] Gabryś-Barker, Danuta, 'What the languages of our dreams tell us about our multilinguality', *The Ecosystem of the Foreign Language Learner: Selected Issues* (2015): p. 3-17.

[263] Grosjean, François, *Life as a bilingual*: p. 204.

[264] Dewaele, Jean-Marc, 'Why do so many bi-and multilinguals feel different when switching languages?', *International Journal of Multilingualism*, 13.1 (2016): 92-105.

[265] Grosjean, François, *Bilingual: Life and reality* (Harvard University Press, 2010): p. 29.

[266] Pavlenko, Aneta, *Emotions and multilingualism*: p. 220.

[267] Tseng, Amelia, 'Identity in home-language maintenance', *Handbook of Home Language Maintenance and Development: Social and Affective Factors*, 18 (2020): p. 114.

[268] Curdt-Christiansen, Xiao Lan, Wei, Li, and Hua, Zhu, 'Pride, prejudice and pragmatism: family language policies in the UK', *Language Policy* (2023): p. 1-21.

[269] Kramsch, Claire, *Language and Culture* (Oxford, Oxford University Press, 1998): p. 77.

[270] Mills, Jean, 'Mothers and mother tongue: Perspectives on self-construction by mothers of Pakistani heritage', In *Negotiation of identities in multilingual contexts*, Aneta Pavlenko, and Adrian Blackledge, (eds), (Multilingualism Matters, 2004): p. 164.

[271] Mangan, Lucy, 'Is it OK for adults to still say "Mummy"?', *The Guardian* (June 5, 2012). https://www.theguardian.com/uk/shortcuts/2012/jun/05/one-wants-ones-mummy

[272] Words can be embodied/disembodied in what Aneta Pavlenko refers to as language embodiment. The moniker, 'Mom' is definitely disembodied for me.

[273] Kouritzin, Sandra, 'A Mother's Tongue', *TESOL Quarterly*, 34.2 (2000): p. 314.

[274] Sedivy, Julie, *Memory speaks: On losing and reclaiming language and self* (Harvard University Press, 2021): p. 3.

[275] Wright, Lyn, L., 'The discursive functions of kinship terms in family conversation', In *Diversifying family language policy* Lyn Wright, and Christina Higgins, (eds), (Bloomsbury Publishing, 2022): p. 17.

[276] Wright, Lyn, L., 'The discursive functions of kinship terms in family conversation', In *Diversifying family language policy*, Lyn Wright, and Christina Higgins, (eds), (Bloomsbury Publishing, 2022): p. 16.

[277] Wright, Lyn, *Critical perspectives on language and kinship in multilingual families*, (Bloomsbury Publishing, 2022): p. 105.

[278] Wright, Lyn, *Critical perspectives on language and kinship in multilingual families*, (Bloomsbury Publishing, 2022): p. 106.

[279] Perry, Nina, 'The universal language of lullabies', BBC News (January 21, 2013). https://www.bbc.co.uk/news/magazine-21035103

[280] Schmid, Monika S., Köpke, Barbara, and De Bot, Kees, 'Language attrition as a complex, non-linear development', *International Journal of Bilingualism*, 17.6 (2013): p. 676.

[281] Personal communication with Catherine Hamilton.

[282] Hamilton, Catherine, and Murphy, Victoria A., 'Folk pedagogy? Investigating how and why UK early years and primary teachers use songs with young learners', *Education 3-13*, (2023): p. 1-22.

[283] Wierzbicka, Anna, 'Two languages, two cultures, one (?) self: Between Polish and English', In *Translating lives: Living with two languages and cultures*, Mary Besemeres and Anna Wierzbicka, (eds), (2007): p. 101.

[284] Wierzbicka, Anna, 'Two languages, two cultures, one (?) self: Between Polish and English': p. 101.

PART 5

[285] Pennycook, Alastair, and Otsuji, Emi, *Metrolingualism: Language in the city* (Routledge, 2015): p. 118.

[286] Pennycook, Alastair, and Otsuji, Emi, *Metrolingualism: Language in the city*.

[287] Samata, Susan, 'Language at Home: A reclaimed heritage', In *Thinking Home*, Sanja Bahun, and Bojana Petric, (eds), (Routledge, 2020): p. 207-223.

[288] Kramsch, Claire, *The multilingual subject: What foreign language learners say about their experience and why it matters* (Oxford: Oxford University Press, 2009): p. 16.

[289] Hoffman, Eva, 'The new nomads', In *Letters of Transit*, André Aciman, (ed.), (New York and London, The New Press: 1999): p. 47

[290] Espinoza, Marco, and Wigglesworth, Gillian, 'Beyond success and failure: Intergenerational language transmission from within Indigenous families in Southern Chile', *Diversifying Family Language Policy*, Wright, Lyn, and Christina Higgins, eds (Bloomsbury, 2022): 277-298.

[291] Fillmore, Lily Wong, 'When learning a second language means losing the first', *Early Childhood Research Quarterly*, 6.3 (1991): p. 342.

[292] Duchêne, Alexandre, 'Multilingualism: An insufficient answer to sociolinguistic inequalities', *International Journal of the Sociology of Language*, 2020.263, (2020): p. 93.

About the Author

Malwina Gudowska is a Polish–Canadian writer, editor and linguist living in London, UK. A National Magazine Award winner, her writing has appeared in *Financial Times*, *Vogue*, *Literary Hub*, *The Globe and Mail* and several book and magazine anthologies. She is a PhD researcher in applied linguistics exploring the emotions of mothers raising multilingual children. Her newsletter, *Motherlingual*, examines the intersection of language and motherhood.